TYPE & IMAGE

Philip B. Meggs

TYPE & IMAGE

The Language of
Graphic Design

 Van Nostrand Reinhold
New York

Van Nostrand Reinhold
115 Fifth Avenue
New York, New York 10003

Chapman & Hall
2-6 Boundary Row
London SE1 8HN, England

Thomas Nelson Australia
102 Dodds Street
South Melbourne, Victoria 3205, Australia

Nelson Canada
1120 Birchmount Road
Scarborough, Ontario M1K 5G4, Canada

16 15 14 13 12 11 10 9 8 7 6 5 4 3 2 1

Library of Congress Cataloging-in-Publication Data

Meggs, Philip B.
  Type and image/Philip B. Meggs.
     p.   cm.
  Bibliography: p.
  Includes index.
  ISBN 0-442-25846-1
  ISBN 0-442-01165-2 (pbk.)
  1. Printing, Practical—Layout. 2. Type and type-founding.
3. Graphic arts.   I. Title
Z246.M44 1989
686.2'24—dc 19   88-21108
                             CIP

For my children,
Andrew Philip Meggs and
Elizabeth Wilson Meggs

Acknowledgments

I deeply appreciate the assistance of numerous people. Dozens of designers and their clients generously provided illustrations and reproduction permissions. I cannot list them here; however, these contributions are acknowledged in the picture credits. At Virginia Commonwealth University, Murry N. DePillars, Dean of the School of the Arts, and John DeMao, Chairman of the Department of Communication Arts and Design, provided encouragement and assistance. In photographing the work, George Nan produced excellent transparencies and prints for reproduction. Diana Lively read the manuscript and made insightful suggestions. Rob Carter provided advice, shared resource materials, and helped solve some difficult content problems. Ellen Lupton, curator of the Herb Lubalin Study Center at Cooper Union, generously contributed to my research.

Lilly Kaufman, design acquisitions editor at Van Nostrand Reinhold, guided this project through its development and completion. Paul Lukas was the editorial supervisor, and Joy Matkowski copyedited the manuscript. Amanda Miller provided editorial assistance and Sandra Cohen was the production manager.

John DeMao, Libby Phillips Meggs, and Julie Sebastianelli worked with me in designing this book. Ben Day provided many excellent observations.

My wife, Libby Phillips Meggs, assisted on a daily basis, helped to select illustrations, critiqued the manuscript, suggested content, and provided encouragement and support. My father, Wallace N. Meggs, provided important research assistance. Research leading to the publication of this book was supported by a grant from the Design Arts Program of the National Endowment for the Arts, a federal agency.

Contents

Introduction

What is the essence of graphic design? How do graphic designers solve problems, organize space, and imbue their work with those visual and symbolic qualities that enable it to convey visual and verbal information with expression and clarity? The extraordinary flowering of graphic design in our time—as a potent means of communication and a major component of our visual culture—increases the need for designers, clients, and students to comprehend its essence.

Traditionally, graphic designers looked to architecture or painting for their model. Certainly, a universal language of form is common to all visual disciplines, and in some historical periods the various design arts have shared styles. Too much dependence upon other arts—or even on the universal language of form—is unsatisfactory, however, because graphic design has unique purposes and visual properties.

Graphic design is a hybrid discipline. Diverse elements, including signs, symbols, words, and pictures, are collected and assembled into a total message. The dual nature of these graphic elements as both communicative sign and visual form provides endless fascination and potential for invention and combination. Although all the visual arts share properties of either two- or three-dimensional space, graphic space has a special character born from its communicative function.

Perhaps the most important thing that graphic design does is give communications resonance, a richness of tone that heightens the expressive power of the page. It transcends the dry conveyance of information, intensifies the message, and enriches the audience's experience. Resonance helps the designer realize clear public goals: to instruct, to delight, and to motivate.

Most designers speak of their activities as a problem-solving process because designers seek solutions to public communications problems. Approaches to problem solving vary, based on the problem at hand and the working methods of the designer. At a time when Western nations are evolving from industrial to information cultures, a comprehensive understanding of our communicative forms and graphic design becomes increasingly critical. I interrupted all other activities for a half-year to study the nature of graphic design; this book is the result.

Chapter One: The Elements of Graphic Design

1-1

The general public does not understand graphic design and art direction. Designers tell the story of a graphic designer trying to explain this job to Grandmother. The designer shows Grandmother a recent project and says, "You were asking me about what I do, Grandmother. I'm a graphic designer, and I designed this."

Pointing to the photograph in the design, the grandmother asks, "Did you draw that picture?"

"No, Grandmother, it's a photograph. I didn't draw it, but I planned it, chose the photographer, helped select the models, assisted in setting it up, art directed the shooting session, chose which shot to use, and cropped the picture."

"Did you write what it says, then?"

"Well, no," the designer replies. "But I did brainstorm with the copywriter to develop the concept."

"Oh, I see. Then you did letter these big words?" asks the grandmother, pointing to the headline.

"Uh, no, a typesetter set the copywriter's words in type, but I specified the typefaces and sizes to be used," responds the designer.

"Well, did you draw this little picture down in the corner?"

"No, but I selected the illustrator, told her what needed to be drawn, and decided where to put it and how big to make it."

"Oh. Well, did you draw this little, what do you call it, a trademark?"

"Uh, no. A design firm that specializes in visual identification programs designed it for the client."

The grandmother is somewhat confused about just what it is that her grandchild does and why credit is claimed for all these other people's work.

The designer's task

The conceptual nature of the graphic design process generates public confusion about the designer's task. The designer combines graphic materials—words, pictures, and other graphic elements—to construct a visual communications *gestalt*. This German word does not have a direct English translation. It means a configuration or structure with properties not derivable from the sum of its individual parts. Figure **1-1** demonstrates this principle. The first set of twelve dots, randomly placed, has no meaning or content beyond the phenomenon of twelve dots printed on the page. By contrast, the second set of twelve dots has been consciously structured into a visual configuration with meaning as a common sign: the letter *H* from the Roman alphabet. In one sense, the letter *H* is not present, but the human eye perceives the dots, and the human mind connects them into a recognizable pattern—the structure of a letterform. In the first configuration, the viewer sees a random dispersion of parts; in the second, the viewer sees the whole.

Organizing these dots into a simple visual gestalt is symbolic of the graphic design process: The designer combines visual signs, symbols, and images into a visual-verbal gestalt that the audience can understand. The graphic designer is simultaneously message maker and form builder. This complex task involves forming an intricate communications message while building a cohesive composition that gains order and clarity from the relationships between the elements.

Another aspect of the designer's task is to infuse content with resonance. A term borrowed from music, *resonance* means the reverberation or echo, a subtle quality of tone or timbre. A violin prized for its resonance creates music with a richness of tone that heightens the expressiveness of sound. Graphic designers bring a resonance to visual communications through, for example, the use of scale and contrast, cropping of images, and choice of typefaces and colors.

A line of type moves to the right.

1-2

The dual life of a graphic form

Almost every graphic form—from a small period at the end of a sentence to the most complex color photograph—has a dual existence: It is an optical phenomenon with visual properties, and it is a communicative signal that functions with other signals to form a message.

The three forms in figure **1-2** illustrate that each has a center located at the point where its horizontal and vertical axes intersect. Even organic forms and forms placed into an unstable spatial dynamic have centers. Perceptual energy is generated by forms in graphic space. Even the static, perfectly balanced letterform *M* in figure **1-2** has energy that is generated by its light -and- dark contrast with the white page. In addition to the *energy of contrast,* which can be produced by contrasts of color, value, or texture between the figure and its ground, a form gains energy from its implied movement and direction. The *M* is static because its horizontal and vertical axes are equal and divide the form into four nearly equal and symmetrical quadrants. The line of type has a long horizontal movement, which propels the viewer's eye toward the right. Some forms radiate energy, and others are passive. Even though the running silhouette has vigorous energy and movement, it maintains equilibrium because its parts are balanced around its axes. These three forms maintain a flat, two-dimensional relationship with the page.

Forms can produce illusions of movement behind the flat page away from the viewer or projected forward from the surface. The perspective diagram demonstrates an *illusion of spatial depth,* a sense of three-dimensional space on the flat surface, and the box suggests projection forward in space toward the viewer. In the last two examples, the implied axes of the forms also move backward and forward in space.

In addition to their optical and perceptual life, graphic forms have symbolic life as signs, symbols, and images that combine with one another to convey a message to the viewer. This communicative role can occur only within a culture, for signals transmit information according to a predetermined system or code. Chinese calligraphy and the English alphabet, for example, are prearranged systems that are understandable only to people who have learned the language.

The dual role of graphic forms is clearly illustrated in Paul Rand's cover for the Spring 1943 issue of *Direction* (fig. **1-3**), a writers' magazine. Two analyses of this cover—as visual design and as graphic communication—clearly demonstrate this duality.

The visual composition can be seen and evaluated almost as an abstract painting (fig. **1-4**). A triangle and a rectangle are placed in a dynamic relationship to each other. Each has an internal, lighter form that creates a pull or tension within the larger form. The darker area of the rectangle duplicates the shape of the triangle and forms a relationship between them. The bold calligraphic line establishes a relationship to the triangle, which seems to pull the gesture toward it almost as though there is a magnetic attraction. Then the gesture moves away to form an angle that echoes the sides of the triangle. A line germinates from each shape. These lines of contrasting weight weave and pull through the space. They divide the white background into three open planes that move and flow with the rhythm of the lines. The lines seem alternately to attract and repel each other as they move through the space. The masthead above is stable, in contrast to the dynamic movement and energy of tilted shapes and flowing lines. Its placement parallels the horizontal edges of the page and unifies them with it. An active yet balanced composition is formed.

A separate analysis approaches the same phenomenon as communication. The masthead tells us that this is *Direction* magazine, and the gestured script below it indicates that this is the first issue of volume 6, published in the spring of 1943. Because *Direction* was a magazine for writers, the triangular photograph of a pen point was interpreted by its readers as a symbol for writers. In the 1980s, the rectangular photograph of a smokestack would be interpreted as a symbol for industrial pollution, but in the early 1940s it was a symbol for heavy industry. The pen point draws an ink line through space to signify the writer's output, and the smokestack produces a bold brush stroke representing smoke as a symbol for industrial production. Inside, *Direction* subscribers learned that a contest for writing by workers in war industry was to be held. The placement of the photographs and the contrast between the lines suggest tension, rather than order and unity, and imply that perhaps discomfort or a difficult adjustment exists for creative writers who are working within war industry.

This magazine cover, produced more than four decades ago by a young designer not yet thirty, clearly demonstrates the important dual role of the graphic designer as message maker and form builder.

Information and communication

Information is knowledge about facts and events, and communication is the transfer of information between people. We live in a world of communication, constantly sending and receiving messages, gathering and disseminating information. With the development of twentieth-century communications technology, a theory of communications or information transmission has evolved. Its central premise is that information can be studied and measured very much like physical quantities such as mass and energy. Shannon and Weaver's basic theory of communication[1] is based on a general communications system (fig. **1-5**) with the following components:

An *information source* that produces the message or raw information to be transmitted

A *transmitter* or *encoder* that transforms this information into a form, called a *signal,* that is suitable for the channel

A *channel* upon which the encoded signal is transmitted to the receiving point. Distortion or interference, such as static in radio reception or "snow" in television, is called *noise,* represented on the diagram by the *noise source.*

The *receiver* or *decoder,* which translates the received signal back into the original message or an approximation of it

The *recipient* or *destination,* which receives the decoded message.

Basic information theory is based on an elemental signal called a *bit* or *binary digit,* the smallest unit of information in a computer or other electronic communication system. A bit consists of one of the two units of the binary code, either one or zero. By reducing the communications process to this elementary level, Shannon and Weaver opened remarkable doors for the development of communications technology. Computers, video recorders, and cellular telephones are examples of technological systems that deliver information by digital technology. Basic information theory addresses the method of communication but not the content or purpose of communication; therefore, it is inadequate to explain communicative art forms including literature, music, or graphic design. Human communication can be subjective, expressive, and aesthetic, but basic information theory is cast in the cold, impersonal logic of the machine. The audience and the complex and rich nuances of graphic signals are aspects of graphic design that are beyond its scope.

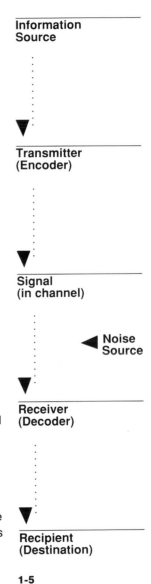

Information Source

Transmitter (Encoder)

Signal (in channel)

Noise Source

Receiver (Decoder)

Recipient (Destination)

1-5

The audience

Complex symbol-making activity dates back at least 300,000 years—the approximate date of the earliest known example of intentional use of symbolism in engraving—to an ox rib found in France that is marked with festooned double-arcs.[2] Early visual language includes: *pictographs,* elemental pictures representing objects; *ideograms,* which signify concepts or ideas rather than specific objects; and *petroglyphs,* which are carved into rock. Figure **1-6**, a rubbing by Rob Carter from a petroglyph carved by Paiute Indians in Grand Wash Canyon, Utah, depicts pictographs of a standing man, a horseman, and a bison. Collectively, these pictographs signify the concept of a hunt, which moves into the realm of the ideogram. From these simple origins, cultures have evolved collective and complex systems of signs and symbols that enable its members to communicate. The ability of the audience to decode and understand a graphic design becomes a major limitation governing its form and content. Milton Glaser observed that "the reason new forms usually don't emerge from the design activity . . . is that design is in many ways a vernacular language. Design-related work assumes that the audience addressed has an *a priori* understanding of the vocabulary," and it "conveys information based on the audience's previous understanding."[3] The audience's language and level of *visual literacy,* which means skill in comprehending and using visual forms, must be taken into account if the designer is to communicate successfully.

A vocabulary develops through trial-and-error experience as a young child learns to talk, to understand the culture's visual language system, such as our alphabet, and to read by using this sign system as a visual equivalent of verbal language. American college students who worked in health-care outreach programs in Nepal observed how the audience's limited visual literacy prevented effective communication. Rural villagers were shown a three-foot-tall illustration of a fly in health-care presentations explaining how a fly deposits infectious bacteria on food. Hopes that the villagers would adopt recommended sanitation procedures were dashed when the villagers left the meetings chuckling that they did not need to worry. After all, their village had no giant three-foot flies, only little tiny ones.[4] Culturally, the villagers had not learned to read pictures and did not comprehend the large illustration as an enlarged image of the common fly. The communicators were naive because they did not know that the intended audience lacked the ability to decode the message.

Within each culture's shared signs and experiences, each individual has a personal "reality world" shaped by unique experiences and learning. This has been illustrated by the example of a man, woman, and child looking at the same street scene. Each perceives it in a slightly different way, consciously perceiving and understanding totally different details of the whole.[5] The woman might notice new dresses in the windows of a fashion boutique, while the child does not even notice this store but observes the antics of a small dog unseen by the woman. Two people reading the same magazine article glean totally different information. Individual experiences shape attitudes and perceptions and create a diverse and pluralistic society. Economic status, ethnic and religious background, social background, and age group all form tribes within our culture. Different tribes respond to different graphic approaches, and graphic style can even be an important means of tribal identification. Graphic approaches used on a Frank Sinatra recording would be totally inappropriate for the audience for a heavy metal rock recording, and vice versa.

1-6

The graphic signal

An important attempt to develop a theory of graphic design as communication was made by Crawford Dunn, who defined three distinct modes of communicative signals and coined a name for each.[6]

Alphasignal is the hard data or primary facts and figures of a communication. *Alpha* is the first letter of the Greek alphabet; it denotes that which is first or primary. Dunn believes that telephone directory listings, stock market quotations, and computer display data are all pure alphasignal. "Alphasignal, then we may say, carries the objective part of the message, without inflecting, without emphasizing, without editorializing, without reinforcing, without propagandizing, maximizing or minimizing—in short, without rhetoric." [7] Alphasignal is the content of the stated message. In figure **1-7** (top), the word *stop* represents the alphasignal of the traffic sign.

Parasignal designates a mode of signal that travels alongside or at the side of the alphasignal to amplify and support it. On a stop sign, the red color and octagonal shape have become accepted through traditional usage as parasignals that support and enhance the alphasignal. Dunn points to the elegant script type and fine engraved printing used on wedding invitations as an example of parasignal, noting that alphasignal alone could be conveyed by typewriter output reproduced by a fast, inexpensive printing service.

Infrasignal is information underlying or beneath the message that can betray the sender. Dunn uses an excuse note forged by a schoolboy who played hooky to define this term. "With effort, he negotiates the alphasignal of the correctly spelled words and—almost—manages the parasignal of his penmanship. A certain unmistakably puerile quality in his handwriting informs the teacher that the note

1-7

is counterfeit." [8] If a planned community installed traffic signs as shown in figure **1-7** (bottom), motorists would know that they were not "official" traffic signs erected by the highway department and might even ignore them. The color is appropriate parasignal; however, the heart shape and script letterforms convey an entirely different meaning. Infrasignal should not be confused with noise, Dunn cautions, for noise is an environmental element or systemic defect that occurs after the message has left the sender and interferes with clear communication between the sender and receiver. Infrasignal is a mode of the signal that is conveyed by the sender along with the alphasignal and parasignal.

Dunn's theory is one useful approach to analyzing and understanding the complexity of graphic forms. Another approach is the philosophy of semiotics,[9] which is a general theory of signs and sign-using behavior.

Signs and their use

A *sign* is a mark or language unit that stands for or denotes another thing. The plus sign for addition, the letter *A* for a specific spoken sound, the word *apple,* and a simple pictograph of an apple are all signs. A sign and its object have a simple connection. They form a pair, bonded by a direct one-to-one relationship. A three-way relationship exists between the signified, the signifier, and the interpreter. The *signified* is the thing that is represented (an apple). The *signifier* is the sign that represents it (the word *apple* or a pictograph of an apple). The *interpreter* is the person who perceives and interprets the sign.

The interpretation of a sign is impacted by the context in which it is used, its relationships to other signs, and its environment. This is demonstrated by three uses of the same red circle. It is the sign of Japan: the country, the people, and their culture are all signified by this simple sign (fig. **1-8**).

In South Carolina, where a state law prevents liquor stores from erecting signs announcing their products, such stores are identified by large red circles or dots painted on the buildings (fig. **1-9**).

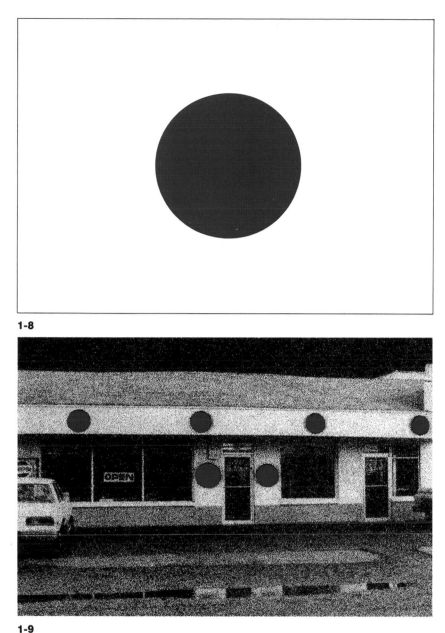

1-8

After Prohibition ended in 1933, a woman in Charleston, South Carolina, was opening a liquor store and hired a painter to paint the building white. After he finished, they were looking at the freshly painted store. The woman stated that she thought it was ridiculous that the state would not allow her to erect a sign and wondered aloud if she could do anything to identify her business. At that moment, the painter lit a cigarette, looked at the red circle on his Lucky Strike package, and suggested that he could paint a big red circle on the building. Soon other stores copied this practice, and a symbolic convention was established. This episode reveals several truths about visual signs. They are often arbitrary, having their meaning assigned by a deliberate decision. Signs can convey their message to only those individuals who have learned the sign or the sign system. A person from the Orient visiting South Carolina might presume that the liquor store was a Japanese facility if he or she had not yet learned that big red circles signified the sale of alcoholic beverages there.

The ability of words to direct the viewer toward the appropriate meaning of a sign or visual form is demonstrated by figure **1-10,** designed by the Russian constructivist El Lissitzky to illustrate a poem by Vladimir Mayakovsky. In this poem, entitled "An Extraordinary Adventure which Befell Vladimir Mayakovsky in a Summer Cottage," the sun visits a desolate Mayakovsky in his cottage for tea and conversation one hot July afternoon. The large red circle signifies the visiting luminary. This layout is from the 1923 book *For the Voice,* noted for Lissitzky's ground-breaking use of elementary geometric elements as illustrations. He assigned them meanings that expressed the subjects of Mayakovsky's poems.

1-9

1-10

Signs can be categorized by types, and one philosopher developed a complex system of sixty-six classes. Signs used in graphic communications normally fall within four basic categories.

An *icon* resembles the thing it represents. A pictorial representation, a photograph, an architect's model of a building, or a star chart are all icons, because they imitate or copy aspects of their subject. Figure **1-11** is an icon representing a bird.

An *index* has a factual or causal connection that points toward its object. Wet streets are a sign that it has rained recently. Smoke signifies a fire. Figure **1-12** is an icon of a nest, but it is also an index signifying bird, because the viewer thinks of a bird upon seeing this image.

A *symbol* has an arbitrary relationship between the signifier and the thing signified. The interpreter understands the symbol through previous knowledge and experience. Spoken or written words are symbols. In figure **1-13,** the word *bird* functions as a symbol. Its designation is arbitrary, for there is no reason for this word to represent a bird instead of a vegetable or a fruit.

A *metasymbol* is a symbol whose meaning transcends the tangible realm of simple one-to-one relationships. History, culture, and tradition all play a role in creating metasymbols, such as the dove with an olive branch as a symbol for peace (fig. **1-14**). For certain audiences, religious and magical signs and symbols take on these properties. The Christian cross and the Hindu mandala are graphic signals possessing this transcendental quality for followers of these religions.

The interpreter brings this expanded meaning to the symbol, as is dramatically demonstrated by the swastika (fig. **1-15**). This symbol has been found in ancient Europe, Asia, and America. In the ancient world it was called *crux gammata* because it is made up of four gammas, the third letter of the Greek alphabet. It is believed to have been a mystic symbol for the sun or fire and, by extension, life. During the early Christian era, it was marked on many tombs as a camouflaged version of the Christian cross. This form was chosen by the Nazi Party in Germany as its official insignia in 1935 under the mistaken belief that it was an ancient Nordic symbol. The swastika's symbolic meaning is now locked into a signification of Nazi Germany, Adolf Hitler, and the Holocaust.

1-11

1-12

1-13

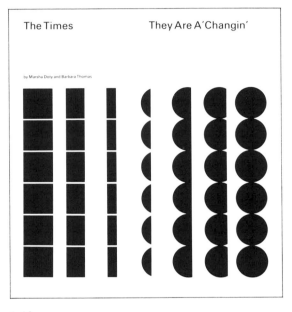

The Times   They Are A'Changin'

by Marsha Doty and Barbara Thomas

1-16

Graphic designers use signs and symbols as powerful vehicles for communication. Elemental forms can be combined to signify content. To illustrate the title of the article "The Times They Are A'Changin'," Dietmar Winkler used a sequence of squares that contract, followed by semicircles that grow into full circles (fig. **1-16**) to give visual form to a concept—change over a period of time.

A letterform, the sign for a speech sound, can be adopted by a graphic designer to signify something else. Lorraine Louie designated the letter *Q* as a sign for a magazine of new American writing, *The Quarterly* (fig. **1-17**). The size, style, and position of the letterform are a constant, but its color, the other forms, and the numeral designating the issue number change with each issue. Readers of this periodical learn this designation rather quickly.

1-15

THE QUARTERLY

SPRING 1987

Q.1

THE MAGAZINE OF NEW

AMERICAN WRITING

$6.95/394-74697-X

Elemental signs can present messages with immediacy and impact. In a folder informing Holiday Inns, Inc., employees that their contributions to higher education would be matched by their employer (fig. **1-18**), Jacklin Pinsler used a pictographic apple, which is a culturally conditioned sign for education ("An apple for the teacher . . ."), with an equal sign on the cover. The equal sign points toward the interior of the folder to prompt the reader to open it and discover that one apple equals two apples. This provocative equation inspires one to read further and learn about the process for multiplying contributions.

Color can carry strong symbolic connotations. Enormous flexibility exists in the meaning of colors. Depending on its context and relationships with other signs, symbols, and images, the color red can connote love, anger, blood, revolution, danger, or Santa Claus. In figure **1-18**, it serves two functions. The red reinforces the signification of apples, and its striking contrast to the black background and white torn-edge contour creates strong visual impact.

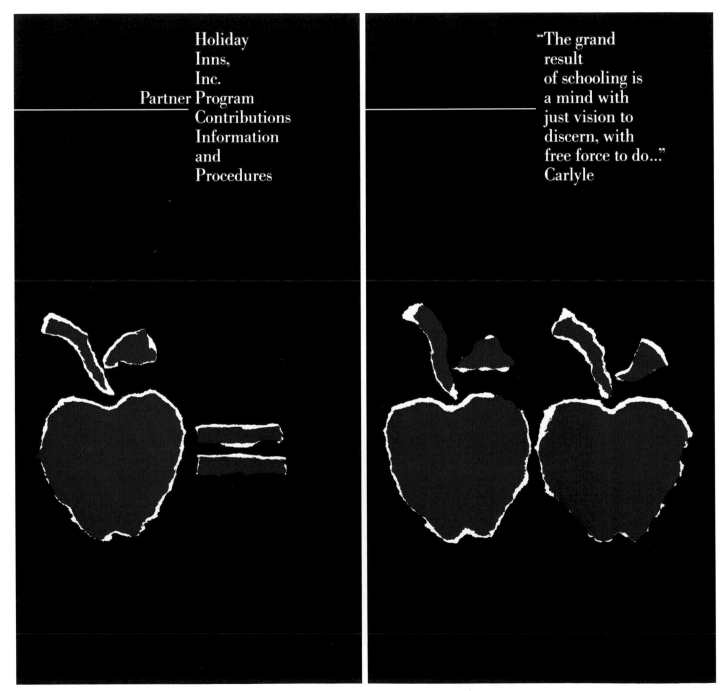

1-18

Lou Dorfsman exploits the fact that an *X* can play the dual roles of a letter in the word *exhilarate* and a symbol for a football player in a diagram to make a powerful graphic statement about football on television (fig. **1-19**).

In the trademark for Ace Chainlink Fence (fig. **1-20**), Joseph Michael Essex drew the letter *A* with lines that resemble wire and linked them together to signify wire fencing.

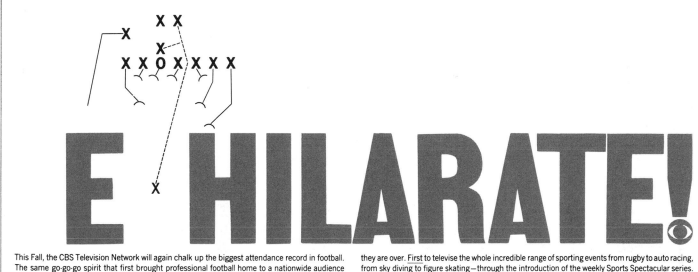

This Fall, the CBS Television Network will again chalk up the biggest attendance record in football. The same go-go-go spirit that first brought professional football home to a nationwide audience (the late National Football League Commissioner Bert Bell attributed the game's phenomenal rise to this network's pioneering coverage) is also responsible for many other CBS Television Network sports firsts. First to give the nation a front row seat at international competitions through exclusive coverage of the 1960 Winter and Summer Olympics. First to use video tape in sports, making it possible to rerun thoroughbred races, crucial golf rounds and scoring football plays as soon as they are over. First to televise the whole incredible range of sporting events from rugby to auto racing, from sky diving to figure skating—through the introduction of the weekly Sports Spectacular series. And throughout the year, this network continues to bring a hundred million television fans such major events of every season as the college bowl games, the Triple Crown, the UN Handicap, the PGA and Masters golf tournaments, and baseball's Major League Games of the Week. Sports play an exhilarating, exciting part in the powerful CBS Television Network line-up, which again this season has the balance, depth and quality to **DOMINATE**

1-19

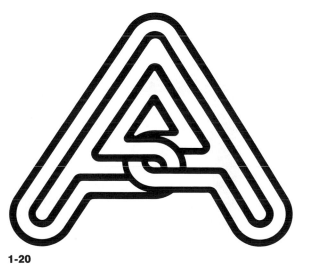

1-20

MATT

M U L L I C A N :

o▼o▼o   Banners, Monuments, and the City

an exhibition of work for public spaces

Signs combine and acquire emblematic properties in William Longhauser's exhibition announcement (fig. **1-21**) for artist Matt Mullican, whose banners and monuments have elemental images such as targets. Mullican's initials and a form from his work are used to create a strong black-and-white configuration. Making one *M* the white of the ground, and the other *M* the black of the target enabled Longhauser to build this image with visual contrasts of positive and negative shapes: white to black, open to closed, and incomplete to complete.

An icon (a pictographic representation of the sun and its radiant energy) and a symbol (the word *sun*) are combined in the trademark designed by Kenneth Love and Richard Felton (fig. **1-22**) for the Sun Company, Inc.

The reader knows immediately that Nat Hentoff's memoir entitled *Boston Boy* (fig. **1-23**) tells about the experience of growing up Jewish in Boston. Designer Janet Odgis combined a symbol (the word *Boy*) and a metasymbol (the Star of David) in such a way that the bookstore browser grasps the context of this book immediately. The symbol becomes the counterform or negative space in the letter *O*.

For the Summit Consulting Group trademark (fig. **1-24**), Frank Armstrong synthesized the initial letter with a triangle, which becomes an icon for the summit of a mountain.

For a public television station's annual fund-raising auction, Dietmar Winkler drew upon the symbolic vocabulary for a motivating concept. The viewer may be very lucky, for sensible bidding may bring a bargain. This concept was accomplished by superimposing the numeral 2—the station's channel number—over a four-leaf clover, which is a traditional symbol for good luck (fig. **1-25**). These diverse examples show the potency of graphic signs and symbols when they are used inventively by designers to construct immediate and direct messages.

1-22

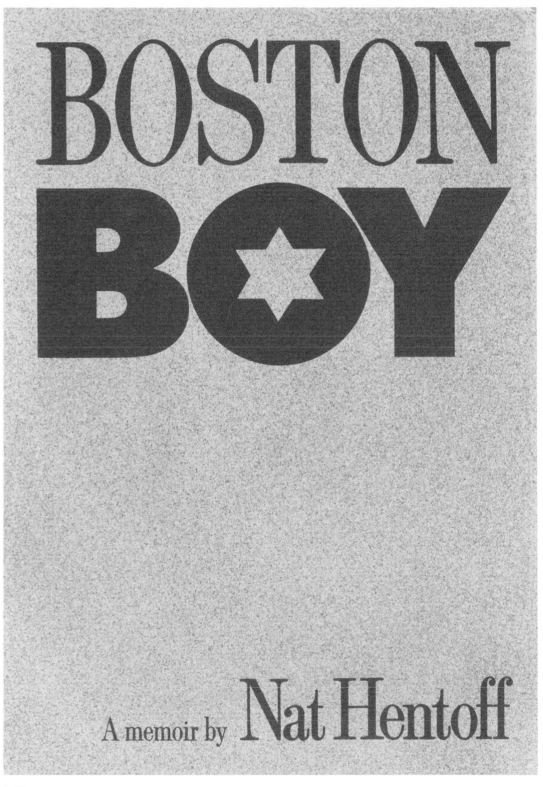

1-23

1-24

1-25

Denotation and connotation

Denotation is the direct meaning of a word, sign, or image. *Connotation,* a second level of meaning, is conveyed or suggested in addition to the denotation. The words *politician* and *statesman* both denote an elected or appointed person who is actively involved in governmental affairs; however, the connotation of each word is very different. *Politician* connotes a person interested in personal gain who promotes narrow interests, and *statesman* connotes an individual who is concerned about the long-term interests of all citizens.

Images also carry powerful connotations. Figures **1-26** and **1-27** are both advertisements with rather straightforward presentations. A headline is centered above a closely cropped portrait photograph denoting men of similar age. Each rests his chin on his fist and looks straight at the viewer. The connotations of each photograph are vastly different.

In figure **1-26** every visual aspect of the photograph connotes a steady, reliable individual worthy of trust as a financial advisor. The man is clean-shaven, and his hair is neatly cut and groomed. He is wearing a conservative business suit and holding a pair of horn-rimmed glasses. The clear, open lighting suggests a brightly illuminated business office.

"I want to be your quarterback."

John Ebey
Merrill Lynch Financial Consultant

"My clients get more than the benefit of my knowledge. They get the knowledge and skill of a whole team of specialists.

"My role is to pull it all together, to fully understand your needs and help you choose the right investment strategy.

"We'll start by looking at your long range goals and deciding what degree of risk is appropriate. Then we'll see where you stand on the basic financial needs—asset management, credit management, insurance, and tax minimization."

John can put the right strategies into action for you because he has all the resources of Merrill Lynch on his side.

Put a professional Financial Consultant like John Ebey, plus all of Merrill Lynch, to work for you. Call 1 800-637-7455, Ext. 9611 for your local Merrill Lynch office.

1-26

By contrast, Dennis Manarchy's photograph (fig. **1-27**), art directed by Chris Baker, connotes a free-spirited rock-and-roll fan. The man is unshaven, and his hair looks shaggy and uncombed. He is wearing a towel around his neck, signifying an interest in physical fitness. The dark, mysterious lighting hides and obscures his face.

These connotations did not occur by accident. The art director and photographer for each of these advertisements chose all of these aspects as deliberately as a newspaper reporter selects either *politician* or *statesman* to describe the subject of an article.

Images convey both a perceptual message and a cultural message. The response to these two advertisements by a fifty-year-old person planning a retirement program who dislikes rock music and by a teenager or young adult who is an avid rock fan will be totally different. When confronted with an image of former president Richard Nixon (see figs. **1-36** to **1-38**), the viewer perceives an image denoting Nixon's physical appearance. Also, the image prompts a conditioned response. Some people feel that he was hounded from office; others believe that he should have been impeached. The viewer's attitudes and opinions about Mr. Nixon, the only president to resign from office, are inescapably bound to the image.

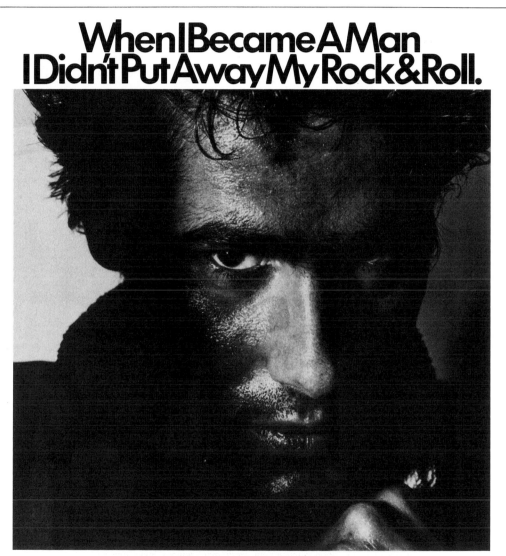

Ein Frag an eynen Müntzer/wahin doch souil Geltz
kumme das man alltag müntzet: Antwort des selben Müntzers/Von dreyen
Feinden vnnsers Geltz/wa wir nit acht darauff haben/werden wir den Seckel zum Gelt an.

Wann wir hetten rechten glauben   Recht Elen/darzü maß vnd gwicht   Einerlay Müntz vnd kain falsch Gelt
Gott vnd gemainen nutz vor augen   Güt frid vñ auch gleich Recht vñ Ghricht   So stünd es wol in aller welt.

Frag an den Müntzer.

Sag lieber Müntzer bistu frumm
Wa mainst das souil gelts hinkum
Daran Teütsch land groß mangel hat
Vnd ir doch müntzet frü vnd spat
Nun ist ye Silbers nicht vil dran
Das man müg gwin am schmeltzen han
Auch wil yetz kainr so hauslich werden
Das er groß schetze grab in die erden
Noch ist kain gelt klagt all welt sehr
Das wundert mich vnd manchen mehr

Antwort des müntzers

Täglich hör ich diß frag vnd klag
Ligt doch die antwort hell am tag
Wañ wir weren sunst als plind
Vnd sehen vnsere gelts drey find
Den Babst/New sitten/frembde wahr
Die vnser land erschöpffen gar
Doch hat der Römisch gwerb ein end
Wa wir wir Teütschen selber wend
Vom anndern so wir nit wölln lon
Werden wirs gelt vmm seckel on

Der Erste Feindt.

Der Babst kan vns gantz höflich satz
Mit Bullen/Abblaß/Dispensatzen
Vmb böß war gut gelt er nimpt
Wie aim geschwinden kauffman zimpt

Auch seind im bstimpt vil groß Annaten
Gend im teütsch Bischoff vnd Prelaten
Welchs alles trifft ein grosse Summ
Ich kans nit glauben ist er frumm
So er gele fordert bey der schwer
Vmb dingt das sunst wol zimlich wer
Noch es jm alle vmbe gelt ist fail
Gnad/Pfründen vnd das ewig hail
Wer mer gibt hat den pessern tail
Er müss ye nit Stadhalter sein
Des ne ren Gots der milch vnd wein
On gold vnd silber diet zukauffen
Baist vns zum gnaden prunnen lauffen
Begert nichts darum dañ dackbars hertz
Er hat selbe tragen vnsern schmertz
Sein plüt vnd rodt zalt vnser schuld
Durch in allain kumpts Vatters huld
Doch wolt der Babst das gelt drum han
Des hat jms glimpfft schier yederman
Glaub mir/Rom het vns gar auß gsogé
Den seckel mit dem gelt entzogen
Het nit der trew Gott gsehen drein
Seine worts vns geben helen schein
In welchem doch gantz klärlich stat
Nit durch die Römisch gulden Port
Sunder Christum den gnaden hort
Drumb hats Babsts grempel yetz ein ent
Wa ich wir Teütschen selber went

Der Annder Feindt.

Den andern Feint nun auch verstand
Ich main den Kauffman der on rü
Frembd vnnütz war vns füret zü
Die vnserm leib so nodt auch thüt
Wies Babsts kram kumpt der sel zügut
Sonder zu lust vnd hoffart raiche
Damit vns teütsch narren laicht
Mancherlay grwürtz vnd welschen wein
Seyden Sammet/sonst rücher fein
Pierredt von rotem scharlach gmache
Darnach ein yeder parr yetz tracht
Der Eltern sitt ist gar veracht
Die vns mit trewen gsparet hond
Das wir so schandelich yetz verthond
Raum ainr Kündsch rock vnd hosen hat
O wie wol stünds/do in ainr stat
Der paurßman trüg ein zwilche Jupp
Für gwürtz war zwibel auff die supp
Lebt rauch/tranck pieren most vñ wasser
Was nit wie yetz ein voller prasser
Satze auff von starcken Filz ein hüt
Was jm für windt vnd kelte güt
Der handwercks man thet jm auch recht
Mit gwand vnd narung was er schlecht
Von lande süch nache der Bürger klaid
Vnd hielt man güten vnterschaid

Der Dritt Feindt.

Yetz kum ich an den dritten finde
New sitten der on zal vil sind
Damit man treibt ein schentlich preng
Yetz kurtz dañ lang/yetz weit dañ eng
Yetz ist es prait/dañ macht mans schmal
Da ist kain maß jnn überal
Was einem yetz an ermeln hangt
Het etwan zü ein rock gelangt
Yetz lest mans gantz/dañ ists zerschnitten
Alweg bringt man ein andern sitten
Vnd müg das heütig morn veralten
Wie möchten wir dañ parschafft bhalten
Wir tragen yetz die welschen schlappen
Seltzam Paret vnd Spannisch kappen
Wo kompt doch einr her über mer
Der vns nit gleich sein sitten lehr
So wol sind wir des wanckeln müts
Warlich ich sorg es bring nit güts
Got werd vns fürn in dise lande
Völcker der wir yetz tragen gwande
Vnd vnser übel grausam straffen
Sein zorn wirdt ye nit alweg schlaffen
Hochfart/Kriegen/füssen/schweren
Mag sich kains wegs ind harr erweren
Vnd dunckt mich es sey an der zeyt
Got wöll ich wäne/es sey noch weyt.

Wolffgang Rösch Formschneyder.

Typography

Our civilization is based on the alphabet and numerals. These elementary marks have no semantic meaning but have been assigned roles as visual substitutes for speech sounds and arithmetic quantities. These simple signs have enabled people to build elaborate philosophies, sciences, and literatures, store this hard-won knowledge as writing or typography, and transcend time and place.

Traditionally, the word *typography* meant the technical process of printing writing through the use of metal types with raised letterforms that could be inked and printed in a process not unlike a rubber stamp. In our electronic age, typography encompasses the transmission and communication of alphabetical and numerical information through a variety of means, including printing, video transmission, computer display, and electric signs. (In this book, a broad definition encompassing alphanumeric communications from gestured crayon writing to neon signs is used.)

In discussing architecture, Ludwig Mies van der Rohe observed that "God is in the details." The same is true of typography, an exact art of measurement and proportion, message and form. Typography involves complex visual relationships of scale and space. Letters become words, which combine to form sentences, paragraphs, and columns. Subtle spatial relationships are critical to legibility and readability.

The designer structures typographic information by giving the units assigned roles, and the reader approaches typography with an intuitive understanding of these functions. This developed early in the history of printing, and major typographic roles can be found in the circa 1530 German broadside proclaiming an indulgence (fig. **1-28**). Typographic units perform the following functions on this early broadside:

The *headline* or *title* is the most significant type in a page's hierarchy of information. Dominant size and position immediately cue the reader that this is primary information, the entry point for the page or article. Research indicates that for every ten people who read the headline in a printed communication, only two read the text.

A *subtitle* is distinguished from a title by smaller type size or weight, indicating secondary information that clarifies or elaborates its headline or title.

Picture captions are the titles, explanations, or descriptions of images. Proximity to the image and type size should unmistakably announce its function. Research has shown that picture captions have from two to four times the readership of the text, making their importance even greater than the traditional role.

Text (also *running text* or *body copy*) is usually the longest unit of typographic material on the printed page and the major source of written information. People who read the body copy are either seriously interested in the subject or prompted by the image or title to seek additional information.

A *heading* is a type unit placed within the text and distinguished from it by contrast of size, weight, or spatial interval. Headings divide text into sections by content. They can break up the gray mass of text, make the text less overwhelming to the reader, and increase readership.

The *signature* identifies a person or organization that wrote or published the material. In our culture we read from left to right and top to bottom; therefore, the logical location for a signature is the terminal point, the lower right-hand corner. This broadside is somewhat unusual because it bears a signature in that location: *Wolffgang Kosch, Woodblock cutter.*

The modern continuation of the role-assignment tradition in typography is demonstrated in the recipe section of a recent book, *Vegetables*, art directed by Kit Hinrichs (fig. **1-29**). The typographic system in the recipe chapter has eleven distinct roles. It has a section title and a brief introductory paragraph in large type that almost functions as a subtitle. In each recipe column, clearly separated from its neighbors by ruled lines, are: the recipe title; a medallion identifying the recipe's ethnic origin and a numeral signifying the number of servings; a small italic notation of the serving yield; the ingredients list; a drop initial; directions; footnotes; and a page number, called a *folio.* The size, style, and color of the units were carefully selected by Hinrichs to create a clear optical separation. The consistency of these elements enables the reader to comprehend quickly the order that the designer has imposed upon the page.

Drop initials are large initial letters dropped into the text. They have been shown to increase readership because they form a focal point at the start of the text to catch the reader's eye and lead it into the copy.

The heritage of typography has an underlying geometric structure. The ancient Greeks based their alphabet on elemental structures of the square, circle, and triangle and established two horizontal guidelines to propel the information forward with rhythmic order. The advent of typographic printing, with metal type locked into an iron chase, further reinforced a horizontal and vertical emphasis. In the twentieth century, the new visual languages of the modern art movements have combined with advanced technology to shatter the limitations of type size and the exclusive reliance upon a horizontal-vertical orientation. ✳ Typography's dual lives as language communication and visual form are not simultaneous. Readers are conscious of type as message and virtually ignore the visual properties. However, the visual properties establish resonance and can invite or repel potential readers. The visual nature of typography is extraordinary for it can combine the time-space sequence and rhythm of music, the linear structure of language, and the dynamic space of painting.

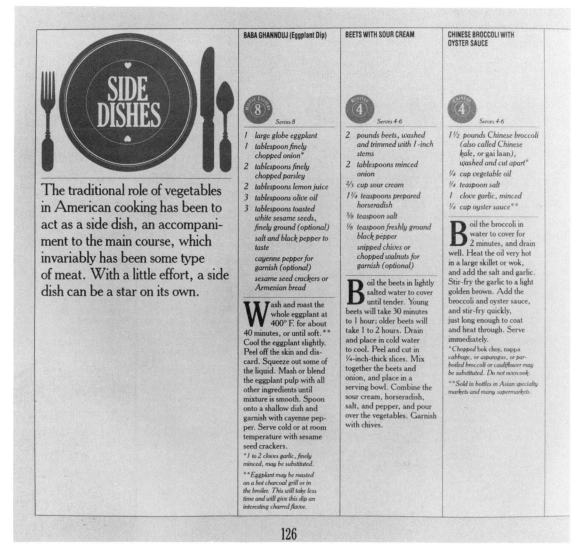

1-29

1-30

1-31

1-32

1-33

1-34

1-35

Images

Images are pictures of all kinds, ranging from simple pictographs to illustrations and photographs. In the earliest printed books, images were simple linear woodcuts printed in black ink along with the type (see fig. **1-28**). Contemporary image making spans a vast range of possibilities including all of the techniques of drawing; painting and illustration; photography, which can now be manipulated and combined through digital editing; and computer-generated imagery. Images can be a substitute reality, an artificial reality, or a new reality. An illustration of Buddha, Mohammed, or Christ demonstrates the power of images as substitution. Images of some religious leaders do not survive from their time: the illustrator's conception becomes a substitute for a lost reality. Followers of these religions project spiritual significance upon these images. Fashion advertising photography presents an artificial reality: the makeup artist, the hair stylist, the photographer with his sophisticated camera and lighting techniques, and the retoucher all conspire to transcend normal human appearance and provide an idealized beauty that does not exist in life.

From the simplest pictograph to realistic illustrations, drawn images are based on a visual syntax. This is the orderly and consistent arrangement of the individual parts (dots, lines, tones, shapes, edges) to give the image cohesiveness. Figures **1-30** to **1-35** demonstrate some of the imaging possibilities from simple notation to full tonal or color representation.

Notation (fig. **1-30**) is linear, reductive, and characterized by economy and brevity. It is the simplest level of image making, for the essence of the subject is captured by minimal graphic means.

A *pictograph* (fig. **1-31**) achieves its presence through the mass and weight of shape. The primary forms of the subject are reduced to elemental geometry, which becomes universal rather than specific.

The *silhouette* (fig. **1-32**) differs from the pictograph because it presents the specific shape of a subject instead of a universal prototype.

A *contour drawing* (fig. **1-33**), like notation, is a linear and conceptual image because imaginary outlines trace the edges or boundaries of forms in space.

Line as tone (fig. **1-34**) depends on the ability of the human brain to construct a gestalt from fragmented data. Black-and-white linear patterning is interpreted as the seamless tone of the image.

Representation (fig. **1-35**), whether tonal or in full color, attempts to replicate the natural appearance of the subject in specific light conditions.

The graphic means used to present an image and its information level become important components of the communication. Although all of these images denote a bird, each one does so in a very different way and becomes a very different communication. The potential for graphic interpretation of any subject is infinite, limited only by the imaginative powers of artists.

In figures **1-30** through **1-35** the level of perceptual information changed, but in figures **1-36** to **1-38** a different type of change in the information level occurs. The illustrator has altered the images to change the connotation. This sequence illustrates the psychological changes in Richard Nixon from the time that he won reelection, to the unraveling of the Watergate wiretapping and burglary, to the Congressional move toward impeachment.

1-36

1-37

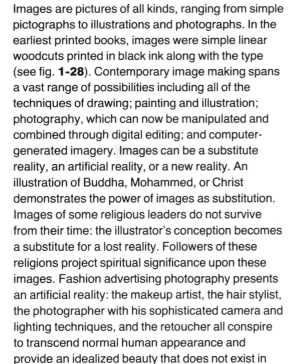

1-38

The persuasive power of photography is based on our preconception that the photograph is a powerful vehicle for denotation: a record of reality that is recorded by a machine. Early photography with its long time exposures and resulting frozen subjects—as well as the photographs on contemporary drivers' licenses—are brute denotation. The century-and-a-half history of photography can be interpreted as the evolution of connotative and aesthetic concerns, which are often related. As figures **1-26** and **1-27** revealed, photography has tremendous connotative power.

Each photograph can reveal its subject as only a single frozen image, and yet each subject contains an unlimited number of potential images for photography.[10] The photographer's selection of viewpoint, lighting, distance, lens, depth of field, type of film, and other aspects combine to form the specific connotative qualities of the image.

Little is known about how we "read" a photograph. Our ability to perceive and understand the world around us is projected onto the photographic image. We see the flat tones or colors of the photograph as translations from the physical world. In a black-and-white photograph taken on the porch of a weathered beach cottage (fig. **1-39**), the contour edge separating the light tone of the sky from the darker band of gray beneath it allows us to interpret this gray plane as a sand dune, and we comprehend the presence of a vast atmospheric space between the porch and the sky. Our reading of this image is spontaneous and automatic, yet the reality of the photograph is a series of flat gray tones and textures. Individuals in primitive tribes have been shown black-and-white photographs, and they could not see the image. They merely perceived a flat sheet of paper with modulated gray tones on it.

1-39

Image transformation

Graphic designers imbue images with expressive and communicative power by altering, exaggerating, and combining them to create a new conceptual reality. The computerized capability of electronic editing, retouching, and combining of images enables contemporary designers to transform images in ways undreamed of in the past.

Image alteration. In a poster for a hospital's culinary workshop (fig. **1-40**), designed by Tom Poth and illustrated by Larry McIntire, a traditional Swiss army knife is altered by replacing the blades with kitchen utensils. The multiple blades connote usefulness, and this concept is transferred to the workshop by association.

Image exaggeration. The American Library Association commissioned illustrator Charles B. Falls to design the poster "Books Wanted for Our Men" (fig. **1-41**) during World War I. Falls emphasized this need and increased the graphic impact of his poster by exaggerating the size of the individual books and the height of the stack carried by the soldier. This exaggeration proved successful, for the campaign to solicit book donations met its objectives.

Image combination. When images are combined, their content becomes additive. To express the theme "Britain Then and Now" (fig. **1-42**), Sibley/Peteet Design combined a traditional portrait of a British monarch—a linear engraving comprised of subtle complex detail—signifying *then,* with a brightly colored, contemporary, flat-shape portrait signifying *now.* The combined image carries concepts of old and new, past and present, then and now.

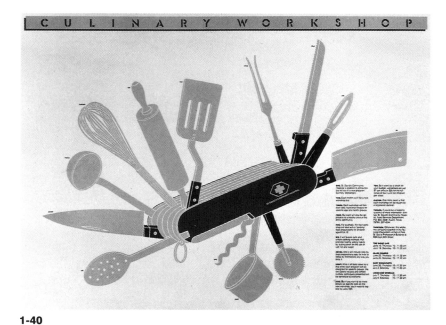

1-40

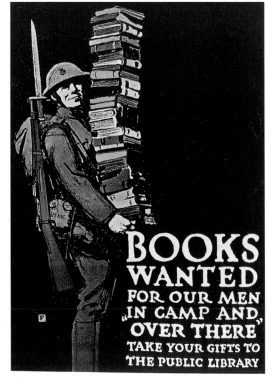

1-41

24

Photomontage. This technique of combining photographic images to invent a new configuration was pioneered by the Berlin Dadaists as early as 1918. It enables designers to express complex ideas in a rapid manner. To signify a lecture entitled "The Engineers' Aesthetic and Architecture," David Colley created a montage from two images that denote architecture (fig. **1-43**). The Greek Ionic capital connotes the aesthetic element, and the geometric grid pattern of the high-rise windows of Mies van der Rohe's Lake Shore Drive apartment buildings signifies engineering.

In publicity for a play entitled *The Gingham Dog* that refers to the civil rights movement and Dr. Martin Luther King, Jr. (fig. **1-44**), Colley juxtaposed period news photographs in a compelling montage. The portrait of Thomas Jefferson, placed on its side to signify that things are out of kilter, is a powerful addendum.

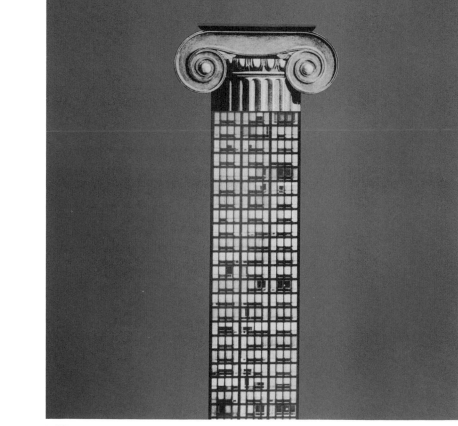

1-43

The Gingham Dog

a production of the play by Lanford Wilson
directed by Kathy Juhl

February 3, 6, 9, and 10 at 8:00 pm 1983
February 4, 5, 11, and 12 at 7:00 and 9:30 pm

the Station Theatre is at 223 North Broadway, Urbana

tickets 4.00 at Record Service in Champaign
or at the door on nights of performance
telephone 384-4000 for reservations

a production of the Celebration Company
at the Station Theatre in Urbana, Illinois

partial production assistance furnished
by the Illinois Arts Council

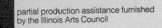

1-44

In a calendar page designed by Jeff Barnes and photographed by Christopher Hawker for Kieffer-Nolde, Inc., montage is used to create jolting scale changes that transform a small Lifesaver candy into a huge life buoy (fig. **1-45**). This image was produced on a Scitex electronic image processor, which permits electronic retouching, combining, and altering of images. A laser scanner tracked across the original photographs, converting them into digital data. A powerful computer was used to resize, edit, and combine these images, which had been converted from photographs to computer graphics. In both still photography and video, advanced capabilities for image alteration are rapidly destroying our traditional faith in the photographic image as absolute truth. In the near future, photography may lose its validity as legal evidence. Deprived of its legitimacy as true fact, its claim to greater truth than illustration and painting will be destroyed.

Art Direction & Design Jeff Barnes, BEO   Photography Christopher Hawker   © 1986 Christopher Hawker

Kieffer-Nolde, Inc.
Offset & Gravure
Graphics
160 East Illinois
Chicago, IL 60611
312-337-5500
Toll Free
1-800-621-8314
In Cleveland
216-344-9170
In New York
212-956-2420
Call or write.
Find out how this
was produced.

	S	S	M	T	W	T	F	S	S	M	T	W	T	F	S	S	M	T	W	T	F	S	S	M	T	W
Nov	1	2	3	4	5	6	7	8	9	10	11	12	13	14	15	16	17	18	19	20	21	22	23	24	25	26
Dec			1	2	3	4	5	6	7	8	9	10	11	12	13	14	15	16	17	18	19	20	21	22	23	24

27	28	29	30	
25	26	27	28	29	30	31

1-45

Camera angle and viewpoint. Ordinary images can be transformed and presented to the viewer in a new way when the designer or photographer sees them in a new way. In a folder for Container Corporation of America providing information about composite cans (fig. **1-46**), Jeff Barnes used wide-angle photography of two cans seemingly balanced on their bottom rims. This arresting and original treatment made conventional objects interesting.

In another fresh and original approach to objects, Jeff Barnes commissioned Dennis Manarchy to photograph furniture tilted onto the floor (fig. **1-47**). When Barnes used these photographs in an advertising campaign for Interna Designs, he aligned the vertical axis of the objects with the vertical edge of the page, which gave the rectangular photographs a diagonal orientation to the page. The reader is arrested by the unexpected nature of these photographs and is challenged to decode the unusual properties.

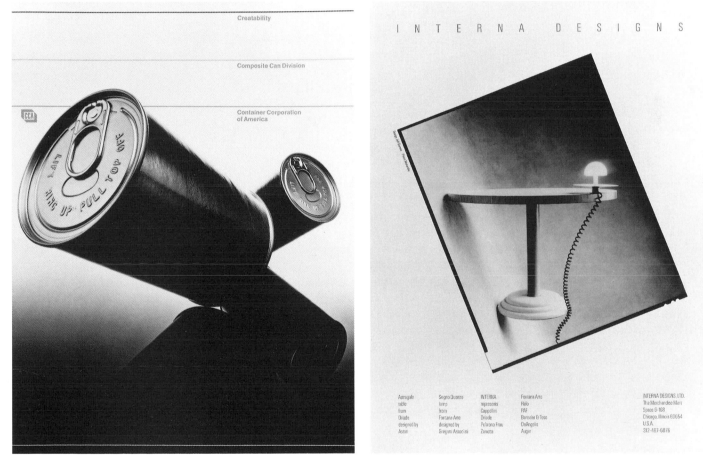

1-46

1-47

Cropping. Cutting off or removing unwanted parts of an image can greatly enhance the effectiveness of routine images. In a simple one-color announcement for a free weekly concert series (fig. **1-48**), Dietmar Winkler took an ordinary photograph of a flutist, converted it to a high-contrast image, and then rotated it so that the viewer appears to be hovering over her shoulder. This unique vantage point combines with the pattern of shapes to transform the ordinary into a more provocative experience for the viewer.

The dynamic effect of cropping upon an image is evidenced by figure **1-49**. In the top version, the racing horse is centered in the rectangle, which creates a static configuration. In the bottom rectangle, the horse is thrusting into the space. This unbalanced composition, combined with the area of open space in front of the horse, more effectively signifies energy and movement.

Noon Hour Concerts
Every Thursday
at 12:10 MIT Chapel
Free Admission

Lute, Recorders
Flute, Bassoon
Harpsichord, Organ
Oboe, Singers
Chamber Chorus

1-48

1-49

1-50

Graphic support elements

Unlike type and images, graphic support elements
are visual materials that do not carry specific
messages but can make a major contribution to the
effectiveness of a design. These elements include
ruled lines, borders, ornaments, patterns, colors,
shapes, and backgrounds. They can structure
space and guide the reader's eye through the
design. Often they play an important role in creating
resonance. The possibilities are limited only by the
imagination of the designer. In a folder for soprano
Joan Heller (fig. **1-50**), Frank Armstrong used rules
and bars to play several important roles: organizing
the typography, structuring and balancing the
space, and creating lively musical rhythms that are
expressive of the content.

1-52

G
GI
GIA
IAC
ACO
COM
OME
MET
ETT
TTI
II

Language as a model for graphic design

A language is a systematic means of communicating ideas or feelings through signs (sounds, visual gestures, or marks) having understood meaning. Our language is our principal communications system, and its grammar and rhetoric are the primary model for other forms of communication, including fine art and hybrid forms that combine pictorial and verbal information: film, video, computer graphics, and graphic design. Graphic design gains richness from the combination of multiple language and optical forms—words, pictures, signs, and colors—into complex communications.

The art of rhetoric, as developed by the ancient Greeks, was a study of principles and rules for preparing and delivering speeches that were effective communication and persuasion. Although many of its ideas have limited application to modern graphic design, its classification of the figures of speech from everyday language and literature is useful because visual symbols and images are often used in the same way. In a presentation at the 1975 Icograda conference, Claude Cossette said, "If we define rhetoric as the science of figures of speech capable of convincing by means of an image, one can imagine that makers of functional images would latch on to this art. . . . " [11] Hanno Ehses uses principles of rhetoric to analyze graphic design. He writes: "Broadly defined, rhetoric is the art that deals with the use of spoken or written discourse. Its object is eloquence, which is defined as effective speech. According to Aristotle, its concern is with 'discovering all the available means of persuasion in any given situation' either to inform (rational appeal), to delight and win over (ethical appeal) or to move (emotional appeal) an audience." [12] Designers should not ignore the vocabulary of rhetoric simply because it uses unfamiliar terms and very precise definitions of similar concepts, for rhetoric actually defines many communications techniques used daily by graphic designers to solve problems.

Figures of speech that show a relationship or resemblance are most important and have graphic parallels in visual communications. Perhaps the simplest of these is the *simile,* which is a comparison or parallel between two unlike things. These sentences contain similes: "The grade on the term paper was like a slap in the face"; and "His heart is as hard as a rock." A visual simile was created in an announcement for an exhibition of sculpture by Alberto Giacometti. Dietmar Winkler configured typography (fig. **1-51**) to look like one of Giacometti's sculptures (fig. **1-52**) by replicating the tall, thin, upward movement. Giacometti's name is made to look like one of his sculptures.

A *metaphor* also points out resemblance, but does so by substitution. "A ship moves through the ocean like a plow through the field" is a simile. "The ship plows the sea" is a metaphor. In a book jacket for William Faulkner's *Light in August* (fig. **1-53**) designed by R. D. Scudellari, the shade pull becomes a metaphor for a noose and, by extension, death. This design works on two levels of understanding. The rain-splashed detail of a window in late afternoon creates a pervading resonance and mood, and the nooselike form signifies impending doom.

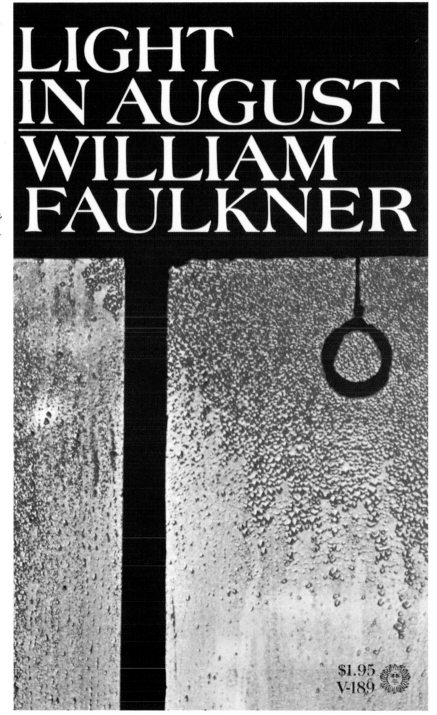

1-53

Personification is the representation of inanimate objects or abstractions by a human image; for example, Cupid signifies love. *Anthropomorphism* is attributing human traits, thoughts, action, and speech to animals or even inanimate objects. John Tenniel's illustration of the White Rabbit from *Alice's Adventures in Wonderland* (fig. **1-54**) demonstrates this concept.

Metonymy is using the name of one thing to stand for another, related thing. When a newscaster states that "the *White House* said today," we know that he means "the president's spokesman said today." The White House is a metonym for the president and his staff. In the poster published by the Twentieth Century Bookstore in Tel Aviv, Israel (fig. **1-55**), headlined "Independence Day," Yehudah Raviv photographed an Israeli flag and a Palestinian flag tied together by a large knot. These intertwined flags become metonyms that stand for the Israelis and the Palestinians, signifying the peaceful coexistence of the two peoples. Daniel J. Walsh of Liberation Graphics observes that May fifteenth is celebrated by the Israelis as their Independence Day, and the Palestinians observe it as the Day of Disaster, the day they lost their land to the Israelis.[13]

1-54

יום העצמאות תשמ"ה

Synecdoche is the use of a part to represent the whole, or vice versa. It achieves a powerful effect in a booklet explaining the movement problems of handicapped people (fig. **1-56**), designed by Frank Armstrong and photographed by Thomas Wedell. A detail of the hands of a person teaching a handicapped person to open a jar represent two people—helper and handicapped—and their relationship.

The essence of a *pun,* observes Eli Kince, is the "phenomena that one symbol can have two or more meanings, or that two or more symbols can have similar or identical images but different meanings." [14] It is the use of words in a way that suggests different meanings or plays upon similar sounds or spellings.

A man approached Dr. Samuel Johnson, the great literary figure of eighteenth-century London, in a restaurant and taunted, "Dr. Johnson, make us a pun!"

Dr. Johnson retorted, "Upon what subject?"

"Er, upon the king!" snapped his challenger.

To gales of laughter from his companions, Dr. Johnson roared, "The king is no subject."

The man walked away believing that Dr. Johnson had failed his challenge, not realizing that Dr. Johnson had only required eight words and two brief sentences to deliver two puns.

Puns can be visual, verbal, or a combination of both. Joseph Michael Essex created a visual pun— a photograph of a child's blocks—in the design of stationery for Ira Block (fig. **1-57**).

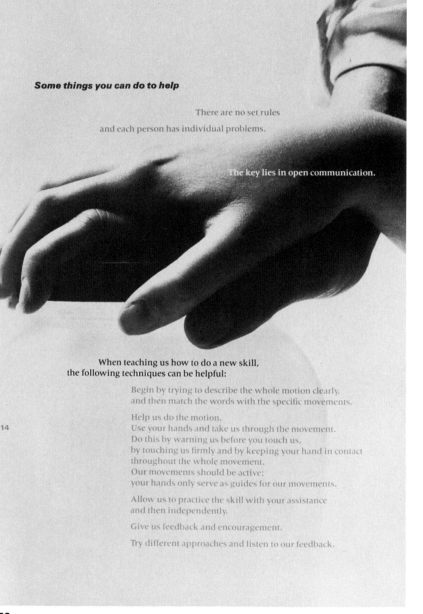

1-56

IRA BLOCK PHOTOGRAPHY, Ltd.   215 West 20th Street   New York, NY 10011   212.242.2728

For those unforgettable evenings...

CHANNEL

N°2

A verbal pun—the similarity between the perfume Chanel No. 5 and the public television station's channel number 2—was used by Chris Pullman to create an arresting advertisement (fig. **1-58**). This is also an example of *parody,* which is a work imitating the style of some other work, often with humorous or satirical intent.

The poster designed by Jim Jacobs Studio for nontraditional productions of classic plays achieves remarkable impact through a visual-verbal pun (fig. **1-59**). Entitled "Uncommon Shakespeare" to express nontraditional productions, the illustration of William Shakespeare is made uncommon by his twentieth-century clothing.

1-59

Lemon.

This Volkswagen missed the boat.

The chrome strip on the glove compartment is blemished and must be replaced. Chances are you wouldn't have noticed it; Inspector Kurt Kroner did.

There are 3,389 men at our Wolfsburg factory with only one job: to inspect Volkswagens at each stage of production. (3000 Volkswagens are produced daily; there are more inspectors than cars.)

Every shock absorber is tested (spot checking won't do), every windshield is scanned. VWs have been rejected for surface scratches barely visible to the eye.

Final inspection is really something! VW inspectors run each car off the line onto the Funktionsprüfstand (car test stand), tote up 189 check points, gun ahead to the automatic brake stand, and say "no" to one VW out of fifty.

This preoccupation with detail means the VW lasts longer and requires less maintenance, by and large, than other cars. (It also means a used VW depreciates less than any other car.)

We pluck the lemons; you get the plums.

1-60

ONE FOR THE ROAD.

Drink and drive, and you may lose something on the way home from the party.

1-61

Hyperbole is exaggeration for the sake of emphasis. Charles B. Falls's poster entitled "Books Wanted for Our Men" (see fig. **1-41**), discussed earlier, achieves hyperbole by exaggerating the image. One soldier would be unlikely to read or carry that many books; however, it emphasizes the need.

The opposite of hyperbole is *litotes,* which is an understatement using a negative as a way to express an affirmative, such as saying "He is not a bad photographer" to mean that he is a good photographer. This can be very effective in visual communications, as evidenced in figure **1-60**. Art director Helmut Krone and writer Julian Koenig described the car with a one-word headline, "Lemon," the most negative thing you can say about an automobile. It implies defective manufacturing. The text explains that this particular vehicle did not pass inspection due to a blemish on the glove compartment chrome strip, so it was not shipped until this minor defect was corrected. A negative understatement becomes the entry point to tout outstanding quality control, inspection, and attention to detail.

Antithesis is the sharp contrast between two opposing ideas or thoughts to intensify their difference. "The revolution promised freedom but brought slavery" is more intense than "The revolution brought slavery." Antithesis, through the sharp contrast between freedom and slavery, increases its emotional fervor. Antithesis is used in a poster directed toward high school students to warn of the hazards of drunk driving (fig. **1-61**). Taking one last drink before departing—"Having one for the road"—contrasts sharply with a photograph depicting the loss of a leg in a traffic accident. Art director Tom Roth and copywriter Steve Trygg created this poster in a national competition sponsored by *Reader's Digest.*

Irony is a deliberate contrast, presenting the opposite of what would be expected. The situation would be ironic, for example, if a fire truck caught fire and burned. For a highly critical *Atlantic* article about American naval strategy, Art Director Judy Garlan commissioned Theo Rudnak to illustrate mighty naval warships as sitting ducks (fig. **1-62**). The cover signifies the irony of naval power that might not be effective in wartime.

An *allegory* is a symbolic representation. A literal device or character is used as a symbol for an idea or principle. The Statue of Liberty is an allegorical figure for freedom. The United States is signified by the allegorical figure, Uncle Sam. In a poster for the Colorado Music Festival (fig. **1-63**), Barry Zaid symbolized the pastoral joy of music by the allegorical figure Pan, ancient Greek god of forests and shepherds who created the first reed pipe, playing music high on an idyllic mountain.

1-62

1-63

Jeremy Campbell observes: "One important property of language is that, while its symbols may be used to bring about physical results in the 'real' world of substance, they need not be used for that purpose. Symbols can be decoupled from physical reality to a greater or lesser extent. Words are not deeds, though they often lead to deeds. Symbols can be manipulated more freely than substance, and they can be manipulated to form new statements and expressions which are only tentative, playful, figurative. Symbols are at liberty to be a little irresponsible and experimental." [15] This potent latitude can be used to entertain and enrich, or it can become deceptive and misleading. As conveyors of information with the power to form and connote it, graphic designers have an ethical responsibility to the audience and should not knowingly create or manipulate signs and symbols to falsely distort truth.

Graphic design is an expressive and creative activity, and each problem has many possible solutions. This chapter has discussed the elements of graphic design: signs, symbols, type, images,

and support elements. Theories about forms and how they communicate, including Crawford Dunn's theory about the modes of graphic signals, the semiotic investigation of signs and their connotations and denotations, and the use of rhetoric to categorize certain types of communicative images are all useful to a deeper understanding of visual communications.

The purpose of graphic design is to convey thoughts, ideas, and feelings between people. Its elements are the common visual and verbal currency of its culture, understood and used in daily life. Signs, symbols, and images are called forth to meet human needs. The peace symbol, shown here in the window of a vacant building awaiting the wrecking ball (fig. **1-64**), was designed by Gerald Holton three decades ago as a public symbol representing a deeply held viewpoint about life-and-death issues of war and peace. In addition to organizing graphic materials into a communicative gestalt, graphic designers sometimes invent new signs and symbols that define human experience and give meaning to our existence.

1-64

Chapter Two: The Union of Word and Picture

2-1

When graphic designers bring word and image together to create visual-verbal messages, two problems must be resolved. First, visual organization is a problem, for two totally unlike systems of communication—language signs and pictorial images—must be merged into a cohesive whole. This ordering of space is discussed in chapter 3. The second problem involves message making: How can these two unlike communication systems come together to reinforce and extend one another?

The interaction of word and picture

Traditionally, the word was dominant and images were used to illustrate or interpret the text. Although word-dominant relationships can still be found, graphics whose imagery merely depicts persons or events from the text are in a distinct minority. The twentieth century, with its fast pace and intense information environment, has radically altered this convention. In an important historical reversal, text often becomes a supporting message used to connote and sharpen the image. Roland Barthes observed: "Formerly, the image illustrated the text (made it clearer); today, the text loads the image, burdening it with a culture, a moral, an imagination." [1]

Text can be a powerful vehicle to alter the meaning of an image or to connote and interpret it for us. This power of words is demonstrated in graphics for a conference entitled "Success and Failure" (fig. **2-1**), designed by Michael Bierut, Vignelli Associates, and photographed by Reven T. C. Wurman. When this graphic is turned so that the word *success* reads correctly, the thumb points upward in an affirmative gesture. When this graphic

is turned so that the word *failure* is oriented correctly, the downward-pointing thumb becomes a negative sign. Bierut used language to "load the image" with a specific meaning. The words *life* and *death* could have been used with this image in a communication about capital punishment or gladiator fights in ancient Rome, or this image could be oriented with the thumb pointing toward the left to illustrate an article about the dangers of hitchhiking. These alternate examples demonstrate the complexity and ambiguity of even a simple image and the ability of words to direct the viewer toward an interpretation. Type has a more specific meaning than an image has; therefore, type can bind an image to a specific meaning. When type directs the viewer toward a specific meaning, individual freedom to form an interpretation is diminished.

The connotative power of words was demonstrated in the newspaper headline from a London tabloid—"They were near to death, their faces prove it"—accompanying a photograph of Queen Elizabeth and Prince Philip leaving an airplane. [2] At the moment the photograph was taken, however, the couple was unaware that they had narrowly escaped a life-threatening accident. Because the readers did not know this, they immediately interpreted the facial expressions as directed by the headline writer.

This connotative power is not limited to the ability of words to connote images, for words can connote other words; images can connote other images reproduced in proximity; and images can connote words. The last can be seen clearly in the cover for the *65th Art Directors Annual* (fig. **2-2**) designed by Bob Gill and photographed by Marty Jacobs. In contrast to the celebratory or visionary images frequently found on creative yearbooks, Gill fabricated an image that implies that art directors' annual competitive exhibitions are "cutthroat, back-stabbing" affairs.

Comparison of the covers for hardcover and paperback editions of James William Gibson's book *The Perfect War*—which analyzes America's involvement in the Vietnam War—reveals the connotative interrelation. The jacket design by Andy Carpenter for the hardcover edition carried the subtitle "Technowar in Vietnam" and an image of soldiers using high-tech equipment to descend to the battlefield (fig. **2-3**). The subtitle and image suggest that the book is about advanced military equipment used in Vietnam. The paperback edition designed by Adriane Stark (figure **2-4**) changed the

2-2

subtitle to "The War We Couldn't Lose and How We Did." It montages two images: a map of Vietnam with pictographs of aircraft superimposed and a young Vietnamese man holding a wounded child. Subtitle and imagery pull this book's meaning and content in a totally different direction to suggest that the author might reveal why the United States could not achieve victory in spite of tremendous technological power. Juxtaposition of the man and child with a prosaic technical map suggests the agony of civilians trapped by impersonal political and military forces.

When shown these two covers and asked to interpret them, a reader noted that the hardcover version was "about all the new technological weapons used in the war." The same person said of the paperback version, "The irony of the title is reinforced. How can there be a perfect war? Nobody wins. It makes me think of what we did to destroy life."

The old adage states: "You can't tell a book by its cover." What actually happens when you look at a book jacket? Its cover design directs you toward an interpretation.

Headlines, titles, captions, and text each have a different relationship to an image. A headline or a title is often on an equal level with the image. If they say the same thing, visual-verbal redundancy results, which can reinforce the message. A record jacket bearing a photograph of the performer and the performer's name in large type is visual-verbal redundancy. Headlines and titles often interact with images to clarify, modify, or extend their meanings.

Captions are seen as subordinate to images and providing information to describe, label, or identify the image. The relationship of images to the running text often fills the traditional role, with the image being perceived as an elaboration or visual description of events, things, or people in the text.

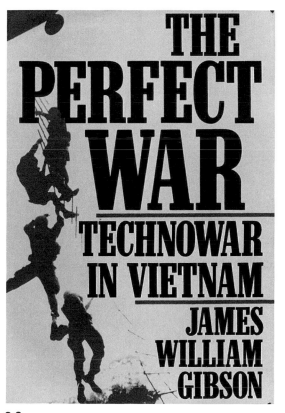

2-3

2-4

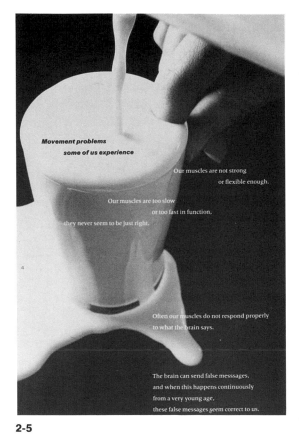

Movement problems
some of us experience

Our muscles are not strong
or flexible enough.

Our muscles are too slow
or too fast in function,
they never seem to be just right.

Often our muscles do not respond properly
to what the brain says.

The brain can send false messsages,
and when this happens continuously
from a very young age,
these false messages seem correct to us.

2-5

The juxtaposition of type and image

The clear separation of type and image, as this text column is separated from the images on this double-page spread, is the conventional visual relationship. Separating the elements permits each one to communicate without interference. Designers often juxtapose or combine type and image in new and unexpected ways, which can intensify their communicative power.

Frequent use is made of type that surprints or overprints an image and type that reverses or drops out from the image. These techniques are used in the booklet "Our Movement Problems," designed by Frank Armstrong and photographed by Thomas Wedell (fig. **2-5**), to create a strong visual hierarchy and effective communication. The size, position, and value contrast of the overprinted headline combine to make it a dominant element. The reader immediately comprehends the overflowing milk glass as a direct result of a handicapped person's movement problems. A cause-and-effect

relationship is established between type and image. The text type is reversed out, and Armstrong has carefully placed it over the simple darker areas of the photograph. Overprinted and reversed type must be planned carefully. Adequate contrast between the image background and the type is critical, because poor legibility can result when the contrast is insufficient or the background is so complex that it interferes with the type.

From the time of the medieval manuscripts, artists and designers have shown great innovation in combining letters with images. These 1890s illustrated initials from the English periodical *The Studio* (fig. **2-6**) demonstrate that letterforms can contain images, be formed by images, or be created by an image that takes the shape of a letter. In a contemporary logo for a book exhibition (fig. **2-7**), William Longhauser transformed letterforms into signs relating to printing production, including a cylindrical press, spiral binding, wire binding, a layout sketch, and an indication for a diecut.

▲
◀ 2-6

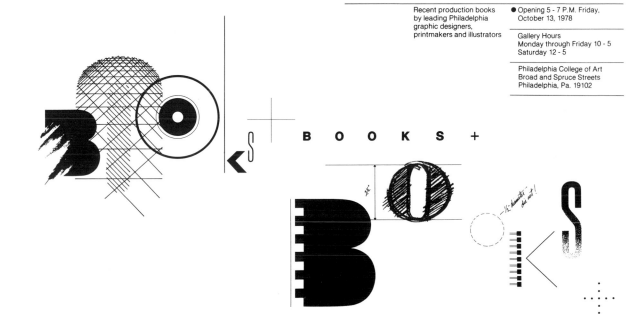

Recent production books by leading Philadelphia graphic designers, printmakers and illustrators

● Opening 5 - 7 P.M. Friday, October 13, 1978

Gallery Hours
Monday through Friday 10 - 5
Saturday 12 - 5

Philadelphia College of Art
Broad and Spruce Streets
Philadelphia, Pa. 19102

2-7

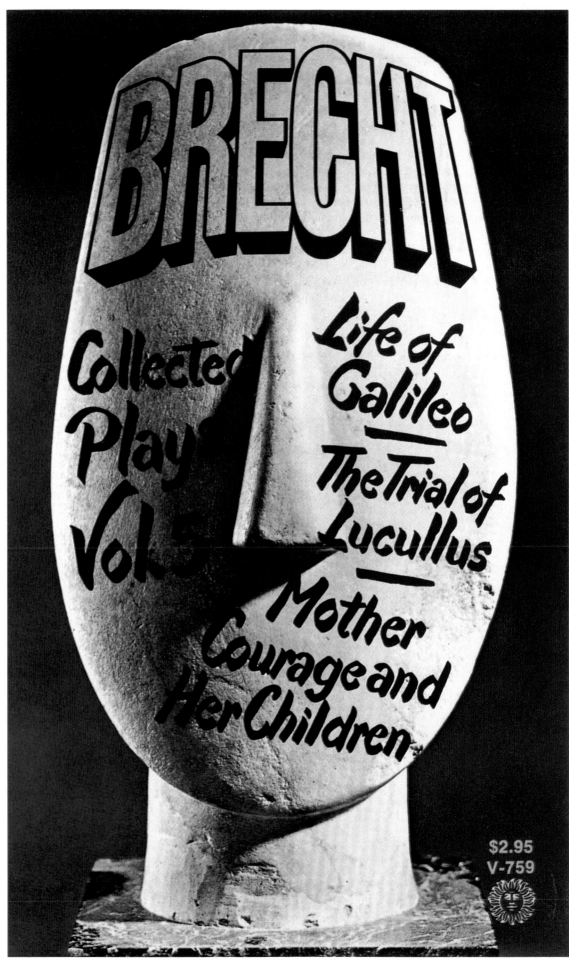

BRECHT

Collected Plays Vol 5

Life of Galileo

The Trial of Lucullus

Mother Courage and Her Children

$2.95
V-759

Dietmar Winkler's typographic homage to Giacometti (see figure **1-51** in chapter 1) is an example of the letterforms in a word combining to become a simile for an image.

An image or object can become the "page" upon which words are applied, as occurs in R. D. Scudellari's cover for *The Collected Plays of* *Brecht, Volume 5* (fig. **2-8**). The reverse can also occur, for type can become the "page" or background environment for an image (fig. **2-9**). Bradbury Thompson used the repeated *Mademoiselle* masthead to form a textural typographic pattern behind a model on this magazine's cover.

2-9

BROTHERS OF PASSAMAQUODIA:

I am glad to hear by Major Shaw, that you accepted the chain of Friendship which I sent you last February from Cambridge, and that you are determined to keep it bright and unbroken…Brothers, I have a piece of news to tell you which I hope you will attend to. Our enemy, the King of Great Britain, endeavored to stir up all the Indians from Canada to South Carolina against us. But our brethren of the six Nations & their allies the Shawanese & the Delawares would not hearken to the advice of his Messengers sent among them, but kept fast hold of the ancient covenant chain. The Cherokees & the Southern tribes were foolish enough to listen to them and take up the hatchet against us. Upon this our Warriors went into their country, burnt their houses, destroyed their corn and obliged them to sue for peace and give hostages for their future good behavior. ¶ Now Brothers never let the king's wicked counsellor turn your hearts against me and your brethren of this country, but bear in mind what I told you last February and what I tell you now. In token of my friendship I send you this from my army on the banks of the Great River Delaware, this 24th day of December, 1776. *George Washington.*

Designed by Dugald Stermer

An even more complex integration of type and image occurs in an editorial layout from *Ramparts* magazine, designed and illustrated by Dugald Stermer (fig. **2-10**). The article discusses relations between the United States and Native American Indian tribes. Stermer set the text of George Washington's message to the Passamaquodia Indians in Times Roman type that fills the page. Type overlaps a black line illustration of George Washington. It reverses out as white against the black image, prints in blue ink over his face and jabot, and prints in red ink in the background.

In a logo designed for the Legname/Bermann film production company (fig. **2-11**), designer Craig Frazier used bold condensed sans serif letterforms to transform the names of the principals of the firm into film sprockets. The shadow cast by the rear-illuminated piece of film has light-struck spots created by light coming through the letter-shaped sprockets. This denotes their transparency.

2-11

On a Stravinsky album cover (fig. **2-12**), Richard Mantel let large Modern-style typography play the dominant role and then used the baseline of the type as an implied stage floor upon which the characters from the performance stand. *U* becomes a doorway, and *Y* and *O* become windows. This places some characters behind the letterforms, which creates a livelier spatial configuration.

Words within images
Pictorial space can contain letterforms and words as elements within it. Words become the image on a cover for *Ms.* magazine designed by Bea Feitler and photographed by Mel Dixon (fig. **2-13**). An editorial message is executed as a neon sign and then photographed to capture the luminous glow radiating against the black background.

2-13

2-12

Ms.

DECEMBER/1973/$1.00

PEACE
ON EARTH
GOODWILL
TO PEOPLE

IND 35185

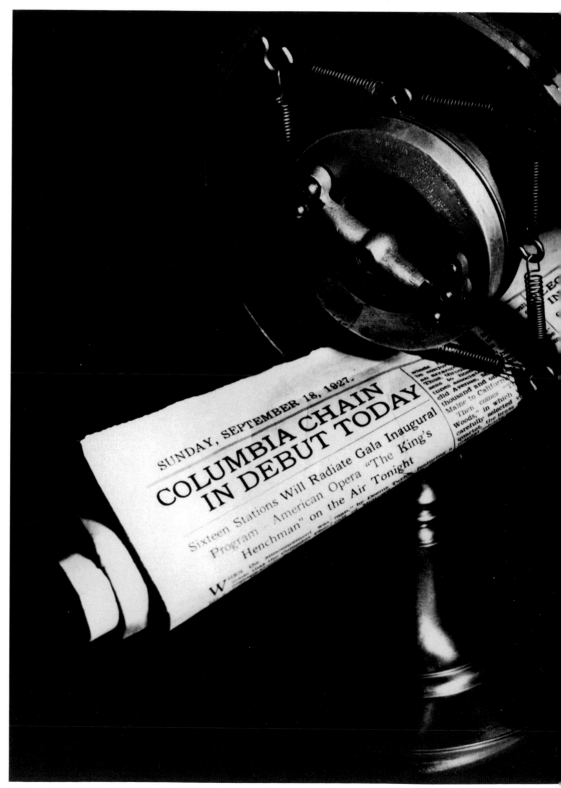

SUNDAY, SEPTEMBER 18, 1927.

COLUMBIA CHAIN
IN DEBUT TODAY

Sixteen Stations Will Radiate Gala Inaugural Program — American Opera "The King's Henchman" on the Air Tonight

A newspaper headline functions as an advertising headline for the Columbia Broadcasting System. Designed by Lou Dorfsman and photographed by Sol Mednick (fig. **2-14**), this advertisement contains an authentic "1927 newspaper story about CBS' first broadcast from the old Metropolitan Opera House. . . . On September 27, 1966, exactly 39 years after that first broadcast," Dorfsman "ran this ad congratulating the Metropolitan Opera on its new move to its new home at Lincoln Center." [3]

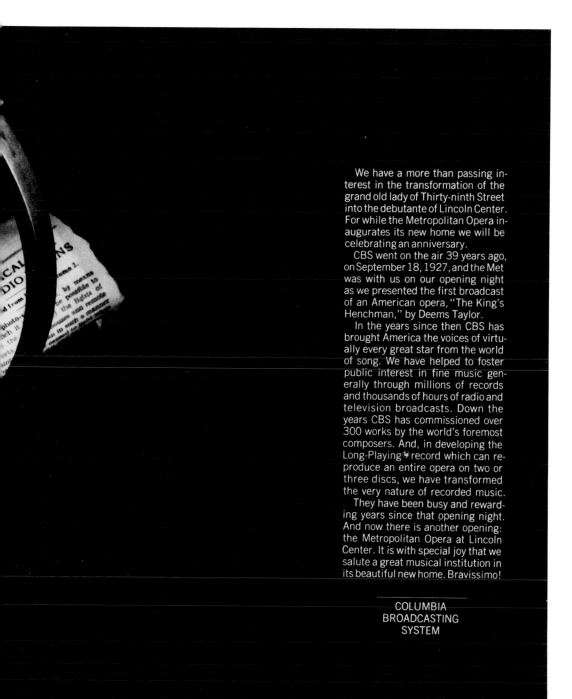

We have a more than passing interest in the transformation of the grand old lady of Thirty-ninth Street into the debutante of Lincoln Center. For while the Metropolitan Opera inaugurates its new home we will be celebrating an anniversary.

CBS went on the air 39 years ago, on September 18, 1927, and the Met was with us on our opening night as we presented the first broadcast of an American opera, "The King's Henchman," by Deems Taylor.

In the years since then CBS has brought America the voices of virtually every great star from the world of song. We have helped to foster public interest in fine music generally through millions of records and thousands of hours of radio and television broadcasts. Down the years CBS has commissioned over 300 works by the world's foremost composers. And, in developing the Long-Playing ♥ record which can reproduce an entire opera on two or three discs, we have transformed the very nature of recorded music.

They have been busy and rewarding years since that opening night. And now there is another opening: the Metropolitan Opera at Lincoln Center. It is with special joy that we salute a great musical institution in its beautiful new home. Bravissimo!

COLUMBIA
BROADCASTING
SYSTEM

STREET INSPIRATIONS

In an illustration entitled "Street Inspirations" (fig. **2-15**), James McMullan integrated words signifying the sounds of a city into the pictorial space. The honk of a horn, "tatat" of workmen, music of a street musician, howl of a dog, and a woman's voice are all articulated graphically. The sidewalk and wall reverberate with city noises and street slang.

The fusion of type and image

The painters of the early twentieth-century futurist movement in Italy believed that "the different aspects of vision could be combined in one 'process of interpenetration—simultaneity-fusion.' " [4] *Simultaneity* means fusing unlike forms so that they exist or occur at the same time. Borrowing a visual technique from their contemporaries, the cubist painters in Paris, futurist artists also used it to mean fusing more than one view of an object into one image. This concept has been useful to graphic designers in building a visual communication.

Image as letter. Through the process of substitution, an image can play the role of a letterform in a word. In an editorial design for the story "Once Upon a Treasure Hunt" (fig. **2-16**), Herb Lubalin superimposed a large headline over a photograph of a beach scene. The blades of two shovels substitute for the letter *U* in the words *treasure* and *hunt.* The headline was printed in metallic gold, which is a symbolic index pointing toward the objective of a treasure hunt.

Letterforms can be constructed from images. In a direct mail folder announcing the grand opening of a new third floor at a Neiman-Marcus department store (fig. **2-17**), Sibley/Peteet Design used silhouette illustrations to spell the word *third*: the *T* is a waiter in the new restaurant; the *H* is a bridal couple signifying the bridal salon; the *I* is a figure representing the lingerie shop; the *R* stands for the section for children's clothing, toys and shoes; and the *D* is a shopper in the new gallery area.

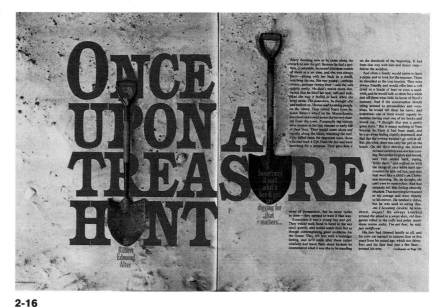

2-16

2-17

2-15

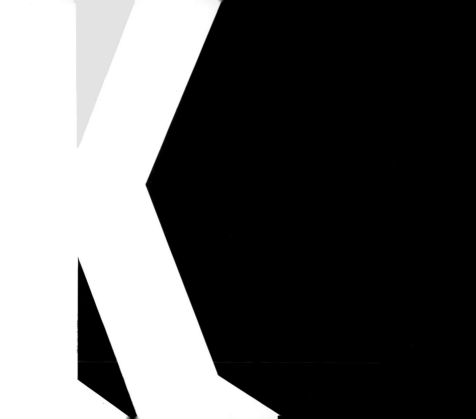

2-18

2-19

KDACDOOR

2-20

Ball

2-21

Letter as image. Letterforms can be altered and manipulated to become simultaneously an image and a letter. In figure **2-18**, a logo designed for Eastside Tennis Club by Diana Graham, the *S* forms are contained in a circle, producing icons representing tennis balls. In these geometrically constructed sans serif letterforms, the round forms are perfect circles, which are critical to the successful blend of *S* and tennis ball.

Simultaneity also occurs in the Knapp Shoes trademark (fig. **2-19**) designed by Tom Geismar. The terminal strokes of the letter *K* sprout feet, which signify the product. The letterform is personified by these feet and becomes a metaphor for a walking person.

Word as image. In human communication, alphabet characters are the atoms, and words are the molecules—the smallest unit of spoken and written communication with a meaning other than signifying a sound. By altering and manipulating the visual form of a word or its substrate, graphic designers expand and extend its meaning.

Diana Graham's logo design for the Backdoor Art Gallery (fig. **2-20**) expresses meaning figuratively by reversing the first part of the word, causing it to read backwards. The exaggerated legs of the *K* and *R* introduce a symmetrical quality and bring a cohesiveness to the configuration.

The trademark for George J. Ball, Inc. (fig. **2-21**), growers and distributors of seeds and plants, was designed by Ivan Chermayeff. It signifies the client on three levels: The word *Ball*—printed in green ink—is the company name; the red circles over the lower case *l*s are signs for balls; and simultaneously, the red circles over green stems signify flowers, which are one of the client's major products.

2-22

2-23

2-24

2-25

2-26

2-27

2-28

2-29

2-30

The rock group Chicago's logo has a warm vernacular form, executed in thick script letters with Victorian swashes in the tradition of sports teams and orange crate labels. In a long series of record albums designed by John Berg, some of which are shown in figures **2-22** to **2-30**, the logo has been applied to varied substrates, and its physical form has been executed in numerous techniques. The word becomes an object and an icon, taking on a physical life as an emblem for this band. James William Guercio wrote about this group: "The printed word can never aspire to document a truly musical experience, so if you must call them something, speak of the city where all save one were born; where all of them were schooled and bred, and where all of this incredible music went down barely noticed; call them CHICAGO." [5]

A visual simile—the corresponding whirls of the logo and a fingerprint—provides the basis for the graphic concept (fig. **2-22**; art by Nick Fasciano).

The rustic texture of weathered wood becomes the substrate, and the logo is incised with wood-carving tools. A strong dimensional and tactile quality results (fig. **2-23**; art by Nick Fasciano).

Leatherwork on cowhide includes historical imagery from the city of Chicago, such as the great fire and the stockades. This cover is printed as a brown halftone over a tan background and embossed to create remarkable fidelity to the original (fig. **2-24**; art by Nick Fasciano).

Embroidery technique duplicates the ambiance of an athletic team's uniform patch. The similarity between the logo and many sports team logos enhances this relationship (fig. **2-25**; art by Nick Fasciano).

A collage of steel-engraved ornaments printed in blue ink on gray paper evokes the character of stock certificates. The photograph is shot with a vertical-line screen to create a compatible engraved quality (fig. **2-26**; art by Nick Fasciano).

The rock group poses as sign painters executing their logo on a wall to the dismay of a resident and policeman (fig. **2-27**; photograph by Reid Miles).

The logo is applied to an antique map of the Chicago area, which continues across the back cover (fig. **2-28**; original map by John Bartholomew & Son, Ltd.).

A candy wrapper is torn away to reveal the logo in relief on a bar of chocolate (fig. **2-29**; art by Nick Fasciano).

The word becomes a tangible, three-dimensional object. It was cut from aluminum and photographed in front of a sheet of brushed aluminum (fig. **2-30**; art by Nick Fasciano).

Text type as image. Setting text type in a shape that becomes a sign or icon has fascinated compositors and designers through the centuries. The February 27, 1834, cover of the French journal *Le Charivari* (fig. **2-31**) parodied King Louis Philippe by depicting his pear-shaped head in the exaggerated shape of that fruit. Another level of meaning is operative as well, because the French term for pear, *la poire,* is also used as a slang term for simpleton or dunce.

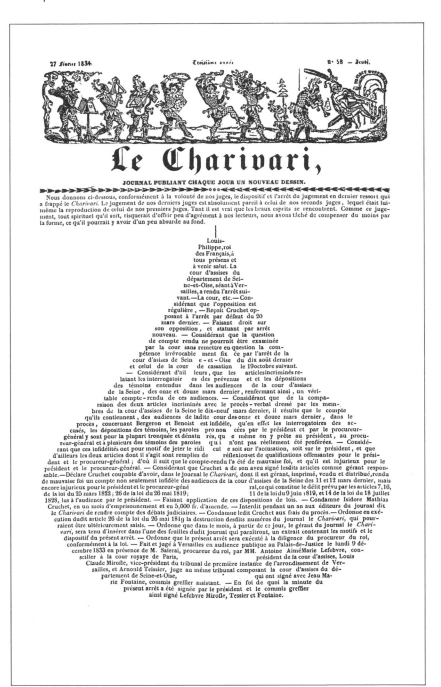

2-31

Type as environmental image
As figure **2-30** demonstrated, typographic forms can become dimensional objects with concrete physical form. Letterforms and words can depart from the two-dimensional information environment to join the three-dimensional world. Michael Manwaring's precast concrete sign for the India Basin Industrial Park (fig. **2-32**) achieves monumentality through scale and mass, becoming sign, sculpture, and artifact. Manwaring relates that after the sign was installed, he ran his hands over and through the letterforms and experienced the organic forms of letters as objects.

2-32

In a poster by Michael Bierut of Vignelli Associates (fig. **2-33**), a two-dimensional drawing creates the illusion of a three-dimensional environment. A graphic sign (the dollar mark) is combined with an interior floor plan to express the subject, a series of seminars for interior designers about the business aspects of that profession.

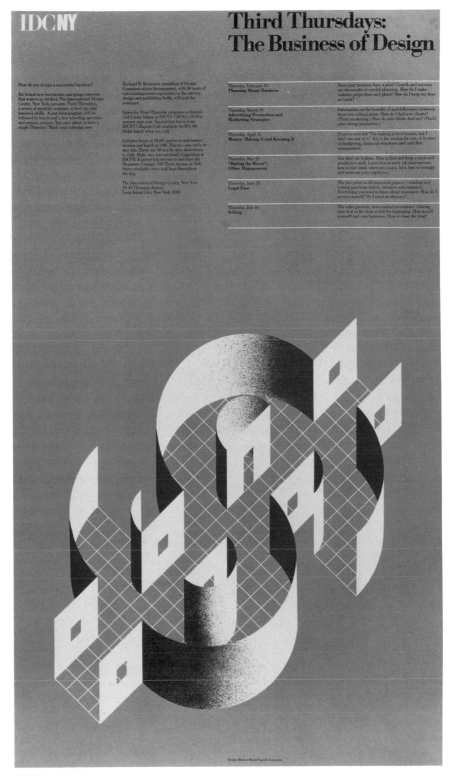

2-33

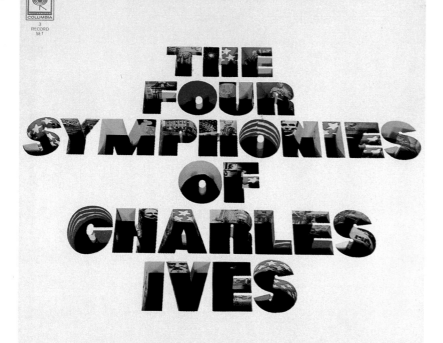

2-34

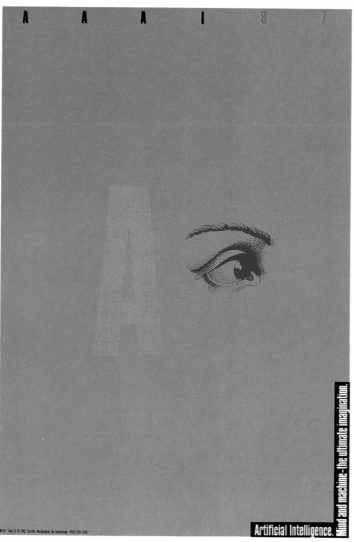

2-35

A different spatial concept is found in the Charles Ives record jacket designed by Virginia Team and Nick Fasciano (fig. **2-34**). Letterforms become voids, sinking into the substrate. Their inner surfaces contain images, signs, and color shapes evoking Ives's Americana themes.

Objective type and image

When type and image are used objectively, they have strong denotative properties and are relatively free of personal bias or strong connotative qualities. The designer uses rudimentary elements of communication to convey meaning. A simple additive process occurs as these communicative signals are placed in proximity to one another.

Letter plus image. The American Association of Artificial Intelligence (AAAI) announced its annual conference, "Artificial Intelligence. Mind and machine—the ultimate imagination" (fig. **2-35**), with a poster. Designer Craig Frazier placed a large letterform *A,* printed in metallic silver ink and embossed with a repetitive pattern of evenly spaced circles, adjacent to an engraved image of an eye. In concert, these forms signify artificial intelligence with immediacy and impact. They are a study in contrast: geometric to organic; machine form to human form; sign to picture; and initial alphabet to rebus. A *rebus* is a representation of words or syllables by pictures of objects whose names resemble the intended words or syllables in sound; for example, a picture of an eye equals the sound *aye* equals the letter *I.*

Word plus image. The power of images to extend and intensify the meaning of a word is demonstrated by the series of informational sheets for the insurance firm Neuenburger Versicherungen[6] by Swiss designer Siegfried Odermatt (figs. **2-36** to **2-41**). The copy line translates, "Between you and adversity, put The Neuenburger Insurance."

Wasser (Water). The water from an overflowing faucet is amplified by the underwater distortion of the word (fig. **2-36**).

Unfall (Accident). The shift in an x-ray of a broken bone is emphasized by the corresponding shift in the type (fig. **2-37**).

Feuer (Fire). A high-contrast photograph of the charred remains of burned wood denotes fire damage; the color of the type connotes fire (fig. **2-38**).

Auto (Automobile). The wrecked automobile slams into jumbled and smashed type (fig. **2-39**).

Glas (Glass). Sharp edges convey danger and damage. The shards cut through the letterforms, but Odermatt has carefully left enough of each letter to permit accurate decoding (fig. **2-40**).

Vol (Burglary). Most of the images in this series are icons, but the fingerprint is an index that points toward the burglar (fig. **2-41**).

2-36

Wasser

Für diesen Fall – die

Neuenburger Versicherungen

Könnte das nicht auch Ihr Wasserhahn sein? Aus Versehen blieb er offen, als Sie die Wohnung verliessen. Der Ablauf ist verschlossen oder hat sich verstopft, so dass jetzt das Wasser überbordet und die Wohnung überschwemmt. Eine schöne Bescherung! Die Wasserschadenversicherung deckt Schäden, die im Innern des Gebäudes entstehen durch Ausströmen von Wasser aus Wasserleitungsanlagen oder durch Eindringen von Regen, Schnee und Schmelzwasser durch das Dach. Die Kosten für das Auftauen eingefrorener Wasserleitungen und deren Reparatur werden ebenfalls von der Versicherung übernommen. Das gleiche gilt für die allfällige Beschädigung von Dritteigentum, was bei Wasserschäden stets zu befürchten ist.

2-37

Unfall

Für diesen Fall – die

Neuenburger Versicherungen

Jeder achte Mensch wird im Laufe eines Jahres von einem Unfall betroffen. Diese Feststellung, die sich aus der Unfallstatistik ergibt, mag Sie verwundern, aber sie stimmt. Beruf, Verkehr und Sport fordern alljährlich eine bestimmte Anzahl Opfer. Durch die Unfallversicherung können die Heilungskosten (Arzt, Apotheke, Spitalpflege usw.), sowie für vorübergehende Arbeitsunfähigkeit ein Taggeld, für dauernde Arbeitsunfähigkeit eine Invaliditätsentschädigung, beim Tod eine Todesfallentschädigung versichert werden. Man unterscheidet zwischen Einzel-, Kollektiv-, Frauen-, Kinder-, Dienstboten-, Auto-Insassen- und Reise-Unfallversicherungen. Der Betriebsinhaber braucht ferner eine Zusatzversicherung zur « Suval ».

2-38

Feuer

Für diesen Fall – die

Neuenburger Versicherungen

Nicht bloss alte Holz- und Riegelhäuser brennen nieder, sondern auch moderne Bauten. Die Feuerversicherung deckt Schäden, verursacht durch Brand, Blitzschlag, Explosionen und Naturkatastrophen. Bei Neuwertversicherung wird auch die Wertverminderung infolge Abnützung usw. ganz oder teilweise vergütet. Bei Haushaltungen und Geschäften können Feuer-, Diebstahl-, Glas- und Wasserschadenrisiken in einer einzigen kombinierten Police versichert werden. Für den Betriebsinhaber ist die Betriebsunterbrechungs-, und für den Hausbesitzer die Mietzinsverlust-Versicherung die natürliche Ergänzung zur Feuerversicherung.

2-39

Auto

Entre vous et l'adversité – mettez

La Neuchâteloise Assurances

Tout détenteur de véhicule à moteur est tenu légalement de souscrire une assurance de la responsabilité civile. Cette assurance garantit aussi la défense du détenteur contre les prétentions injustifiées. L'assurance Casco complet ou partiel et celle des Occupants d'automobiles sont les compléments indispensables à l'assurance de la responsabilité civile. L'assurance Casco complet couvre tous les dégâts au véhicule du détenteur, y compris la perte. L'assurance Casco partiel est limité au vol, à l'incendie, aux bris des glaces, et aux forces de la nature. Les occupants d'automobiles sont assurés contre les accidents, sans tenir compte de la responsabilité. Les proches parents du détenteur, exclus de l'assurance de la responsabilité civile, sont couverts par cette assurance.

2-40

Glas

Für diesen Fall – die

Neuenburger Versicherungen

Scherben bringen Glück, sagt der Volksmund; meistens aber kosten sie eine Menge Geld! Das Glas spielt im modernen Geschäft, in der modernen Wohnung eine immer grössere Rolle, womit natürlich auch die Gefahr des Glasbruches ständig zunimmt. Die Glasversicherung deckt Bruchschäden an Gebäude- und Mobiliar-Verglasungen.

2-41

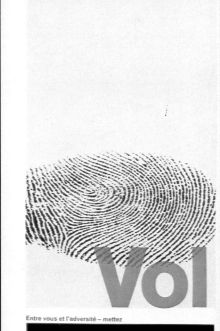

Vol

Entre vous et l'adversité – mettez

La Neuchâteloise Assurances

La plus belle empreinte digitale ne garantit pas l'arrestation du voleur et la restitution des choses subtilisées. La seule protection efficace contre la perte due à un vol est une bonne assurance. L'assurance couvre les dommages dont auraient à souffrir votre patrimoine ou les locaux que vous habitez, par suite d'un vol avec effraction; vous pouvez l'étendre au cas de vol simple et de vol de bicyclettes.

Visual-verbal synergy

Visual-verbal synergy is the cooperative action of words and pictures used together to create a meaning that is greater than the individual signification of the parts. This concept was advocated by copywriter Bill Bernbach of the Doyle Dane Bernbach advertising agency. This agency's Volkswagen campaign is a classic example of the technique. Figure **2-42**, created by Art Director Helmut Krone, Copywriter Rita Seldon, and Photographer Wingate Pinge, demonstrates this principle. Without the image, the headline is incomplete, for the statement, "It was the only thing to do after the mule died," calls for clarification and completion. What was the only thing to do after the mule died? The photograph provides resolution—purchase a Volkswagen.

Without words informing the reader about the mule dying, the photograph is perceived as merely a snapshot of a rural couple with their house and car. Each individual reader could project personal interpretations onto it based on their background and experience. The headline, as discussed earlier, binds the image to a specific meaning. (Figure **1-60** in chapter 1 is from the same advertising campaign. It achieves its *litotes* or understatement through visual-verbal synergy.)

"It was the only thing to do after the mule died."

Three years back, the Hinsleys of Dora, Missouri, had a tough decision to make.

To buy a new mule.

Or invest in a used bug.

They weighed the two possibilities.

First there was the problem of the bitter Ozark winters. Tough on a warm-blooded mule. Not so tough on an air-cooled VW.

Then, what about the eating habits of the two contenders? Hay vs. gasoline.

As Mr. Hinsley puts it: "I get over eighty miles out of a dollar's worth of gas and I get where I want to go a lot quicker."

Then there's the road leading to their cabin. Many a mule pulling a wagon and many a conventional automobile has spent many an hour stuck in the mud.

As for shelter, a mule needs a barn. A bug doesn't. "It just sets out there all day and the paint job looks near as good as the day we got it."

Finally, there was maintenance to think about. When a mule breaks down, there's only one thing to do: Shoot it.

But if and when their bug breaks down, the Hinsleys have a Volkswagen dealer only two gallons away.

2-42

Visual-verbal synergy can be charged with powerful emotional impact. Figure **2-43**, a poster to warn high school students about the potential dangers of drunk driving, rationalizes that "Not everyone who drives drunk dies." The larger-than-life photograph of a teenager with a horribly scarred face is in shocking contrast to the headline. This poster, selected in the national competition sponsored by *Reader's Digest,* is by the creative team of Art Director Sal DeVito and Copywriter Jamie Seltzer.

2-43

The Big Apple Opens in Orange County

Sponsored by State Mutual Savings and Loan
and Jann Church Advertising and Graphic Design, Inc.

VIA AIR MAIL

FIRST CLASS MAIL

FIRST CLASS MAIL

CONTENTS:
The New York Art Directors Club Show.
Featuring 1200 examples of the best advertising and
graphic design in the U.S.A. Categories include:

SHIPPED:
From the New York
Art Directors Club on
loan for 14 days only.

Newspaper Advertising, both black and white and color; Newspaper Editorial; Magazine Advertising, including Consumer Ads, Public Service Ads, Political Ads, and Public Service or Trade Ads; Television Consumer and Public Service Spots; Film Titles and Logos, and Film Promos; Promotional and Graphic Design, including Booklets, Brochures, Annual Reports, Sales Kits, House Organs, Capabilities Brochures, Packaging, Record Albums, Calendars, Letterheads, Logos,

Corporate Identity Programs; Posters, both Public Service, Promotional and Political; Books and Book Jackets; Art Graphic and Illustrative, including Advertising, Promotion, and Editorial; and Photography including Advertising, Public Service, Promotion, Editorial; and more.

January 22 thru February 1, Monday thru Friday 9 to 4, at
4001 MacArthur Blvd, Newport Beach, (714) 833-8383.

Visual-verbal synergy isn't limited to advertising. A poster announcing a traveling exhibition from New York City (fig. **2-44**), designed by Jann Church and photographed by John Lawler, announces: "The Big Apple Opens in Orange County." The indefinite headline is given more specific meaning by the photograph. The opening of a parcel containing a framed photograph of an apple decodes the headline. Reading word and picture together, we learn that an exhibition from New York City will be opening in Orange County.

Type or image alone

Effective and complete graphic communications can be created by type without images or by images without type. On the jacket designed by Lou Dorfsman for a book about the first moon landing (fig. **2-45**), a color photograph of the first moonwalk was tipped onto gray paper embossed with the crater-textured surface of the moon. Typographic explanation is unnecessary, for the imagery immediately communicates the subject of the book.

The opposite strategy was used by Herb Lubalin in an early newspaper advertisement for a clearance sale (fig. **2-46**). In contrast to the crowded space of a newspaper, Lubalin used brackets to show what will be left after the clearance sale—absolutely nothing. In a sense, the absence of imagery functions the way images normally do. Although the combination of word and image has tremendous potential for interaction and synergy, these two examples demonstrate their ability to convey potent messages when used individually.

This chapter has examined the relationships that can exist between type and image as they enhance the message and generate unexpected visual combinations. The written word and pictures are totally different means of communication. By transforming and integrating letters, words, and images, graphic designers expand and extend our language possibilities.

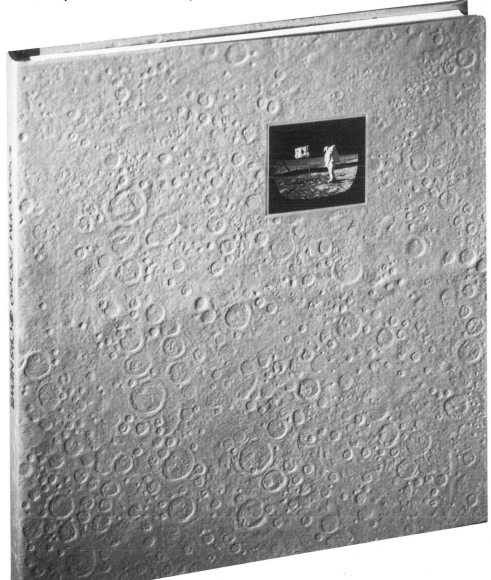

2-44

2-45

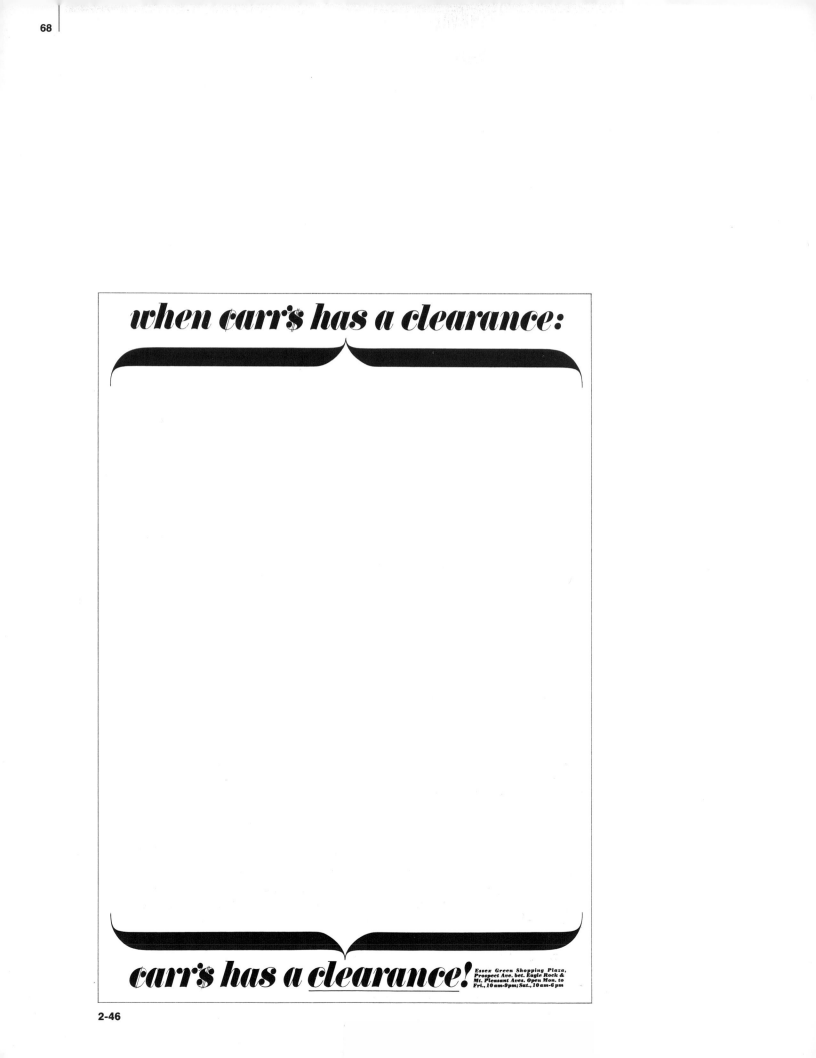

when carr's has a clearance:

carr's has a clearance! Essex Green Shopping Plaza, Prospect Ave. bet. Eagle Rock & Mt. Pleasant Aves. Open Mon. to Fri., 10 am-9 pm; Sat., 10 am-6 pm

Chapter Three: Graphic Space

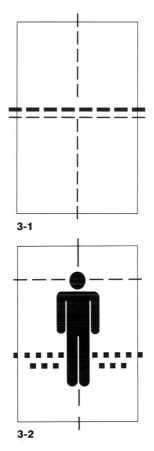

3-1

3-2

Thoroughly understanding graphic space requires considering the characteristics of the spatial field and the nature of human vision. Every graphic design occurs in an area of space that is usually a flat two-dimensional plane bounded by the four edges of a sheet of paper or other substrate, such as the film, video, or computer image. The designer organizes the visual and verbal components of the message upon this surface and composes unlike elements into an ordered unity. The horizontal and vertical edges of the page determine the area and are the design's first four lines, containing and controlling the composition. Forms can either align with the edges to create stability and order or be composed in opposition to the edges to create an energetic forcefulness.

Every graphic surface has a horizontal axis and a vertical axis. The geometric center where these two axes cross is potentially a powerful focal point. The *optical center,* which is the point that appears to be the center to the human eye, is slightly above the *geometric center,* which is the center arrived at by measurement (fig. **3-1**).

The human factor
People have a strong horizontal and vertical orientation (fig. **3-2**) that is innate to our very nature and experience. The force of gravity—a vertical pull toward the earth's center—and a person's vertical upright posture in opposition to it create a vertical orientation. The horizon line is seen as horizontal because our human scale and height are so small relative to the size of the earth that the curvature of the earth is flattened. Our architecture, furniture design, and city planning all reinforce the horizontal and vertical orientation.

The way human vision works is important to the experience of graphic communications. The human eye focuses sharply upon a very small area. Focus upon a word in the middle of a line of text and notice how quickly the words on either side lose their definition. Toward the end of the line of type, the words become indistinct gray blurs. This drop in sharpness is acute: At two-and-one-half degrees from the point of greatest sharpness, visual acuity

decreases fifty percent; at forty-five degrees from the point of greatest sharpness, the acuity has fallen to two-and-one-half percent.[1]

Our vision becomes indistinct and fades at its periphery. Hold your arms outstretched to the side so that they cannot be seen, and then, while slowly moving them forward, observe your difficulty in determining exactly when and where you become aware of them. They appear indistinct until they begin to move in front of the body.

Our eyes are constantly in rapid motion as they scan, shift, and select. Although graphic space is usually fixed and two-dimensional, it should not be thought of as being static, for eye movement generates energy and motion as it traces a kinetic linear path upon the surface. A static line of type is transformed into a dynamic continuum of verbal meaning and visual rhythm by the reader's eye. Despite the breaks in the continuity of our visual awareness as our eyes dart from focal point to focal point, we usually consider our vision to be a seamless continuum.

Another visual phenomenon that affects design is the *afterimage.* After looking at a pattern of bright color and then looking at a white surface, we see the complementary color of the bright pattern. Intense value or color contrast creates a sensation of flickering. The perception of the brilliance, lightness, or darkness of an area is not absolute because it is influenced and determined by the color and value of surrounding or adjacent areas. Under dim illumination, colors and value contrasts dim and fade into nothingness.

Objects appear smaller in the distance, and parallel lines appear to become closer and merge as they move away from us in space. *Atmospheric perspective,* the tendency of atmosphere to make objects appear cooler in color and lighter in value as they become more distant from our vantage point, alters our perception. All of these visual phenomena have an impact upon the experience of information in graphic space.

In drawing, dark seems close to viewer...light seems further away!

By habit and custom going back to the ancient Greeks, written and typographic communications in Western cultures have a sequence of horizontal lines moving from the upper left-hand corner to the lower right-hand corner. This movement is our basic orientation toward graphic space (fig. **3-3**).

People seek order and clarity in environments and communication. Anthropologist Edmund Carpenter observes: "Man is the great pattern-maker and pattern perceiver. No matter how primitive his situation, no matter how tormented, he cannot live in a world of chaos. Everywhere he imposes form."[2] The audience's need for order must be addressed and satisfied by the graphic designer through his or her approach to spatial organization.

Form relationships in graphic space

Forms establish relationships to one another in space through identifiable principles. These principles are used by the designer to turn disparate elements into a cohesive whole.

Alignment. When forms, their edges, or their central axes align with one another, relationships and connections between them are established (fig. **3-4**).

Continuation. Forms generate eye movement on a page. Linear elements, such as a line of type, generate an eye movement that continues beyond the end of the line—just as a boat continues slowly forward in the water after the motor is cut off—unless it is deflected by another focal point. Continuance can create alignments and relationships (fig. **3-5**).

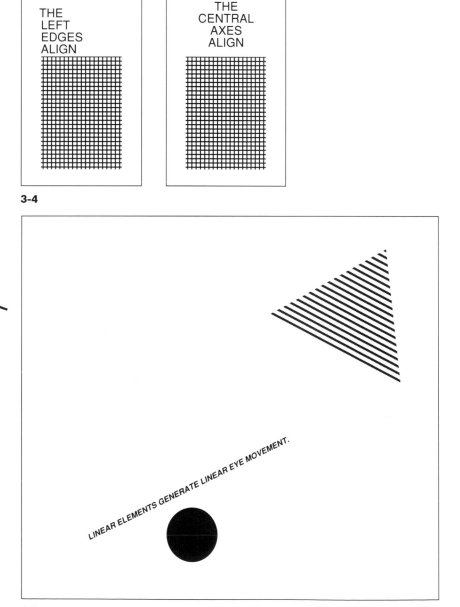

LEFT TO RIGHT READING
LEFT TO RIGHT READING
LEFT TO RIGHT READING
LEFT TO RIGHT READING
LEFT TO RIGHT READING
LEFT TO RIGHT READING
LEFT TO RIGHT READING
LEFT TO RIGHT READING
LEFT TO RIGHT READING
LEFT TO RIGHT READING
LEFT TO RIGHT READING
LEFT TO RIGHT READING
LEFT TO RIGHT READING
LEFT TO RIGHT READING
LEFT TO RIGHT READING
LEFT TO RIGHT READING

3-3

THE LEFT EDGES ALIGN

THE CENTRAL AXES ALIGN

3-4

LINEAR ELEMENTS GENERATE LINEAR EYE MOVEMENT.

3-5

Proximity. Forms that are located close to each other in graphic space form a relationship to each other. In figure **3-6**, the two numbers in the top diagram form a relationship due to their proximity; however, when other numbers are introduced with closer proximity to the first two numbers, new relationships are formed. The interval of space between the first two numbers—which connected and joined them in the first diagram—now separates them.

A designer has successfully employed the principle of proximity when the reader instinctively reads the correct caption for each illustration on a page. If the reader becomes confused about which caption goes with which illustration, the designer has failed to take this principle into account.

Correspondence. When forms have corresponding visual properties, such as similar size, shape, color, tone, texture, or direction, they develop a relationship or correspondence. In figure **3-7**, the three geometric forms in the top diagram are very different and are seen as three dissonant, unrelated forms. In the bottom diagram, similar properties of alignment, size, tone, and texture permit the viewer to perceive them in a meaningful relationship. Like properties attract and unify forms in graphic space, and different properties conflict and repel.

3-6

3-7

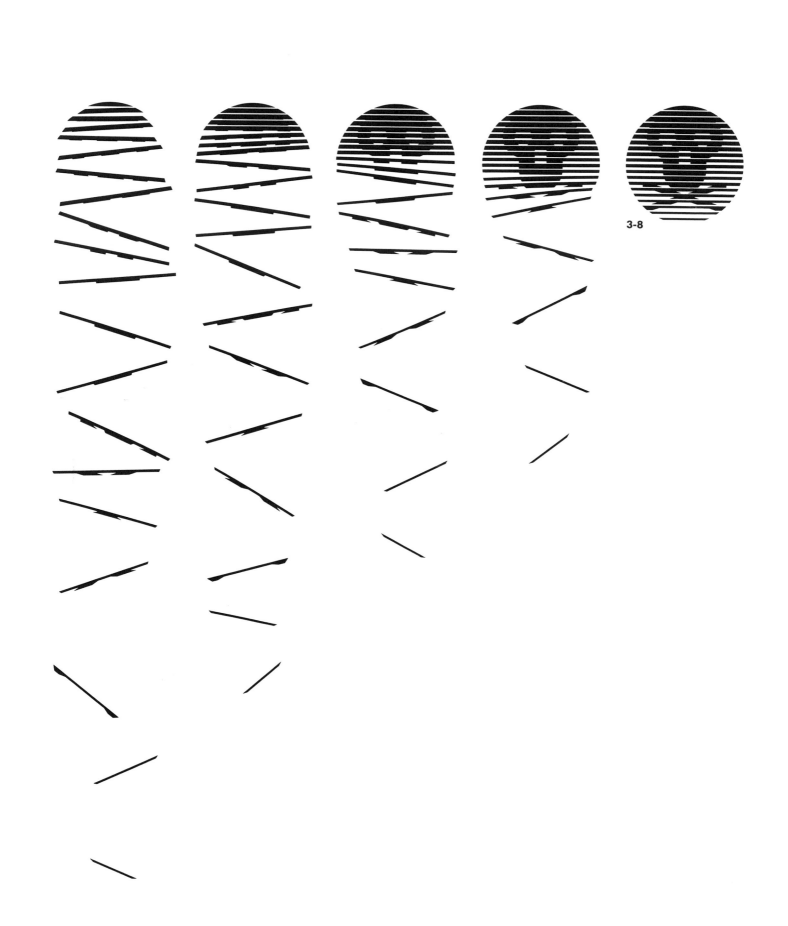

3-8

Completion. When elements have sufficient relationships through alignment, continuation, proximity, and/or correspondence, a person sees them as a complete form or unified whole. The dots in figure **1-1** became an *H* through the ability of the human eye to perceive implied relationships. The logo for The National Campaign Against Toxic Hazards (fig. **3-8**), designed by the author, is composed of twenty separate linear elements. Their similar properties (direction, tone, shape) and alignment enable the viewer to perceive not twenty bars, but a circular configuration. The thick-and-thin areas of the bars are combined by the viewer, who perceives the traditional index signifying poison emerging from the circle.

Audience participation can become a factor in the communications process when the designer provides incomplete information, allowing the viewer to participate by deciphering the message. In Dietmar Winkler's poster for a brass ensemble concert (fig. **3-9**), the viewer combines the left and top edges of a typographic configuration with a stark white line to form the silhouette of a brass horn. Perhaps some viewers will not be able to perceive the image at first glance. The text and the brass color of the type are cues that assist the viewer in completing the image.

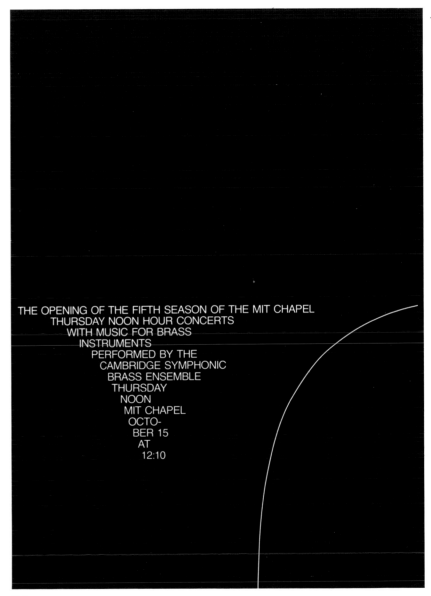

3-9

Symmetry and asymmetry

The word *symmetry* has two meanings. Its general use denotes well-proportioned and balanced parts, with a beauty resulting from the ordering of the parts to form a whole. More specifically, it means the similarity of form or arrangement on either side of a dividing line or plane. The symmetry found in nature, including the symmetrical character of the human body and face, is a powerful impetus for symmetry in art and design. *Bilateral symmetry* is the placement of equal form and weight on both sides of a dividing line. The size, shape and position of elements correspond (fig. **3-10**). Early printers used bilateral symmetry as an organizing principle to bring order and unity to the printed page (see fig. **1-28**), and many advertising art directors favor it to produce a symmetrical sequence of image, headline, and body copy (see figs. **1-60, 1-61, 2-42,** and **2-43**).

On the book jacket for *Vegetables* (fig. **3-11**), photographed by Tom Tracy and designed by Kit Hinrichs, D. J. Hyde, and Lenore Bartz, strong bilateral symmetry is present. The composition of the photograph has light-valued vegetables bleeding off the page above and below the central complex and extending the symmetrical axis.

Other forms of symmetry are found in design and nature. In *radial symmetry,* the elements radiate from a central axis or point, as in a sunburst pattern (see fig. **1-22**, whose sunburst illustrates radial symmetry, which has an asymmetrical relationship with the word). *Rotational symmetry* occurs when the elements rotate around a central point and divide the 360-degree circle into equal portions, such as a five-pointed star with each point occupying seventy-two degrees of the circle. *Ornamental* or *crystallographic symmetry* involves the dense packing of similar forms in space. The hexagonal pattern of tiles on a bathroom floor is an example of ornamental or crystallographic symmetry on a two-dimensional plane, and the complex process of crystal formation in nature is an occurrence in three-dimensional space.

3-10

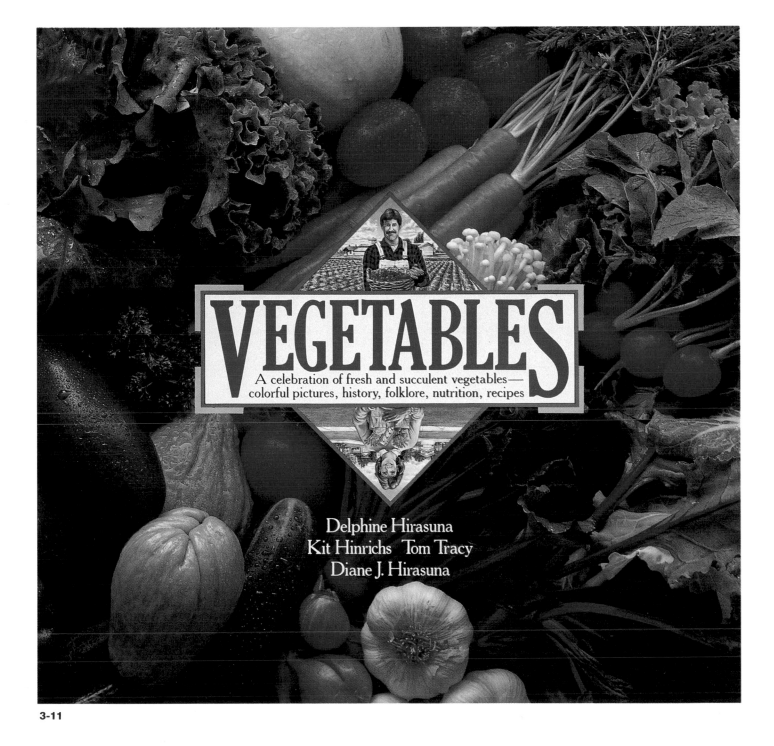

VEGETABLES

A celebration of fresh and succulent vegetables—
colorful pictures, history, folklore, nutrition, recipes

Delphine Hirasuna
Kit Hinrichs Tom Tracy
Diane J. Hirasuna

The modern art and design movements of the early twentieth century rebelled against symmetrical balance and embraced *asymmetry,* which traditionally meant the lack of proportion between the parts of the whole, or the lack of symmetry. Asymmetry has been redefined as dynamic equilibrium or the creation of order and balance between unlike or unequal things. The order and dynamic that can be achieved through asymmetric balancing of unlike elements is seen in two *Boston Globe Magazine* covers designed by Ronn Campisi. In figure **3-12**, a typographic list of people that Alfred Eisenstaedt has photographed is positioned on the left, balanced by a small photograph of Eisenstaedt on the right. Horizontal rules define the space and give structure to the page.

ALSO: ENERGY FROM SPACE

The Boston Globe Magazine

June 21, 1981

WITNESS TO OUR TIME: Alfred Eisenstaedt has photographed Hitler meeting Mussolini, Thomas Mann, Joseph Goebbels, Günter Grass, Hedy Lamarr, Rainer Werner Fassbinder, the Great Depression, Leni Riefenstahl, John F. Kennedy, Sophia Loren, George Bernard Shaw, Igor Stravinsky, Vladimir Horowitz, Joseph Stalin, Hiroshima, Yehudi Menuhin, Bing Crosby, Joan Crawford, Fred Astaire, Marilyn Monroe, Tallulah Bankhead, Katharine Hepburn, Lyndon Baines Johnson, Henry Kissinger, Marlon Brando, Charlie Chaplin, Richard Nixon, Nikita Khrushchev, Winston Churchill, W. H. Auden, Robert Frost, T. S. Eliot, Charles Lindbergh, Harry Truman, Franklin Delano Roosevelt, Ernest Hemingway, Bertrand Russell, Ronald Reagan's ranch, V-J Day, Albert Einstein, Alec Guinness, the eyes of Edward Teller, Sinclair Lewis, James Cagney, General Douglas MacArthur, Jomo Kenyatta, Fidel Castro, Clare Boothe Luce, Harold Macmillan, Mikhail Baryshnikov, the Blue Nile Falls in Ethiopia, Rachel Carson, Salvador Dali, Judy Garland, Judge Learned Hand, Dwight D. Eisenhower, General Hideki Tojo, Shirley Temple, Clement Attlee, Queen Elizabeth II, Thornton Wilder, Nelson Rockefeller, Walt Disney, Josephine Baker, the Graf Zeppelin, General George C. Marshall, Dame Edith Evans, Andrew Wyeth, Paul Dudley White, Edward R. Murrow, Leonard Bernstein, Dag Hammarskjöld, Adlai Stevenson, Arthur Rubinstein...

3-12

3-13

In figure **3-13**, the photograph of author Jean Stafford is placed in the lower right and balanced against the typography on the upper left. The vertical line of dots to the left of the display type is a critical compositional element, for it relates the informal typographic complex to the vertical edges of the page and the photograph. The axes of the lower typographic lines shift toward the right, as if the photograph has a magnetic pull of energy, and create a diagonal movement that echoes the diagonal lines of the book.

"Symmetry signifies rest and binding," observes Dagobert Frey, and asymmetry signifies "motion and loosening, the one order and law, the other arbitrariness and accident, the one formal rigidity and constraint, the other life, play and freedom." [3] A decision to use symmetrical or asymmetrical composition should grow out of the subject matter and design intent, for both can be effective approaches to graphic space.

Comparison of Lance Hidy's poster (fig. **3-14**) for the Hewlett Library with a calendar page (fig. **3-15**) for Kieffer-Nolde, Inc., designed by Jeff Barnes and photographed by Dennis Manarchy, demonstrates how powerful symmetrical and asymmetrical spatial organization can be. Hidy uses absolute bilateral symmetry to suspend a moment in time, creating a dignified commemorative about the naming ceremony for a theological library. Barnes uses dynamic asymmetry to express the energetic forces of nature during springtime and evoke the winds of March and sprouting of springtime flowers. Hidy effectively uses absolute bilateral symmetry to achieve monumental order, and Barnes achieves unquelled energy with asymmetrical elements in dynamic equilibrium.

3-14

MARCH/APRIL

kn

KIEFFER-NOLDE, INC. Offset & Gravure Graphics, 160 East Illinois, Chicago, IL 60611
312-337-5500 Or Toll Free 1-800-621-8314, In Cleveland 216-344-9170

Modular relationships

A *module* is a basic elementary unit that can be combined and repeated to become the basis for the whole. The physical world with its molecular and crystal structure, all life with its cellular structure, and much art and design are based on modular relationships. The most frequent use of modular structure in graphic design is the use of a modular grid of horizontal and vertical linear divisions. A grid structure can take many forms: a regular sequence of squares or rectangles; a format of columns for publications design; and complex modular relationships that allow for diverse typographic treatments and a large variety of image sizes and shapes.

A *visual program* is a system of parameters used consistently to unify a series or sequence of designs. Grid structure, consistent use of type sizes and styles, placement of page numbers, and a color plan are factors that might be included. Russian constructivist designers of the 1920s made important contributions to the development of visual programs. The trilingual 1925 book, *The Isms of Art,* designed by El Lissitzky, is a milestone in the use of a modular grid structure and mathematical measurement to bring order to complex visual material. Lissitzky carefully planned a visual program that gives order and consistent graphic properties. This book is organized into two sections: an eleven-page typographic section, followed by a forty-eight-page pictorial portfolio presenting major European art movements from 1914 until 1924.

Lissitzky executed his layouts on graph paper, which imposed the order of modular structure into his work. He specified sans serif type, for he and other members of the modern movement believed

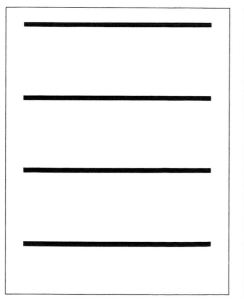

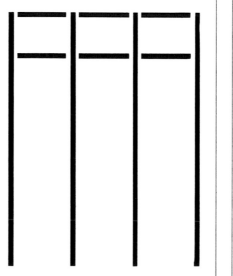

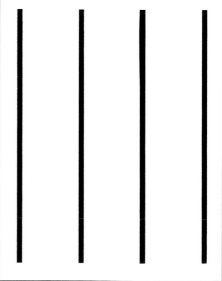

that it best expressed the rationalism of the scientific and technological era. Pictorial portfolio pages are anchored by heavy black rules in their top outside corners, adjacent to the name of the movement. Page numbers align with the outside vertical grid line. Visual continuity and immediate identification result, for readers quickly learn to look at the outside top corner for this information. By stripping away their backgrounds to silhouette many of the photographs, Lissitzky gives them a strong "object quality." Picture numbers are large, which makes them concrete forms in the design organization. These numbers are composed in counterpoint to the illustrations. Lissitzky makes generous use of white space as an important compositional element.

Figure **3-16** reproduces major typographic pages above their geometric structure, which Lissitzky emphasized by subdividing the space with black rules. The title page has horizontal bars to create a three-part grid structure for the trilingual text. The contents pages are divided with a central horizontal or vertical bar.

The text pages have a three-column vertical grid containing German, French, and English versions. The two sets of horizontal bars in the top portion of page VIII are important to Lissitzky's program for the pictorial portfolio. The highest set establishes the top of the live area and aligns with the titles placed on each portfolio page. The lower set establishes a flow line. This horizontal grid line is used consistently in many pages, bringing continuity to the format. Figure **3-17** superimposes the grid structures used in the typographic pages. I think that Lissitzky used this grid system from the typographic pages to bring order and structure to the illustrated portfolio.

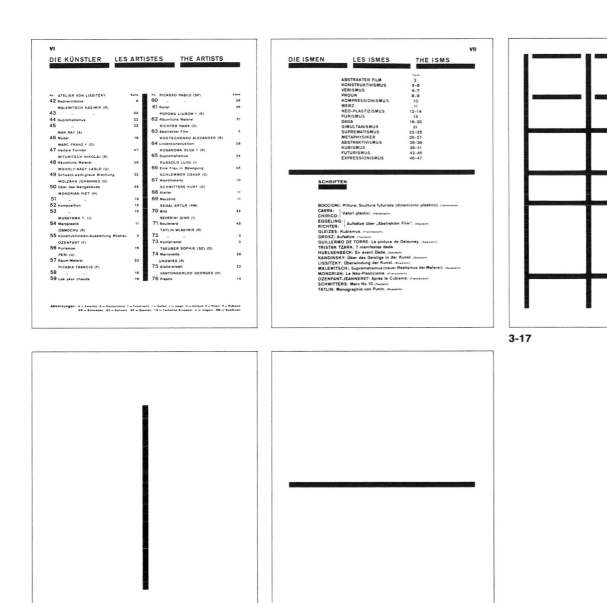

3-17

Figures **3-18** through **3-21** show double-page spreads from the portfolio with the grid superimposed on the lower reproduction. In page after page, the alignment of images to the grid is unmistakable. Lissitzky was flexible in his attitude toward the system. He would optically adjust images within the grid and even violate it to create a more balanced or dynamic layout.

Figure **3-18** illustrates pages 2 and 3. On page 2, an organic photomontage of a filmmaker, actress, and equipment is aligned in the first column, and two angles created by strips of film are placed in the second two columns. On page 3, the large halftone image is two columns wide and the smaller one is one column wide. Lissitzky moved them to the right to create a connection between the large photograph and the title and bar and to produce a more balanced page and spread.

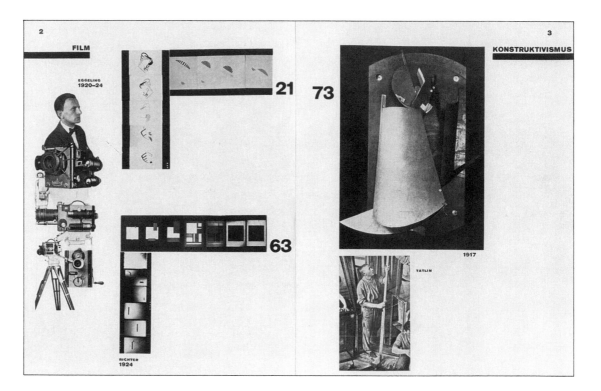

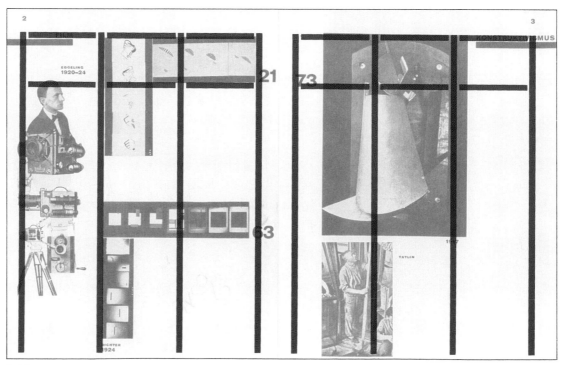

3-18

One observes that the alignments between the grid, type, and images are not always perfect, and some images are sized wrong. *The Isms of Art* was printed by letterpress, and the printer assembled type and halftone blocks on the press bed according to Lissitzky's layouts. Subtle size errors when shooting the negatives to make the halftone blocks and in aligning and placing type, bar rules, and the blocks on the press bed were inevitable considering the exactitude that Lissitzky sought from 1920s letterpress printing technology.

Pages 12 and 13 present the work of Mondrian (fig. **3-19**). The large painting is two columns wide, the small painting is one column wide, and the silhouette photograph is optically adjusted, with the arm and coattail extending just beyond the grid line. If Lissitzky had aligned the left edge of the coat with the left edge of the painting, it would have appeared to be too far to the right. Cohesion is achieved by the movement of forms in space, as indicated on the lower reproduction. The figure numbers play an important role as connecting forms.

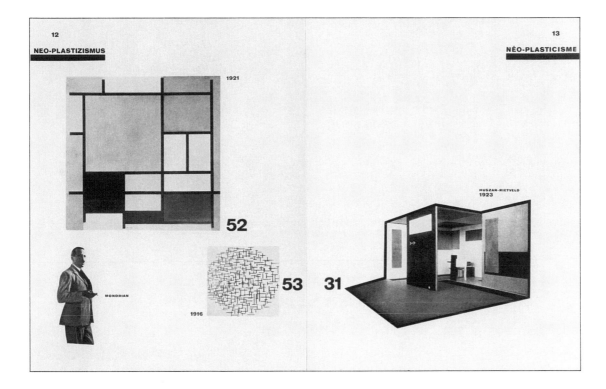

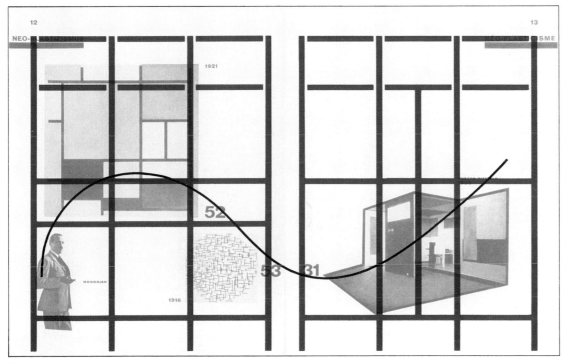

3-19

On page 14, the diamond-shaped painting is about
two columns wide, as is the top painting on the
opposite page (fig. **3-20**). Lissitzky made an optical
adjustment by allowing the top corner of the
diamond shape to thrust up above the top edge of
the opposite painting; otherwise, the diamond
shape would have appeared too low on the page.
On page 14, the balance and relationship between
the painting and the sculpture are carefully
considered, as is the relationship of the dark vertical
form in the painting to the sculpture.

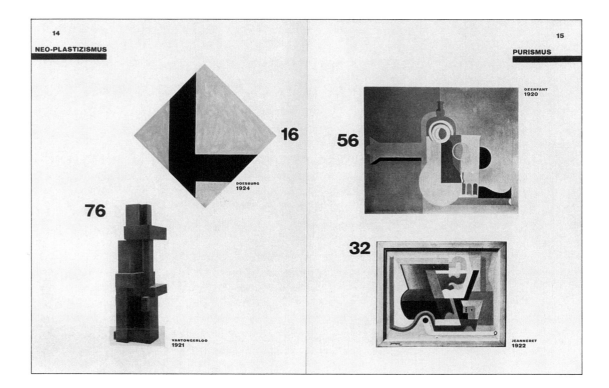

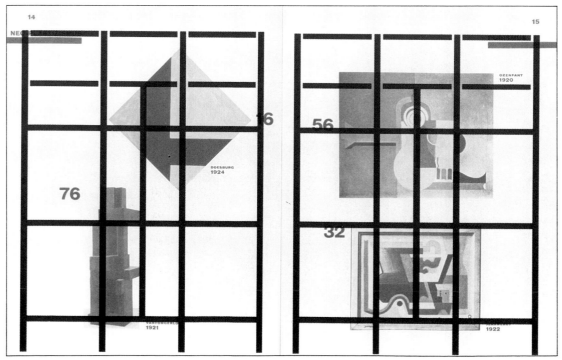

3-20

On page 22, Lissitzky sized and positioned the two paintings on the grid and placed the photograph of Malevich in a balanced relationship with them (fig. **3-21**). Page 23 is typical of pages that reproduce just one painting: Lissitzky centered the images, taking care to use the grid to create alignments with material on the opposite page. Here the top horizontal edges of two Malevich paintings are placed on the flow line. This relationship unifies the double-page spread.

The importance of El Lissitzky to twentieth-century graphic design led typographer Jan Tschichold to write in 1965 that there is a new "generation that has never heard of him, and yet stands on his shoulders." [4] He was truly one of the great innovators of graphic design, for his pioneering work in applying grid structure to visual organization was just one of his many important contributions.

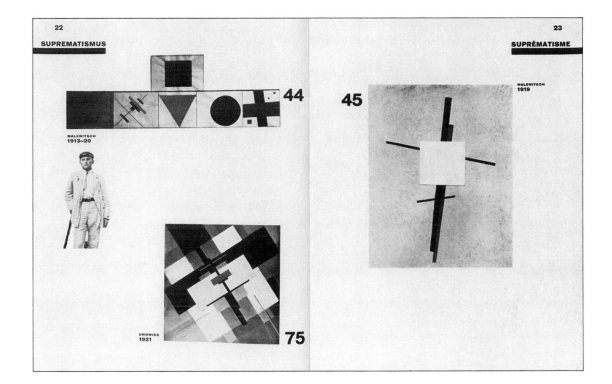

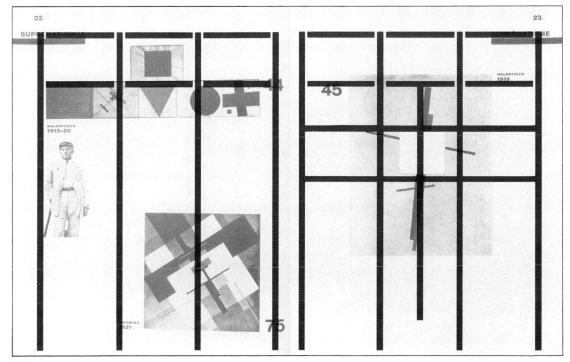

3-21

While El Lissitzky's approach to the grid allowed for a degree of flexibility, the Swiss architect, painter, and designer Max Bill placed emphasis upon absolute mathematical order in many of his graphic designs. In the series of *Moderne Schweizer Architektur (Modern Swiss Architecture)* folios from the early 1940s, the placement of photographs and typography conforms to a rigid modular system (fig. **3-22**). The first grid was used for the photographic pages with two columns for photographs. The left-hand column can contain three photographs that are eight units[5] square, and the second column can hold three horizontal photographs that are twelve units wide by eight units high. This grid accommodates both square format and 35 mm format photographs. The horizontal margins are two units deep, and the vertical margins are one unit wide. The second grid—used for the text pages printed on the back of the photographic pages—is a mirror image of the first: the wider column is on the left.

Figure **3-23** is a typical typographic page in this trilingual publication intended primarily for a German audience. The German text is set in a larger point size on the wider column, and the English and French translations are set in smaller type in the narrower column. Switzerland is multilingual, so formats with a controlled typographic structure were vital and the development of grid formats was hastened. Wherever possible, Bill aligned the top of type columns with the horizontal grid lines to relate text pages to the photographic pages.

Bill's grid format can accommodate from one to six photographs. The two-unit horizontal margin below the photographs provides space for captions. A ruled line, two units from the bottom of the page,

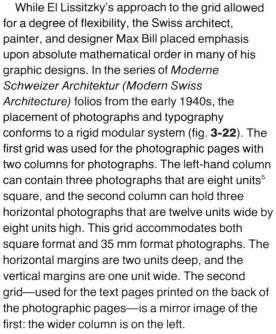

3-22

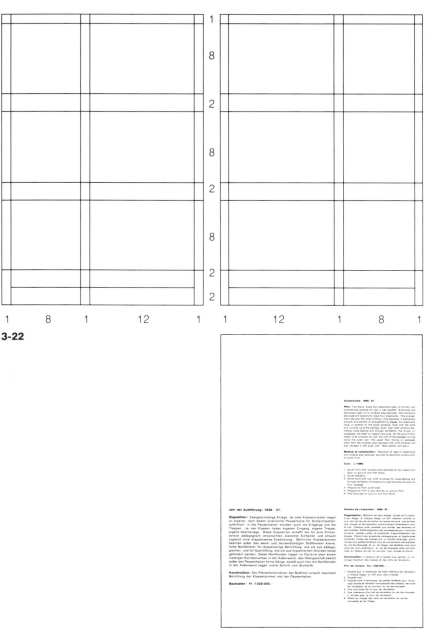

3-23

is above the building's name which aligns with the left margin, and the architect's name aligns with the grid line for the left edge of the larger photographs and their captions. The six photographs in figure **3-24** fill the grid. The intervals of white space created by unfilled grid sections (fig. **3-25**) infuse variety into the folios.

Large images are placed on the grid structure by joining several modules into one rectangle (fig. **3-26**). The white space in this layout provides relief for the viewer by rendering the page open and spacious. It separates the images from their environment just as a mat isolates artwork from its environment. The placement of the church steeple (on the left in the top photograph, and on the right in the lower photograph) produces a satisfying asymmetrical balance. If the bottom photograph had been placed to the left, or if the designer had switched the size and position of the two photographs, this balance would have been disrupted.

In response to the subject matter, a systematic departure from the primary grid structure is permitted. In figure **3-27** the top horizontal photograph is twelve units deep, and the two smaller photographs are placed four—instead of two—units above the hairline rule. This produces better balance on the page. Moving down the page, the mathematical division of space is satisfying. The top photograph equals twelve units; the open space equals six units; the lower photograph equals eight units; and the margin below them equals four units for a 12 : 6 : 8 : 4 ratio. The vertical edges conform to the grid, and alterations are consistently made in two-unit increments. As a consequence, these pages are fully compatible with the overall program.

3-24

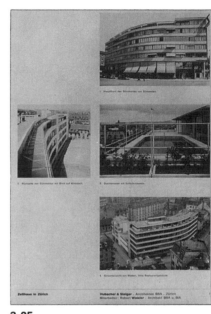

3-25

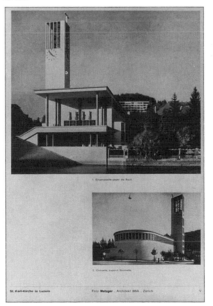

3-26

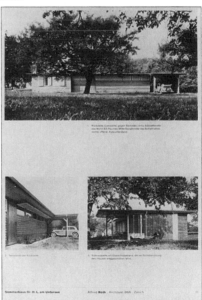

3-27

Order and clarity are achieved by a grid structure. Attention is focused, not upon the designer's manipulation of space, but upon the content. Over two hundred photographic pages in these folios were designed over several years. The grid structure brings efficiency to the process, for the designer organizes material on each page within established spatial and typographic parameters. Without this graphic program, the designer would have to develop a design plan for each page. Much time would be consumed, and the pages would be inconsistent. Bill achieved tremendous variety within this format. Four other examples from scores of page layouts are diagramed in figure **3-28**.

Even the most rigorous grid is no substitute for the designer's sensitive eye for balance. The grid provides a framework, but the designer still must make careful decisions about the size and placement of the elements and their relationship to one another.

By changing the parameters of the grid, designers can alter the visual properties of the page. By using a very narrow vertical grid with twelve 5-pica-wide columns on a tabloid page, John DeMao creates lively and unusual page layouts (fig. **3-29**). Typographic units and photographs are one to six columns wide. As the pages were designed, horizontal alignments began to form. The result is informal and dynamic, using the grid as a point of departure. Torn-edged collage elements and initial letters further express the energetic dissonance of modern dance, turning a grid-derived page into a field of tension, as discussed below.

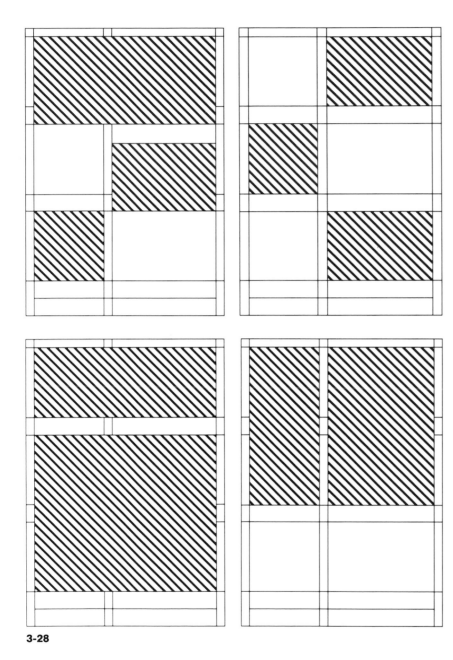

3-28

■ *Dance and Choreography*

Majors in this department prepare to become performers, choreographers, teachers, or participants in the many fields related to dance.

A daily modern technique class is part of the core curriculum. Ballet is studied concurrently with modern technique, but the choreographic emphasis of the program is on modern techniques. By the junior year, students choose either performance or choreography as an emphasis area. The senior project is a public presentation in either the performance or the choreographic area.

The department has a professionally active faculty of five full-time and ten part-time members. A Visiting Artist also joins the faculty each semester. Dance majors have opportunities to study with many other guest teachers and lecturers in the weekly meeting of Dance Workshop.

Included in the curriculum are technique courses in modern, ballet, folk, ethnic, jazz, and tap, improvisation, teaching methods, choreography, production, dance history, and music for dancers. The active production calendar of VCUDANCECO, the performing organization of the department, provides many practical experiences in performing, choreographing, and staging.

The Department is housed in a newly renovated building with eight fine studios, one of which is equipped as a performance space. Other campus performances are given in the Music Recital Hall and in the new Concert Hall. Off-campus performances are given in the Empire Theatre, Dogwood Dell Amphitheatre and public schools in and outside of the Richmond area. The VCUDANCECO calendar for 1983-84 will include two major collaborative productions with the Department of Music, one of which is to be televised.

Admission to the major program is by audition, and consideration is given to the applicant's previous training and performing experience. The Department also offers a minor in dance, and most of the dance courses are open to non-majors as well as majors. The Evening College curriculum offers T'ai Chi and Improvisation as well as dance technique courses.

●

This "time line" section of the Best Products Employee Annual Report describes in words and images a remarkable year in the history of our company. Within the span of one fiscal year—February 1982 to January 1983—Best nearly doubled its number of showrooms and employees.

Today the catalog showroom industry's biggest retailer employs more than 17,000 people in 27 states, has yearly sales of $1.6 billion and operates 189 showrooms under eight different names: Basco, Best, Dolgin's, Great Western, Jafco, LaBelle's, Miller Sales and Rogers.

Until recent years, through the dedication and hard work of its employees, Best had been able to increase profits and career opportunities by rapidly opening new showrooms bearing the Best name. But changing economic forces—including high interest rates and sluggish sales—called for changing that strategy: The Best solution was to acquire existing chains of showrooms from other retailers.

1982: the Year of Acquisition
In September, Best acquired Modern Merchandising, the 75-showroom chain based in Minnetonka, Minn. It was the most important merger in the history of the catalog showroom industry and dominated headlines in industry publications for several months.

More than 7,000 employees became part of the Best family as a result of the acquisition, working in showrooms and regional offices throughout the West and mid-West under the Dolgin's, Great Western, Jafco, LaBelle's, Miller Sales and Rogers names. The acquisition was a perfect geographic fit for Best, which has directed its expansion along the East Coast, in Texas and in California.

The Modern merger was preceded by the acquisition in July of Basco, a 19-showroom chain located in the Philadelphia, Pittsburgh and Cleveland areas. While some of these showrooms were closed and others continued to operate under the Basco name, most were converted to Best showrooms bearing the Best logo. Showrooms in the Modern network continue to operate under the six names known to customers in their various markets.

The Best-Modern-Basco union brought together employees with a history of collaboration: Creative Merchandising and Publishing Co., a subsidiary of Modern and now of Best, has published the Best catalog since 1959 and had printed the Basco catalog from 1961 until this year. Founded by Harold Roitenberg, who serves as Creative's chairman and is also on the Best board of directors, Creative was the foundation upon which Roitenberg built Modern, largely by acquiring other showroom chains.

Late in 1982, President Andrew M. Lewis announced plans to consolidate the corporate structures of Best and Modern with the goal of creating a new organization combining the strengths of the two. Employees in all locations maintained a high level of customer service during this transition period, which continues into 1983.

New Showrooms
Although overshadowed by the eventful Modern acquisition, Best opened six new showrooms in fiscal 1982, signaling the company's continued interest in Sunbelt locations and experiments in showroom design. In El Paso, Texas, and Pinole, Calif., 67,000-square-foot showrooms were opened and in Sandusky, Ohio, Best opened its first suburban mall sales center, a 30,000-square-foot showroom where all merchandise is displayed under glass.

Also opening this year were three showrooms in the West: two under the LaBelle's name, one in Farmington, N.M., and one in Salt Lake City; and a Jafco in Eugene, Ore.

In January 1983, Best opened a new central distribution center in New Haven, Ind., a 200,000-square-foot facility designed to serve 18 showrooms in the East and mid-West and to replace the CDC at Chicago. Also in fiscal 1982, construction began on another CDC, located in Las Vegas, Nev., now serving the company's West Coast showrooms.

Extensive renovations in the company's four Dallas-area showrooms brought a new look for customers there.

and thanks to the flexibility of Best employees, were accomplished without closing for business.

Improved Service
While historic changes were taking place in the company's corporate structure, important showroom modifications increased the quality of customer service. "Point of order," also known as POO, was introduced in several Best showrooms. This computerized inventory system—which enables employees to determine prices, stock levels and alternative merchandise selections—is much like the progressive Tel-O-Serv system in place at Basco at the time of acquisition.

In 1983, POO is scheduled to be installed in 66 more Best showrooms where it will reduce waiting time for customers and help buyers respond to the needs of individual showrooms.

1982

February   March   April   May   June   July

The No. 6 seller for 1982: the Winnersville Slender Cycle.

Novella D. Morris, a data entry operator at Ashland, Va., is one of 149 Best employees receiving awards for perfect attendance.

Best films a TV commercial in Spanish for the Florida market.

The company opens its first Data Base store in Richmond, Va., selling microcomputers for the home and office.

Best acquires Ashby's, a Richmond, Va.-based eight-store chain selling brand name women's clothing at discount.

Point of order, a computerized inventory system, is tested in several showrooms. Its successful trial leads to plans for company-wide adoption.

Lori Anderson poses for People magazine, wearing jewelry purchased by Burt Reynolds from the Best showroom in Tyson's Corner, Va.

The No. 8 seller for 1982: Brother's Correct-O-Ball 7300 XL-1 electric typewriter.

A Best Products Foundation donation to the Anaheim, Calif., Red Cross helps victims of the worst fire in that city's history.

Central returns areas are installed company-wide to streamline the returns process.

The No. 5 seller for 1982: the Extend-A-Phone cordless telephone, model EX 3000.

The No. 10 seller for 1982: Sharp's Microwave Oven, model 5d-1226.

The No. 2 seller for 1982: the Canon AF35M Sure Shot 35 mm autofocus camera.

The names of 17 or more than 17,000 Best employees have been hidden on this time line. How many can you find?

The No. 7 seller for 1982: Coleco Midway's Pac-Man portable arcade game.

Dr. Frank S. Royal, a member of the Best board of directors, is named one of the "100 Most Influential Black Americans" by Ebony magazine.

The Best Products Foundation helps establish a job internship program for troubled adolescents through the Settlement Club Home in Austin, Texas.

Best brings air conditioners back to its merchandise mix.

Best Chairman Sydney Lewis and Executive Vice President Frances A. Lewis conduct the annual stockholders' meeting in the absence of President Andrew M. Lewis, who is in Minnetonka, Minn., for the final negotiations leading to the Modern Merchandising acquisition.

Domestic soft goods make their debut in selected showrooms.

Montklair, Calif., showroom manager Steve Shroder and his wife Gwynne celebrate their 15th wedding anniversary with daughter Melissa, adopted with the help of the company's adoption assistance plan.

BASCO

Hayet A. Rist of Ashland, Va., retires from Best for a life of gardening and deep sea fishing.

The 19-showroom Basco chain is acquired; some showrooms are closed with special sales.

Jimmy Connors defeats Bjorn Borg in the Best Summer Challenge tennis tournament in Richmond, Va.; President Andrew M. Lewis presents the trophy.

Best sews up a deal with Singer to become the first retailer outside a Singer franchise to sell the popular sewing products.

SINGER

The grid approach is particularly useful when a large number of images and typographic units must be organized in a graphic space. In a one-year timeline for Best Products, designers Rob Carter and Tim Priddy used a vertical grid to divide the space into chronological zones representing twelve months (fig. **3-30**). The grid structure is followed closely by the typography, but it is violated in the lower area where a lively composition of images moving at angles to one another is in contrast to the more structured upper portion.

The discipline and limitations of the grid should not be seen as a creative straitjacket, for designers using it can achieve flexibility and originality. In a Container Corporation of America Annual Report (fig. **3-31**), John Massey used a modular grid of almost two hundred half-inch squares to contain twelve color photographs of CCA employees. Careful placement enabled Massey to relate forms, colors, and tones so that the photographs blend into each other along some edges but have abrupt linear edges and corners at other junctions. This graphic vitality combines with the variety of sizes and the dynamic diagonal edges of the overall configuration to create a cohesive and intriguing cover.

Multiple-image design

Composing type and images on a grid is but one method for designing complex, multiple-image layouts. Any structural principle can be adopted and used as an organizing theme. In a double-page design presenting "Things to Do and See" (fig. **3-32**), Don Trousdell has used a rhythmic alignment of vertical images as a unifying principle by making the vertical axes of the images parallel. From the myriad possible images to signify each of ten activities, Trousdell carefully selected vertical ones: a baseball bat for the Cooperstown Baseball Museum, an ear of corn for the Farmer's Market, an ostrich for the zoo, a doll for antique collecting. Typography is related to the images by carefully aligning type units with an illustration's left edge or a prominent feature such as the fish's mouth or by aligning the central axes of type and image.

Other potential themes might have been the selection of objects that fit within square spaces (a baseball glove, a basket of strawberries, a profile of an elephant, a squat antique chair), horizontal spaces, or circular spaces. The designer's imagination is the only limitation constraining the invention of an organizational schema and appropriate images.

Establishing a dominant image is another effective method to structure complex pages. Figure **3-33**, a double-page spread from a Nature Company catalog designed by Kit Hinrichs and Natalie Kitamura, has no discernible grid. Images are presented in a variety of sizes, some are silhouetted, and four of them overlap the deep navy blue borders. Type units are varied. Some are set flush left and ragged right, some are flush right and ragged left, and others wrap around the photograph. Order is achieved in spite of the complexity of ten images and lengthy captions because a major focal point is created by the dominant African antelope mask. The other images form relationships with this large image and the borders. Through the principle of proximity, each unit of type forms a clear relationship with its image.

Container Corporation of America   Annual Report 1967

3-31

3-32

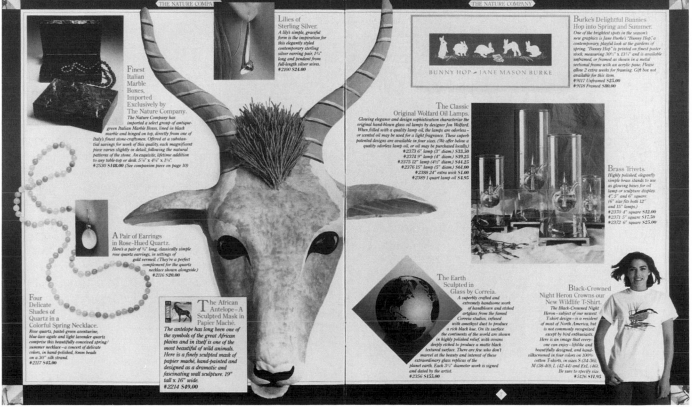

3-33

Field of tension

Another approach to organizing graphic space is to transform it into a dynamic field of tension. This effect is achieved by creating taut relationships between the elements of the design and between the elements and the edges of the rectangle. Often, diagonal movements and countermovements and forms that bleed and run off the page are used to create this spatial dynamic. Extreme contrasts of size and scale can play an important role in creating this tension.

Piet Zwart of the Netherlands, who like Lissitzky was a pioneering graphic designer of the 1920s, mastered this spatial concept. In pages 26 and 27 from his 1928 catalog for the NKF cableworks (fig. **3-34**), four photographs and a cross-section diagram are combined on the left-hand page with dynamic scale and spatial contrasts. A red arrow slashing across the page runs from the cable on a large industrial crane to a cross-sectional photograph of the cable. This arrow echoes the diagonal movement of type on the right-hand page, where a dynamic composition of red and black type moving at angles and open white spaces provides a lively contrast to the complexity of the montage page.

Printed in red and black on tan paper, the "New Dutch Graphics" poster by Cheryl A. Brzezinski (fig. **3-35**) uses a variety of complex graphic techniques and relationships to transform the space into a dynamic field of tension. The space is divided into tan and black zones, but unity occurs in spite of the intense division because the stacked letterforms at the top (the *N* and *I*) pull weight into the light area, while the tan *D,* gray *E,* and tan word *GRAPHICS* pull light into the black area. In the lower half of the poster, the largest tulip performs a similar spatial reversal. It is split into a duotone photograph against the tan, and a stark line drawing against the black background.

Windmills and tulips, traditional images signifying Holland, are used in repetition to energize the space. Three windmills become dynamic forms, their axes shifted in diagonal counterpoint to the vertical format. A rotational pattern of arrows and dotted lines signifies the wind and the rotary action of the windmill blades and activates the top portion of the space. Although the windmills are printed in the same screen tints, the one on the right appears lighter by its contrast with the black background.

The row of five tulips thrusting upward from the bottom are executed in different graphic techniques: a black line drawing, a pink halftone, a red line drawing, a soft duotone, another black line drawing, and a pink linear image against a red shape. Transparency and overlapping serve to unify these dissonant images. They attract one another due to the similar subject matter and organic floral forms, but repel each other because of the contrasting color, value, and technique. Brzezinski provides the viewer with a complex, multilayered experience.

3-34

3-35

The *Boston Globe Magazine* cover designed by Ronn Campisi and illustrated by Gene Greif (fig. **3-36**) has a dominant image, the photograph of George Frazier, which is placed in a lively tension with the second most prominent image, a portion of a page whose wavelike lower edge signifies smoke from the cigarette. A series of carefully planned relationships brings unity to this design with an open structure. The typewriter creates a movement from the head, to the major display typography, to the top of the page. The ruled line above the secondary display typography becomes a connector from the cigarette to the photograph of Richard Nixon. The poison pen image creates a linear movement from the horizontal base to the lower corner of the Richard Nixon photograph. Images bleed off each of the four sides of the design, creating a lateral expansion.

In an advertisement for the Granfalloon furniture store designed by Jeff Barnes and photographed by Robert Keeling (fig. **3-37**), graphic support elements transform the magazine page into a field of tension. The photograph of the white furniture against a black floor emphasizes the furniture design and material and is shifted at an angle to the page. Rules with rounded terminals contain the typography. Dot patterns echo the pattern of circular holes in the metal furniture. One sequence forms a drop shadow; another overlaps the photograph. The dot patterns pull weight into the white areas of the page. Their three different size and scale relationships create a sequence of overlapping planes that imply depth. Barnes has achieved unity by aligning the dot patterns and bars with the axes of the photograph and through the repetition of circles and arcs in the photograph, its curved corners, and the graphic support elements.

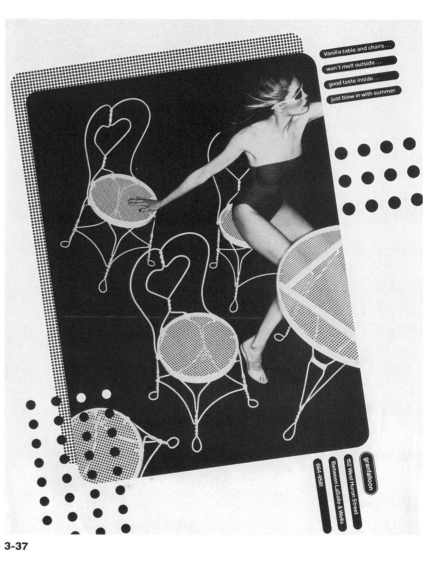

3-37

3-36

3-38

Repetition and rhythm

Repetition is repeating identical or similar forms in a consistent spatial relationship and creating an overall pattern of equal weight. Contrast occurs when unlike elements are introduced into the repetitive sequence. *Rhythm* is repeating similar elements with a variety of forms or spatial intervals and creating variety in repetition. It possesses the ebb and flow of recurring elements in space. Alfred North Whitehead observed that "the essence of rhythm is the fusion of sameness and novelty; so that the whole never loses the essential unity of the pattern, while the parts exhibit the contrast arising from the novelty of their detail. A mere recurrence kills rhythm as surely as does a mere confusion of differences. A crystal lacks rhythm from excessive pattern, while a fog is unrhythmic in that it exhibits a patternless confusion of detail." [6]

Whitehead's "essence of rhythm" is found in a poster presenting Chihuly Indian glass cylinders (fig. **3-38**), designed by Malcolm Grear and photographed by Gene Dwiggins. Careful organization of the artifacts into four rows against a black background enabled Grear to create a lively and satisfying rhythm. Identifying captions are reversed out of the background at a forty-five-degree angle, creating a secondary rhythm in lilting counterpoint to the horizontal rows of vertical objects.

Visual continuity

Single-surface visual communications, such as a poster or book jacket, are independent entities, but multiple-surface graphic designs introduce the additional problems of continuity and visual flow. A sense of belonging, of being part of the larger whole, should be expressed by pages in a publication, book jackets in a series, and packages for a family of products. At the same time, each design should have its unique identity, for too much sameness or redundancy becomes boring. The designer develops strategies to link the sequence by determining what will be alike and what will be different. Visual characteristics (for example, size, position, color) of typography and images can be repeated to create continuity. Grid structure, repetition, rhythm, and alignment that occur on the two-dimensional surface now occur in time and space as many pages or a series of designs are experienced by the viewer.

According to one of his former assistants, Leo Lionni once observed that if the pages in a publication design were not unified, the designer could just go back through and draw a mustache on all the men in the photographs to create visual continuity.[7] The underlying principle advocated by Lionni is that any element or graphic quality recurring within a sequence of pages or designs becomes a unifying force that generates visual continuity.

The cover and inside spread for a direct mail folder, designed by Jacklin Pinsler for Adesso (figures **3-39** and **3-40**), demonstrate this principle. The angled headline repeats itself, and the rectangular photograph in the interior of the folder repeats the size, position, and angle of the pitcher in the cover photograph. The red bar in the upper right-hand corner of the cover appears at the fold inside. Two units of text type in the interior relate to the size, measure, and position of the cover text type.

These unifying factors are complemented by variation. The cover headline is white reversed from black and the inside headline is black on the white page. A new element—a red bar running along the left-hand edge—is introduced on the interior spread. An appropriate balance between continuity and diversity is created between this folder's cover and interior.

Adesso.

For the fire of red. Sizzling.

Festive. Joyful. Bold.

The excitement of ceramics.

From dinnerware to

one-of-a-kind. To celebrate

the special and everyday

occasions of life.

ADESSO IS EXCITEMENT

3-39

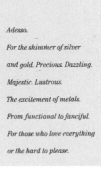

Adesso.

For the magic of black.
Dramatic. Mysterious.
Provocative. Elegant. The
excitement of glass. From
unique barware to delicate
stems. To delight others or
treasure yourself.

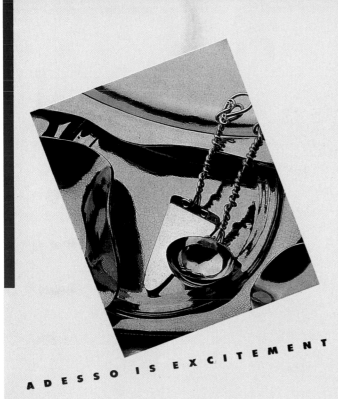

A D E S S O   I S   E X C I T E M E N T

Adesso.

For the shimmer of silver
and gold. Precious. Dazzling.
Majestic. Lustrous.
The excitement of metals.
From functional to fanciful.
For those who love everything
or the hard to please.

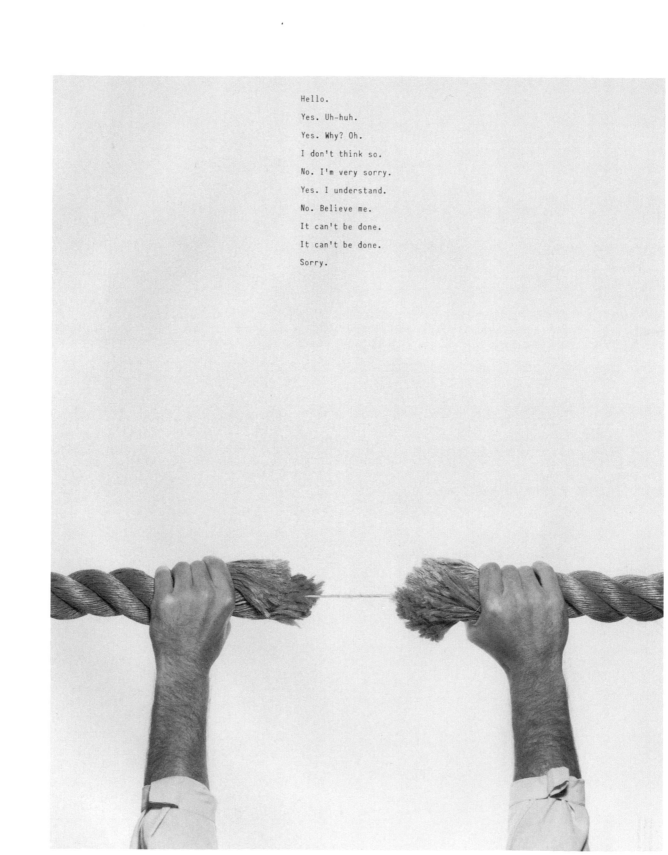

Hello.
Yes. Uh-huh.
Yes. Why? Oh.
I don't think so.
No. I'm very sorry.
Yes. I understand.
No. Believe me.
It can't be done.
It can't be done.
Sorry.

The kinetic experience of turning the page can be used to present a sequence of events, contrast images, or develop concepts. Sequential right-hand page advertisements illustrate the dilemma of a customer who is "hanging by a thread" because a supplier cannot meet a need (fig. **3-41**). The reader turns the page to learn that the customer has found a sturdy rope (fig. **3-42**), a metaphor for the support that is being offered.

Hello.
Yeah. Look.
Yeah. Listen to this:
they can do that.
That's what they do.
I don't know. That's
just what they do.
Yeah. Thanks. I know.
Thanks. Sure. Anytime.

Kieffer-Nolde's
Electronic Pre-Press
Imaging System

Kieffer-Nolde,Inc.
Offset & Gravure
Graphics
160 East Illinois
Chicago, IL 60611
312-337-5500
Or Toll Free
1-800-621-8314
In Cleveland
216-344-9170
Call or write for
our complimentary
color calendar.

3-42

Rhythmic continuity in the time-space experience of the viewer paging through an extended design sequence is called *visual flow.* In a promotional brochure presenting American flag artifacts (fig. **3-43**), Kit Hinrichs achieved visual flow through the repetition of layout ideas. Double-page spreads filled with a large image alternate with spreads having a full-page image opposite a page with centered typography, a small image, and generous white space. Some of these layouts have the full-page image on the left and others have it on the right. This rhythm is broken twice: One layout depicts three cigar band flags; the center spread mirror-images two postcards with typography

centered above and below and then folds out to reveal a multiple-image layout. The repetition of the Stars and Stripes motif is a unifying device, the ultimate example of Lionni's mustache paradigm.

Whereas visual flow describes the continuity within a multiple-page visual communication, *serial design* involves a series of independent but related items. In effective serial design, the designer establishes parameters that define a spatial structure, typographic system, and color scheme. These parameters must be tight enough to insure immediate identity with the series but flexible enough to allow variation and identification of the individual designs within the series.

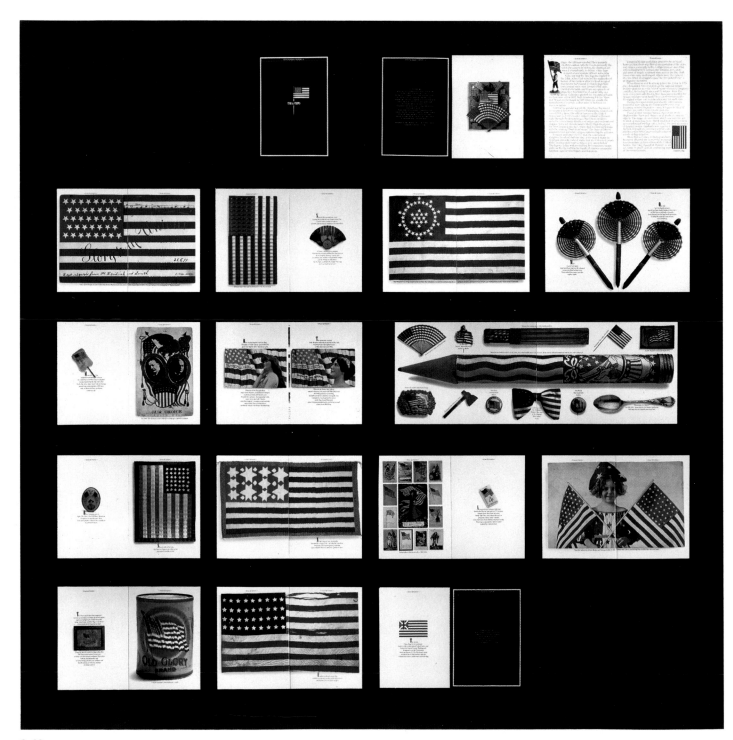

3-43

For the Vintage Contemporaries extended series of fictional works (fig. **3-44**), Lorraine Louie developed a format that allows the viewer to recognize immediately that each volume belongs to the series but permits the flexibility necessary to accommodate differences. Each jacket contains the same elements: the title, author's name, an illustration, a critical quotation about the book, and the series logo and signature. The format developed by Louie (fig. **3-45**) is based upon a geometric division of space into rectangular zones keyed to a vertical grid line to the left of the center, consistent typographic treatment, and a sequence of carefully planned alignments.

On each cover, the author's name appears in all capitals, set in a variation of Kabel Bold, with the first and last names letterspaced to align left and right. It is reversed from a colored rectangle in the upper right-hand corner. The title appears below this rectangle, set in all-capital Kabel Bold and printed in color with a gray screen-tint drop shadow. The title is also letterspaced to flush left and right, aligning with the edge of the illustration on the left and the author's name on the right. The letterspacing of the authors' names and the titles becomes exaggerated when very short words appear, but legibility is not significantly diminished. Three sizes of type are used for titles in the series. Books with one-line titles have the largest size, and books with three-line titles have the smallest size. A rectangle composed of small dots is keyed to the lower left corner of the top rectangle and runs behind the title and illustration. This form is critical to the composition, for it becomes a visual connector unifying the three major elements. In the bottom space, a critical comment and logo align with the major vertical grid line.

Flexibility is needed because some titles only contain one word and others contain two, three, or four words and must be set as two or three lines. Louie adjusts the depth of the title area and the illustration to accommodate this variation. Another subtle adjustment from the standard format is required on some covers because the quotations at the bottom of the page vary from two to eight lines.

The illustrations are surreal and iconographic, suggesting a theme or location rather than depicting a narrative event from the story. Because most have a single major object or animal in an environment, good impact in the point-of-purchase environment is achieved. In figure **3-44**, illustrations in the top two rows are by Rick Lovell, and the photo illustrations in the bottom row are by Marc Tauss.

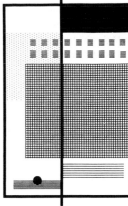

3-45

3-44

Planes in space

When planes or forms are placed in front of or behind one another, the forward forms can appear opaque or transparent. When the frontal forms are opaque, they overlap the ones behind them and create a sense of depth. On the murder-mystery book jacket for *The Artful Egg* (fig. **3-46**), designed by Louise Fili and illustrated by Robert Goldstrom, the space is constructed by overlapping planes. The relationship between the rectangles of the envelope, typographic area, sunlit walls, and rug create a taut relationship. We peer over the postman's shoulder as the victim's body is discovered, partially obscured from us by the postman's envelopes.

In the cover for *Divide the Night* (fig. **3-47**), designed by Louise Fili and illustrated by Susannah Kelly, we look down from a high vantage point at the perspective of a night street scene. The horizontal and vertical axes of the widely letterspaced type align with the perspective of the illustrations, creating a remarkable unity. The smaller size of the author's name, along with its proximity to the sidewalk, places it on the ground plane, while the title appears to hover above the scene.

The phenomenon of overlapping planes opens unexpected possibilities when, instead of overlapping one another, the planes or forms interpenetrate and create an illusion of transparency. In the magazine cover illustration for "The Vanishing Nurse: Why She Has Become an Endangered Species" (fig. **3-48**), designed and illustrated by Dugald Stermer, the transparency of the figure reveals the masthead behind her to become a graphic statement illustrating the title. There is no typography on this cover: Stermer often letters the words in the same pencil and watercolor technique used for the image.

3-46

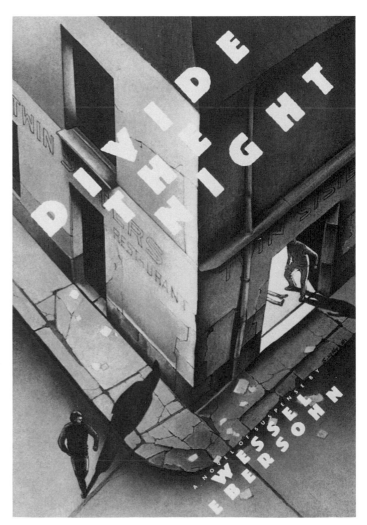

3-47

3-48

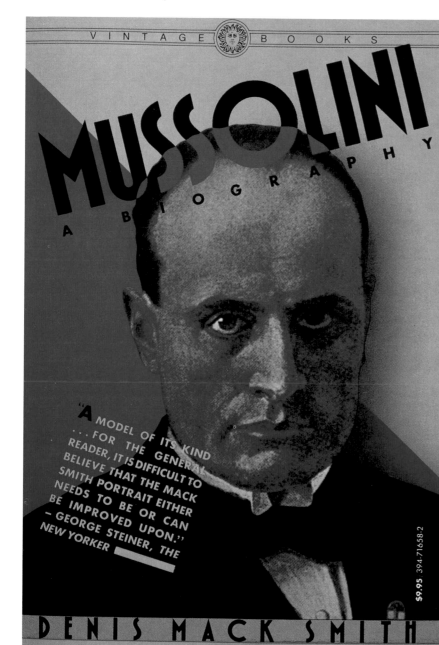

3-49

A very different graphic quality occurs when the head of Mussolini intersects the name in the book jacket designed by Carin Goldberg (fig. **3-49**). The letters turn blood red, echoing the red in the bottom half of the diagonally divided red and orange background. Goldberg has created a tight relational composition of overlapping planes: The orange quotation from a review overlaps the portrait, which overlaps the background planes. An ambiguous relationship between type and image exists, for it is unclear whether the word *Mussolini* is in front of the head, behind the head, or fused with the head. This intensifies the emotional power of the design, as does the fierce stare of the dictator, whose illuminated right eye becomes a strong focal point as a result of its central position and strong value contrast.

Two vastly different types of imagery are combined in Dietmar Winkler's poster for a Bach concert (fig. **3-50**). A traditional portrait of the composer is overlapped by a precise geometric configuration of arcs organized on a grid structure. This pattern is a graphic interpretation of the almost mathematical structure of Bach's compositions. Transparent printing inks permit the portrait to be seen through the red and blue arcs, which change color where they overprint the darker tone of the figurative image. This poster signifies Bach, the man, and the intrinsic qualities of his music. The display type is based on Fraktur types of the sixteenth century,[8] which have baroque curvilinear flourishes and were still widely used in Germany during Bach's era. The alignment of the four units of display type with the vertical edges of the geometric pattern creates unity between these graphically disparate elements.

j.s. bach   the art of the fugue

lionell rogg   organist

Wednesday
October 29
8:30 pm
Kresge
Auditorium
MIT

Tickets
at the door
$2.00
MIT Students
$0.50

Scale and visual hierarchy

The size of an element within the graphic space and its size relationship to other elements in the design are significant perceptual and communicative factors. A recent magazine advertisement presented an automobile that appeared to be a midsize vehicle, but in the showroom it proved to be a small compact. The people photographed with the automobile were unusually short, conveying through scale contrast an impression of a larger vehicle.

Figure **3-51** demonstrates a range of scale relationships between a typographic element and an image. In this sequence of nine variations, the image size decreases by about ten-percent increments while the type size increases by ten-percent increments. An important consideration in the development of scale relationships is the establishment of a visual hierarchy, which means a group of visual elements arranged according to emphasis. In this sequence, the image is dominant in the first composition, and the type is clearly dominant in the final compositions. Other factors influencing visual hierarchy include value, color, position, and proximity. Elements become focal points in the design. Attention to their relative position in the visual hierarchy enables the designer to guide the viewer's eye as it scans the space.

3-51

The following three designs demonstrate very different solutions to the problem of scale relationships. In Ronn Campisi's *Boston Globe Magazine* cover "Prized Fighting" (fig. **3-52**), the article begins on the cover. Large text type occupies about fifty percent of the total area. However, the title—reversed from an intense red area—is the dominant element. The photograph remains a powerful element in spite of its small size.

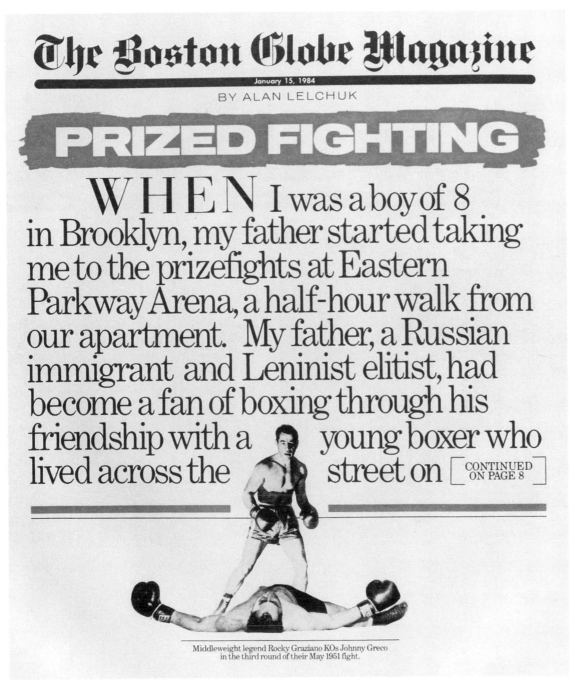

3-52

The Best Running & Fitness Day

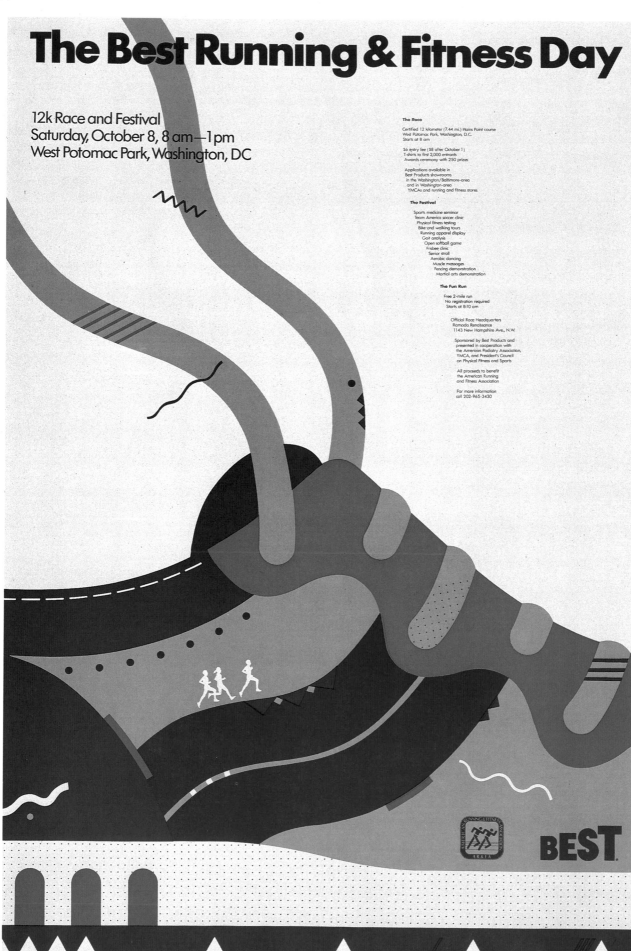

12k Race and Festival
Saturday, October 8, 8 am—1pm
West Potomac Park, Washington, DC

The Race

Certified 12 kilometer (7.44 mi.) Hains Point course
West Potomac Park, Washington, D.C.
Starts at 8 am

$6 entry fee ($8 after October 1)
T-shirts to first 2,000 entrants
Awards ceremony with 250 prizes

Applications available in
Best Products showrooms
in the Washington/Baltimore-area
and in Washington-area
YMCAs and running and fitness stores

The Festival

Sports medicine seminar
Team America soccer clinic
Physical fitness testing
Bike and walking tours
Running apparel display
Gait analysis
Open softball game
Frisbee clinic
Senior stroll
Aerobic dancing
Muscle massages
Fencing demonstration
Martial arts demonstration

The Fun Run

Free 2-mile run
No registration required
Starts at 8:10 am

Official Race Headquarters
Ramada Renaissance
1143 New Hampshire Ave., N.W.

Sponsored by Best Products and
presented in cooperation with
the American Podiatry Association,
YMCA, and President's Council
on Physical Fitness and Sports

All proceeds to benefit
the American Running
and Fitness Association

For more information
call 202-965-3430

BEST

A giant running shoe dominates the visual hierarchy in a poster for a running and fitness day (fig. **3-53**) designed by Rob Carter and Tim Priddy. The low, "worm's eye" vantage point, the tight cropping of the shoe, and the small size of the silhouette runners all intensify the graphic impact of the image. The correspondence between the curvilinear shoelaces and body text unifies these unlike elements.

Competition for ascendency in the visual hierarchy can create a dynamic tension between elements. On the book jacket for *The Enigma of Arrival,* designed by Lorraine Louie (fig. **3-54**), competition exists between the author's name and the de Chirico painting. The name has dominant scale, but the painting has dominant color and value contrast. The importance of elements as part of the message should determine their hierarchical relationships. For example, the cover of a new book by a well-known author should emphasize the author's name rather than the not-yet-known title.

Graphic support elements play a vital role in the overall spatial structure of this design. A green rectangle of graded texture behind the title unifies it and, through alignment, relates the title to the two brown ruled lines on the left and the yellow building in the painting. The gray tone fading in from the bottom of the page further animates the space. The ruled lines play an important structural role and contribute rhythm and unity to the overall design.

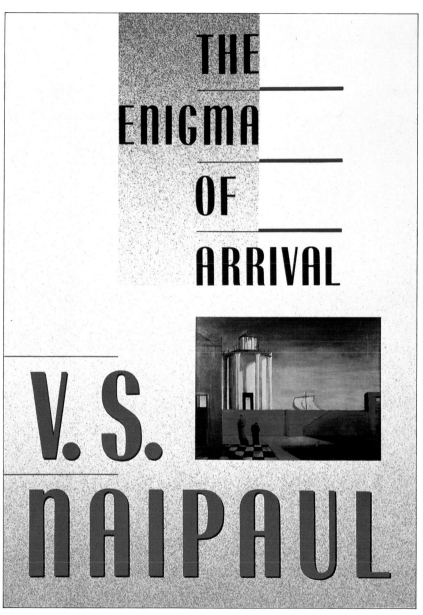

3-54

Bold condensed display type combines through alignment with an illustration to form the dominant configuration in the *Saturday Evening Post* editorial spread designed by Herb Lubalin (fig. **3-55**). The text type between the words *AND* and *RUN* is printed in red to connect them, creating a horizontal thrust across the pages that bleeds on both sides. John Falter's illustration of a victim's hand on the pavement suggests the terrible violence of the accident. The principle of synecdoche, using a part to represent the whole, is found here.

Motion and implied motion

The interpretation of movement and motion on a two-dimensional surface has been a preoccupation of twentieth-century visual thinking from the early years of the century. Artists confronted the speed of motor cars and airplanes and cinematography's

42

ONE MOMENT OF PANIC TURNED THE DRIVER INTO A HUNTED KILLER

By JOHN D. MACDONALD

HIT AND RUN

Painting by John Falter

Twenty-eight days after the woman died, Walter Post, special investigator for the Traffic Division, squatted on his heels in a big parking lot and ran his fingertips lightly along the front-right fender of the car which had killed her. It was a blue and gray four-door sedan, three years old, in the lower price range.

The repair job had probably been done in haste and panic. But it had been competently done. The blue paint was an almost perfect match. Some of it had got on the chrome stripping and had been wiped off, but not perfectly. The chrome headlight ring was a replacement, with none of the minute pits and rust flecks of the ring on the left headlight. He reached up into the fender well and brushed his fingers along the area where the undercoating had been flattened when the fender had been hammered out.

He stood up and looked toward the big insurance-company office building, large windows and aluminum panels glinting in the morning sun, and wondered where Mr. Wade Addams was, which window was his. A vice president, high up, looking down upon the world.

It had been a long hunt. Walter Post had examined many automobiles. The killing had occurred on a rainy Tuesday morning in September at 9:30, in the 1200 block of Harding Avenue. It was an old street of big elms and frame houses. It ran north and south. Residents in the new suburban areas south of the city used Harding Avenue in preference to Wright Boulevard when they drove to the center of the city. Harding Avenue had been resurfaced a year ago. There were few traffic lights. The people who lived on Harding Avenue had complained about fast traffic before Mary Berris was killed.

Mr. and Mrs. Steve Berris and their two small children had lived at 1237 Harding Avenue. He was the assistant manager of a supermarket. On that rainy morning she had put on her plastic rain cape to hurry across the street, apparently to see a neighbor on some errand. It was evident she had not intended to be gone long, as her two small children were left untended. The only witness was a thirteen-year-old girl, walking from her home to the bus stop.

Through careful and repeated interrogations of that girl after she had quieted down, authorities were able to determine that the street had been momentarily empty of traffic, that the death car had been proceeding toward the center of town at a high rate of speed, that Mary Berris had started to cross from right to left in front of the car, hurrying. Apparently, when she realized she had misjudged the speed and distance of the car, she had turned and tried to scamper back to the protection of the curb.

Walter Post guessed that the driver, assuming the young woman would continue across, had swerved to the right to go behind her. When she had turned back, the driver had hit the brakes. There were wet leaves on the smooth asphalt. The car had skidded. Mary Berris was struck and thrown an estimated twenty feet through the air, landing close to the curb. The car had swayed out of its skid and then accelerated.

The child had not seen the driver of the car. She said it was a pale car, a gray or blue, not a big car and not shiny new. Almost too late she realized she should look at the license number. But by then it was so far away that she could only tell that it was not an out-of-state license and that it ended, in her words, "in two fat numbers. Not sharp numbers like ones and sevens and fours. Fat ones, like sixes and eights and nines."

Mary Berris lived for nearly seventy hours with serious brain injuries, ugly contusions and abrasions and a fractured hip. She lived long enough for significant bruises to form, indicating from their shape and placement that the vehicle had struck her a glancing blow on the right hip and thigh, the curve of the bumper striking her right leg just below the knee. The fragments of glass from the lens of the shattered sealed-beam headlamp indicated three possible makes of automobile. No shellac or enamel was recovered from her clothing. It was believed that, owing to the glancing impact, the vehicle had not been seriously damaged. She did not regain consciousness before death.

For the first two weeks of the investigation Walter Post had the assistance of sufficient manpower to cover all places where repairs could have been made. The newspapers co-operated. Everyone in the metropolitan area was urged to look for the death car. But, as in so many other instances, the car seemed to disappear without a trace. Walter Post was finally left alone to continue the investigation, in addition to his other duties.

And, this time, he devoted more time to it than he planned. It seemed more personal. This was not a case of one walking drunk lurching into the night path of a driving drunk. This was a case of a young, pretty housewife—very pretty, according to the picture of her he had seen—mortally injured on a rainy Tuesday by somebody who had been in a hurry, somebody too callous to stop and clever enough to hide. He had talked to the broken husband and seen the small, puzzled kids, and heard the child witness say, "It made a terrible noise. A kind of—thick noise. And then she just went flying in the air, all loose in the air. And the car tried to go away so fast the wheels were spinning."

Walter Post would awaken in the night and think about Mary Berris and feel a familiar anger. This was his work, and he knew the cost of it and realized his own emotional involvement made him better at what he did. But this was a very small comfort in the bitter mood of the wakeful night. And he knew there would be no joy in solving the case because he would find at the end of his search not some monster, some symbol of evil, but merely another victim, a trembling human animal.

His wife Carolyn endured this time of his involvement as she had those which had gone before, knowing the cause of his remoteness, his brutal schedule of self-assigned work hours. Until this time of compulsion was ended, she and the children would live with—and rarely see—a weary man who kept pushing himself to the limit of his energy, who returned and ate and slept and went out again.

Operating on the assumption that the killer was a resident of the suburban areas south of the city, he had driven the area until he was able to block off one large section where, if you wanted to drive down into the center of the city, Harding Avenue was the most efficient route to take. With the co-operation of the clerks at the State Bureau of Motor Vehicle Registration, he compiled a discouragingly long list of all medium and low-priced sedans from one to four years old registered in the name of persons living in his chosen area, where the license numbers ended in 99, 98, 89, 88, 96, 69, 86, 68 and 66. He hoped he would not have to expand it to include threes and fives, which could also have given that impression of "fatness," in spite of the child witness's belief that the numbers were not threes or fives.

With his list of addresses he continued the slow process of elimination. He could not eliminate the darker or brighter colors until he was certain the entire car had not been repainted. He worked with a feeling of weary urgency, suspecting the killer would feel more at ease once the death car was traded in. He lost weight. He accomplished his other duties in an acceptable manner.

At nine on this bright October tenth, a Friday, just twenty-eight days and a few hours after Mary Berris had died, he had checked the residence of a Mr. Wade Addams. It was a long and impressive house on a wide curve of Saylor Lane. A slim, dark woman of about forty answered the door. She wore slacks and a sweater. Her features were too strong for prettiness, and her manner and expression were pleasant and confident.

"Yes?"

He smiled and said, "I just want to take up a few moments of your time. Are you Mrs. Addams?"

"Yes, but really, if you're selling something, I just —— "

He took out his notebook. "This is a survey financed by the automotive industry. People think we're trying to sell cars, but we're not. This is a survey about how cars are used."

She laughed. "I can tell you one thing. There aren't enough cars in this family. My husband drives to work. We have a son, eighteen, in his last year of high school, and a daughter, fourteen, who needs a lot of taxi service. The big car is in for repairs, and today my husband took the little car to work. So you can see how empty the garage is. If Gary's marks are good at midyear, Wade is going to get him a car of his own."

"Could I have the make and year and model and color of your two cars, Mrs. Addams?"

She gave him the information on the big car first. And then she told him the make of the smaller car and said, "It's three years old. A four-door sedan. Blue and gray."

"Who usually drives it, Mrs. Addams?"

"It's supposed to be mine, but my husband and Gary and I all drive it. So I'm always the one who has it when it runs out of gas. I *never* can remember to take a look at the gauge."

"What does your husband do, Mrs. Addams?"

"He's a vice president at Surety Insurance."

"How long has your boy been driving?"

"Since it was legal. Don't they all? A junior license when he was sixteen, and his senior license last July when he turned eighteen. It makes me nervous, but what can you do? Gary is really quite a reliable boy. I shudder to think of what will happen when Nancy can drive. She's a scatterbrain. All you can do is depend on those young reflexes, I guess."

He closed his notebook. "Thanks a lot, Mrs. Addams. Beautiful place you have here."

"Thank you." She smiled at him. "I guess the automobile people are in a tizzy, trying to decide whether to make big cars or little cars."

"It's a problem," he said. "Thanks for your co-operation."

He had planned to check two more registrations in that immediate area. But he had a hunch about the Addams's car. Obviously Mrs. Addams hadn't been driving. He had seen too many of the guilty ones react. They had been living in terror. When questioned, they broke quickly and completely. Any questions always brought on the unmistakable guilt reactions of the amateur criminal.

So he had driven back into the city, shown his credentials to the guard at the gate of the executive parking area of the Surety Insurance Company and inspected the blue-gray car with the license that ended in 89.

He walked slowly back to his own car and stood beside it, thinking, a tall man in his thirties, dark, big-boned, a man with a thoughtful, slow-moving manner. The damage to the Addams car could be coincidence. But he was certain he had located the car. The old man or the boy had done it. Probably the boy. The public schools hadn't opened until the fifteenth.

He thought of the big job and the fine home and the pleasant, attractive woman. It was going to blow up that family as if you stuck a bomb under it. It would be hell, but not one tenth, one hundredth the hell Steve Berris was undergoing.

He went over his facts and assumptions. The Addamses lived in the right area to use Harding Avenue as the fast route to town. The car had been damaged not long ago in precisely the way he had guessed it would be. It fitted the limited description given.

He went into the big building. The information center in the lobby sent him up to the twelfth-floor receptionist. He told her his name, said he did not have an appointment but did not care to state his business. She raised a skeptical eyebrow, phoned Addams's secretary and asked him to wait a few minutes. He sat in a deep chair amid an efficient hush. Sometimes, when a door opened, he could hear a chattering drone of tabulating equipment.

Twenty minutes later a man walked quickly into the reception room. He was in his middle forties, a trim balding man with heavy glasses, a nervous manner and a weathered golfing tan. Walter stood as he approached.

"Mr. Post? I'm Wade Addams. I can spare a few minutes."

"You might want to make it more than a few minutes, Mr. Addams."

"I don't follow you."

"When and how did you bash in the front-right fender of your car down there in the lot?"

Addams stared *(Continued on page 88)*

3-55

kinetic movement in time and space. One approach is symbolic. For example, the speed lines drawn behind a car or plane in comic books, which signify the disturbed atmosphere where the moving object has just passed, are an index of speed and motion.

Photography's remarkable ability to provide a record of motion is demonstrated in another page from the booklet "Understanding Our Movement Problems" (fig. **3-56**), designed by Frank Armstrong and photographed by Thomas Wedell. A double exposure effectively conveys a human action. Other photographic methods for expressing movement on a two-dimensional surface include multiple printing of an image, blurred motion by time exposure, and multiple stop-action sequences created by using strobe lights to stop motion in a series of exposures on one piece of film.

3-56

CALL FOR ENTRIES
THE MEAD LIBRARY OF IDEAS
INTERNATIONAL ANNUAL REPORT COMPETITION
DEADLINE: JUNE 8, 1981

THE MEAD
LIBRARY OF IDEAS

A sequence of still images can imply that movement has occurred. In a poster designed by Jann Church and photographed by Walter Urie (fig. **3-57**), the opening of an exhibition is signified by the progressive turning of pages through a series of four photographs. The viewer perceives these four images as a sequence; the camera captured four moments in time.

Unity through correspondence

Similar visual properties create relationships that can unify words and images into a whole. Color can be a potent force for unifying typography and images. On the book jacket for *Preserving the West* (fig. **3-58**), designers Louise Fili and David Tran keyed the colors of the typography and its background to the colors in Lowell Georgia's sunset photograph of Mission San Xavier del Bac, Arizona. The dark brown headline type echoes the dark brown windows and mountains, the putty-colored type reflects the earth tones of the clouds and architecture, and the tan background is keyed to the sky. The glowing blue drop shadows of the title reflect the vibrant patches of blue sky. They used a similar treatment in the cover design for *Preserving New England* (fig. **3-59**). The blue title typography echoes the deep blue sky in Ellis Herwig's night photograph of a New England lighthouse. The smaller red type repeats the glowing red reflections from the light, and the pink background reverberates with the warm glow of the subtle pink tones reflected in the light tower and on the buildings. The yellow drop shadows under the blue headline type glow with the same vibrancy as the window lights. The designers responded to the color of the photographs and used the same palette typographically to capitalize on the dynamic contrasts of warm and cool colors.

Lettering and image are unified in Dugald Stermer's cover for *Once in Europa* (fig. **3-60**) through correspondence of multiple qualities: the texture of the pencil technique used to render both the image and lettering; the subtle red and blue applied to the lettering, which echoes the blue feathers and red breast of the bird; and the diagonal movement of the axis of the lettering, which corresponds to the diagonal axis of the bird's body.

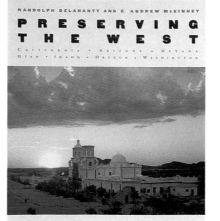

3-58

3-59

3-57

3-60

3-61

3-62

The Azalea Ball logo designed by Woody Pirtle (fig. **3-61**) uses a consistent graphic element, a single-weight line, to draw stencil letterforms, a logo combining a stylized icon of an azalea blossom with the letter *A*, and ruled lines structuring and dividing the space.

Visual elements within an image can correspond to shapes and forms in the surrounding space to create unity. In a poster for an educational program in historic preservation (fig. **3-62**), designer Willi Kunz uses an exquisite James B. Abbott photograph of an architectural detail. Shapes and edges within a complex gray-green form correspond to similar elements within the photograph: wavy lines, incised horizontal stripes, and round forms. The rectangles in the photograph are echoed in the stair-step edge of the gray-green form and black bars in the left corners of the poster. Typography aligns with horizontal and vertical lines in the photograph, which establish a grid for the poster.

Organizing graphic space into a cohesive totality is a complex process. The vitality of contrast must be weighed against the unity of correspondence. Decisions about symmetrical versus asymmetrical organization, establishing a grid system, or creating a field of tension with forms in dynamic equilibrium should evolve from the designer's analysis of content and message, for communication and composition should be viewed as an organic and inseparable whole.

Chapter Four:
Graphic Resonance

The importance of resonance in graphic communications parallels its importance in speech communication. The body language, tone of voice, facial expressions, and the like that accompany talking have been rated by one researcher as carrying sixty-five to seventy percent of the social significance of a conversation or verbal presentation.[1] About these nonverbal signs, another observes, "Vigor of voice, timbre, stress, pauses and speech velocity, facial expression, the gestures and physical bearing . . . are . . . signs accompanying speech, which can, but need not, be isolated, and are comprehended by the name 'paralinguistic component.' "[2]

The power of verbal resonance was demonstrated in the 1980 television debate between presidential candidates Jimmy Carter and Ronald Reagan. This joint appearance was followed by a pronounced shift in the polls and then Reagan's landslide victory. Many observers credited Reagan's expression and delivery, rather than any policies or proposed solutions to national problems, as the crucial elements for victory.

In a famous television commercial for the Wendy's restaurant chain, Clara Peller demanded, "Where's the beef?" This simple line became a national catch phrase and increased Wendy's revenues by thirty-two percent. The line had been used in an earlier commercial with little notice or effect. The balding, middle-aged gentleman in the first commerical projected the image of a critical complainer; in contrast, Peller came off as an underdog, an indignant grandmother concerned about getting a fair deal.

Only limited attention has been given to the vital importance of the accompanying gestures, intonations, and expressions in speech communication, just as little attention has been given to visual resonance in graphic communications. These qualities are critical to successful message transmission, but their expressive and ambiguous nature makes explaining and defining them hard. Scientific information theory enables us to transmit data from a space probe cruising by Saturn, but it cannot explain the expression and resonance of human dialogue.

The nature of graphic resonance

In Chapter One, *graphic resonance* was defined as a term borrowed from music. It means a reverberation or echo, a subtle quality of tone or timbre. A violin prized for its resonance creates music with a richness of tone that heightens the expressiveness of sound. Graphic designers bring a resonance to visual communications through the interaction of the connotative qualities of type and images and the expressive power of the visual vocabulary, that is, color, shape, texture, and the interrelations between forms in space. Mass communication is given an aesthetic dimension that transcends the dry conveyance of information, intensifies the message, and enriches the experience of the audience.

The aesthetics of signs and messages often determines their effectiveness because the aesthetic dimension can create receptivity in an audience jaded by the overcommunication of contemporary society. From a marketing standpoint, the decision to purchase commodities, including grocery store products, records, books, and computer software, is often prompted by an individual's response to graphic resonance. Other factors are involved, as anyone will testify who has ever decided between purchasing premium-priced shampoo in a beautiful package and an identical product, priced lower but in a mundane package.

Every visual nuance and every decision made by the designer contributes to the overall resonance of the design. Typeface selection, scale and cropping of images, the denotative *and* connotative properties, color, and spatial organization all play roles. Figures **4-1** through **4-9** provide an elementary demonstration of the role of resonance in effective graphic communications.

Figures **4-1** through **4-3** are identical except for the copy line. Each example has the ordinary photograph of a man above a copy line set in a commonly used typeface. The typography defines the image by giving us information about the man. The spatial organization is simple bilateral symmetry. The level of resonance is very low.

In the middle row of designs, the lighting, clothing, environment, and facial expressions change. Each image now has connotations relating to and enforcing its copy line. Figure **4-4** has dramatic lighting that generates an aura of prominence. The model's expression is dignified. His noble bearing and conservative suit connote this man as a noteworthy public official.

Figure **4-5** has the bland, flat lighting of straightforward mugshots typified by drivers' licenses and police files. The model's expression is blank and unfeeling. The gray shirt, identification number, and height stripes in the background convey an impression that the man was in custody when this photograph was taken.

Figure **4-6** is illuminated with natural outdoor light. The model's expression is relaxed and happy. The lakeside environment, clothing, and fish amplify the copy line.

In the final row of designs, the type style, size, and weight are changed to more appropriately express the content. The spatial organization and the relationship of type to image are different in each example and contribute to the resonant qualities of each design. The supporting elements that have been added in two of the designs further differentiate the communications.

Figure **4-7** becomes an almost cliché example of the political poster. A bold sans serif typeface is used for its reach and graphic impact on small outdoor posters and bumper stickers. Although the actual area of the photograph is decreased somewhat, its impact and importance are increased by the large scale and close cropping on the face.

Figure **4-8** actually has decreased graphic resonance. The photograph is smaller. Because condensed, all-capital, sans serif type is often seen in bureaucratic communications, it has a convincing authenticity. Bland symmetrical composition implies that this communication was assembled by a government print shop with limited concern for design organization. The small type identifying this as Bulletin J-4327 adds to the impression of a law enforcement "wanted" announcement.

Figure **4-9** has an expansive, outdoor quality, produced by the open landscape that bleeds on all four sides. Bold slab serif type is used in varying sizes to create a dense rectangle. Its size and weight lend a quality of importance and immediacy. The fish image and its measurement lines add another level of visual information about the subject.

These very simple visual communications—printed in one color and containing only a photograph and copy line—demonstrate how the resonant properties of image, typestyle, scale, elemental support elements, and spatial relations add strength and intensity to the message. In more complex graphic designs, the addition of color, elaborate support elements, and multiple levels of meaning further intensify resonance.

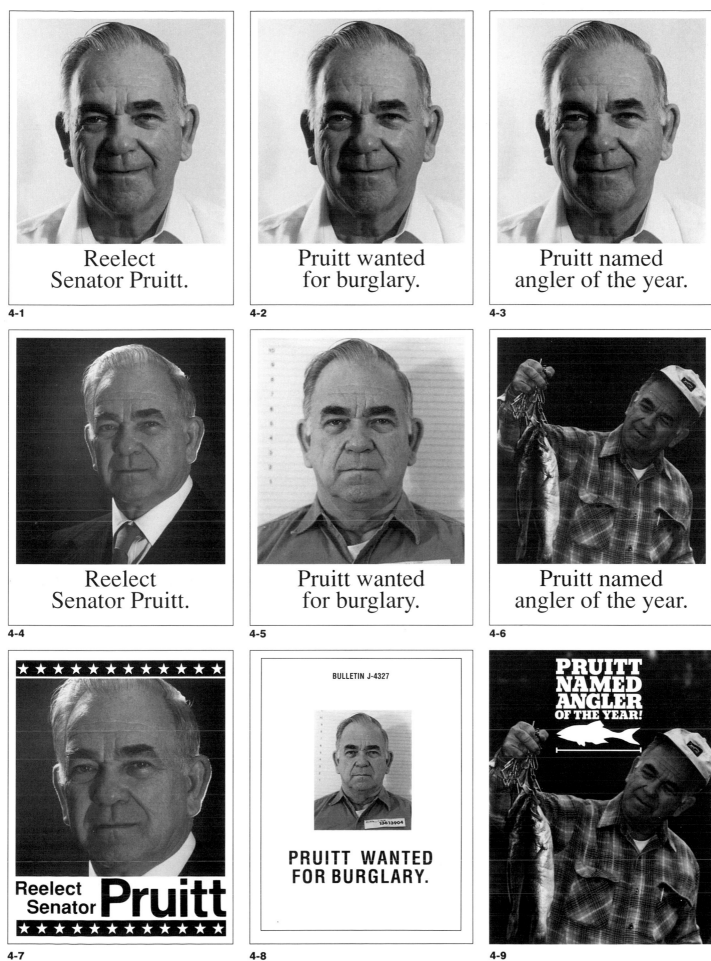

Reelect Senator Pruitt. 4-1

Pruitt wanted for burglary. 4-2

Pruitt named angler of the year. 4-3

Reelect Senator Pruitt. 4-4

Pruitt wanted for burglary. 4-5

Pruitt named angler of the year. 4-6

Reelect Senator **Pruitt** 4-7

BULLETIN J-4327

PRUITT WANTED FOR BURGLARY. 4-8

PRUITT NAMED ANGLER OF THE YEAR! 4-9

Typographic resonance

Typographic resonance is generated by the cultural, stylistic, and connotative properties that typefaces possess in addition to their function as alphabet signs. A typeface gains these resonant qualities through historical tradition, associations relating to its typical use, and its optical properties. In 1902, German designer and architect Peter Behrens observed that "next to architecture, [typography gives] quite the most characteristic picture of a period, and the strongest testimonial of the spiritual progress of development of a period."[3] Behrens compared reading written or typeset material to observing the flight of a bird or gallop of a horse. One perceives the motion as a rhythmic whole instead of focusing on each detail. The motion of a horse and a bird are very different phenomena that produce very different perceptual and emotional responses in the viewer. Likewise, typeface designs span a broad range of expression.

Before the widespread use of photodisplay typesetting in the 1960s, the exorbitant cost of introducing new typefaces and making them available in many sizes of hand-set metal display type slowed the introduction of new designs. The explosion in typeface designs over the past three decades stems from more than just the remarkable cost-effectiveness of introducing fonts for photographic and digital typesetting or the entrepreneurial instincts of equipment manufacturers intent upon marketing new fonts. Typeface designers' fascination with the resonance and expression of letterforms and the interest of graphic designers in achieving resonance through typeface selection are powerful factors. From classical beauty to outrageous novelty, the extraordinary range of typographic variations available today provides a virtually unlimited range of possibilities. This abundance is a two-edged sword. It provides the designer with unfettered opportunities for achieving resonance and expression; however, the vast type library includes both refinements and mediocre versions of classic typefaces, and many novelty fonts lack order or cohesive design. These fonts seek attention through flamboyant shapes and garish texture. As many weeds grow in the typographic garden, a strong personal sense of typographic excellence is required.

The relationship between typeface form and semantic content is demonstrated in a series of exercises (figs. **4-10** though **4-15**). Word combinations are set in typefaces selected to connote their meanings.

In figure **4-10**, stroke weight conveys a sense of lightness and boldness, emphasizing a *whisper* and a *shout.* Contrast between the two typefaces plays an important role, for resonance is relative to context and juxtaposition. For example, if the size and style used here for *shout* had been used for *whisper,* and foot-high letters were used for *shout,* this size and weight would appear small and subtle.

To *mumble* is to garble words by speaking in a low, indistinct manner, and the spasmodic repetition of vocal sounds is a *stutter* (fig. **4-11**). The use of a word that imitates natural sounds or whose sound suggests its meaning is called *onomatopoeia.* This same principle can apply to the visual appearance of a word.

In figure **4-12**, sharp diagonal points cover *criticize* with visual barbs. *Praise* is presented in a dignified and restrained manner, and *flatter* is embellished with a visual sugar coating.

In figure **4-13**, *sweet talk* is set in an elegant florid script, *straight talk* is in a medium-weight sans serif type without ornament or flourish, and *double talk* is executed in a novelty face whose dual characters defy spatial logic.

Figure **4-14** is more subtle. *Explain* is set in Helvetica Medium, a clear, articulate sans serif typeface. *Teach* is set in Century Schoolbook, a type that has been widely used in elementary textbooks because of its outstanding legibility and character differentiation.

Synonyms for *brag* include strut, swagger, flaunt, and flourish. These properties are all suggested by the plump vernacular script used for this word in figure **4-15**. *Exaggerate* is executed in a typeface whose capital swashes are outlandish, making them appear added to the letters instead of being part of the form.

Figure **4-14** is the antithesis of figure **4-15**. The former uses time-honored typefaces whose clarity and legibility express positive human activities directed toward others, and the latter uses outlandish typefaces to express flamboyance.

Designer Louise Fili (see figs. **4-32**, **4-35**, and **4-48**) observes that as she designs a book jacket, the book "cries out for a typeface that will give it the right tone. . . . I'm the detective that tries to find it, and very often, it's a face that doesn't even exist." Some of the measures Fili will take in searching for the face that has the appropriate resonance are: having the job set in a typeface related to the forms she wants, then altering them radically; resurrecting old faces by having characters missing from the specimen relettered; or even making up a new typeface and having it hand-lettered.[4]

SHOUT!

4-10

4-11

criticize

PRAISE

FLATTER

4-12

Sweet Talk

STRAIGHT TALK

DOUBLE TALK

4-13

explain

Teach

4-14

Brag

Exaggerate

4-15

The Truth About Energy

A report on the world's energy resources from Mobil

4-16

BURLINGTON

1963 Annual Report

4-18

A letter denotes only one thing—its sound—until its connotative power is extended and intensified by the designer. Tom Geismar transformed a capital *E* into a symbol for energy in the booklet cover for "The Truth about Energy" (fig. **4-16**). A bold italic sans serif letterform was realigned so that its stem became vertical; then it was cut diagonally and its parts were shifted. This treatment creates a kinetic angularity that connotes lightning and power. Overlapping warm colors—black, brown, red, and yellow—gain intensity through their contrast with the cool blue background.

The meaning of a word can be expressed through imaginative execution. Graphic resonance can reinforce the existing meaning of a word, or it can generate an ambiance for a word used as a trade name. The masthead for the Munich tabloid *Revolution* (fig. **4-17**), published briefly during the World War I era, is executed with the vigorous brush calligraphy of street graffiti. This spirit of raw energy is also found in Richard Seewald's expressionistic woodcut depicting a line of soldiers firing upon demonstrators in the streets.

In an annual report cover designed by George Tscherny and photographed by John Naso (fig. **4-18**), the company logotype for Burlington Industries—a company that manufactures cloth and fabrics—was woven into fabric, then photographed. Texture, color, and folds that move in space all become parasignals, relating the word *Burlington* to its products.

A new word for a new retail store, *Chiasso* (fig. **4-19**), provided designer Jeff Barnes with an opportunity to express the store's varied and unique products and convey the possibility of a wild and unconventional shopping experience. Unity is achieved in the face of tremendous dissonance because the horizontal axis of each letterform is optically centered on an implied line. The correspondence of stroke weights, between the *H* and *O* and the *C* and *A,* for example, lends further unity.

CHIASSO

4-19

Revolution

Auflage 3000　　　**Zweiwochenschrift**　　　Preis 10 Pfg.

Jahrgang 1913　　　　　　　　　　Verlag: Heinrich F. S. Bachmair

Nummer 1　　　　　　**München**　　　　　　15. Oktober

Richard Seewald: Revolution

(Original-Holzschnitt)

Inhalt:

Mitarbeiter:

Adam, Hugo Ball, Johannes R. Becher, Gottfried Benn, Franz Blei, Max Brod, Friedrich Eisenlohr, Engert, Leonhard Frank, John R. v. Gorsleben, emmy hennings, Kurt Hiller, Friedrich Markus Hübner, Philipp Keller, Klabund, Else Lasker=Schüler, Iwan Lazang, Erich Mühsam, Hemrich Nowak, Karl Otten, Sebastian Scharnagl, Richard Seewald und andere.

4-17

When Bob Gill was commissioned to design a title for a television situation comedy about a dumb secretary entitled "Private Secretary" (fig. **4-20**), he "redefined the problem, emphasizing that part of the problem which communicated something which was unique: How can an image which says one thing (private secretary) *also* say something else (that she is stupid) without *actually* saying it?" [5] Gill achieved resonance through a direct logic that is elegant in its simplicity. The most appropriate way to signify *private secretary* is to type it, and the best way to suggest that she is incompetent is by making blatant errors.

Gill's attitude toward letterforms argues for the potential value of the entire spectrum of letterforms found in the environment, including vernacular signs, drafting lettering sets, low-resolution computer graphics, and eccentric handwriting. In a similar vein, the late Herb Lubalin plumbed all levels of contemporary expression for appropriate solutions. For a 1961 article about baseball manager Casey Stengel, Lubalin paraphrased the black metal squares with white letters and numerals used to display scores and other information at ball parks (fig. **4-21**).

4-20

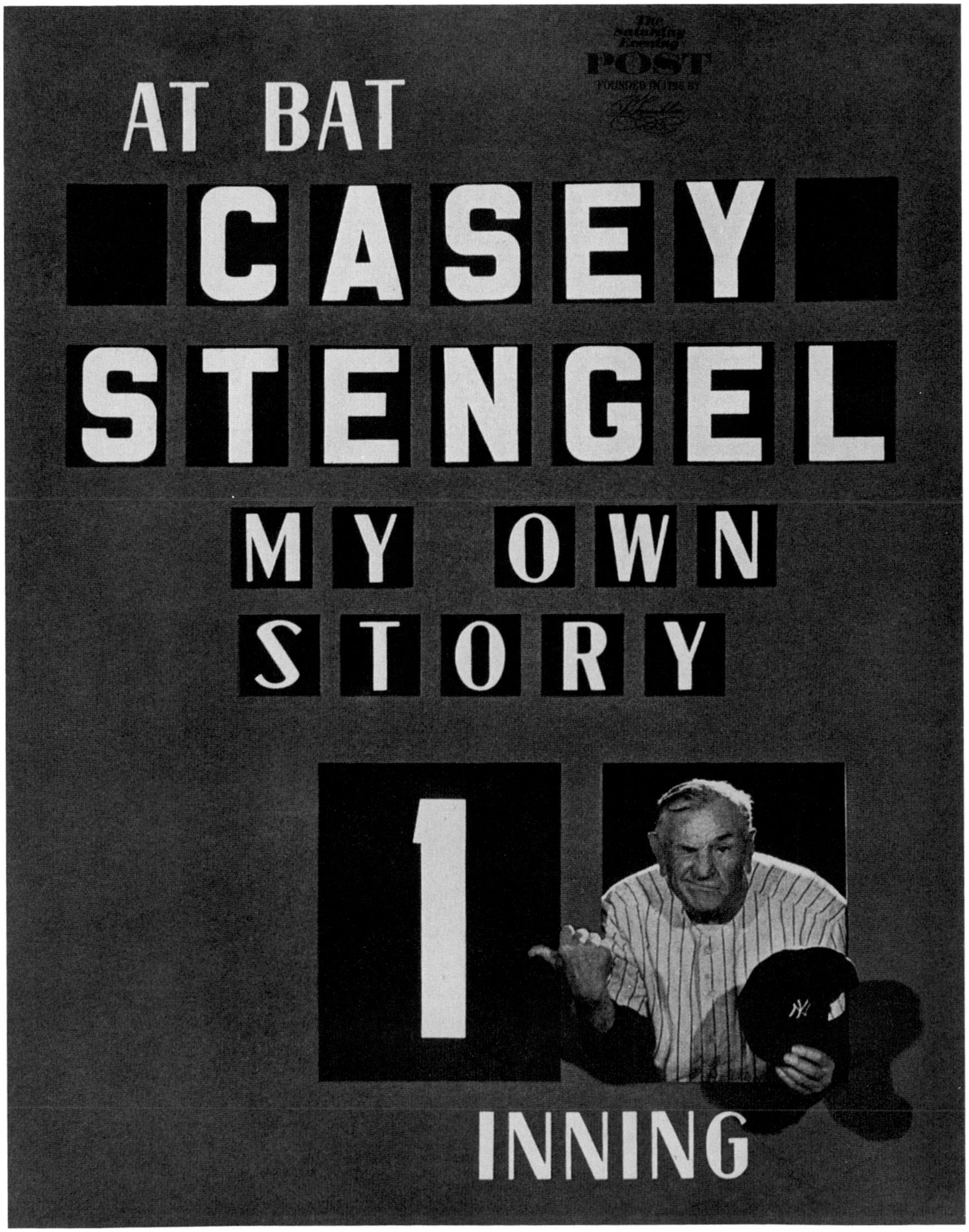

4-21

An intuitive selection process is critical to the search for typographic resonance. Selection of a typeface, its size, color, and weight, and its relationship to images and support elements all contribute to the resonance of the design. Editorial designs for *The Boston Globe Magazine* by Ronn Campisi show this clearly. In figure **4-22**, a lengthy sentence about American mercenaries joining terrorists in Libya functions as the title. Campisi selected a bold, condensed, modern-style typeface and filled the page with this statement to create a heavy, almost ominous feeling. Form correspondence between the type and the arches in the photograph is a unifying factor. Both are vertical black forms, and the arcs of the rounded letterforms relate to the arcs of the arches. Both have contrasting thick and thin elements. The initial *T*, the ruled line around the photograph, and the bar with letterspaced sans serif type reversed from it are all printed in red ink. These red areas become focal points that create graphic tension analogous to the tense subject. The eight vertical green lines play an important spatial role in relating the heavy central complex to the edges of the page and corresponding to the vertical stress of the condensed type and the arches.

4-22

The Boston Globe Magazine

August 26, 1984

On Boston Light

North America's oldest lighthouse,
on Little Brewster Island, has withstood time, tides,
and acts of war. It remains one of the few stations
where lightkeepers have not been replaced
by machines.

Resonance and the Chinese boxes

"On Boston Light" (fig. **4-23**), a cover designed by Campisi featuring an article about America's oldest lighthouse, has a remarkable openness; this layout is as clear and crisp as the lighthouse by the sea on a sunny spring day. A slightly condensed, highly legible font from the Century family reverberates with the same clarity and honesty found in the subject. Scale and spatial relationships between the color photograph, the title, and the subtitle are carefully resolved to create an asymmetrical repose. Focal points of color—the bright red roof, red *O,* and yellow spot of light behind the initial *N*—form a dynamic triangular relationship. The axial movement of elements shifts to the left, then to the right. The dotted line forms a subtle vertical that unifies and stabilizes the elements.

Resonance is created by the generous, open white space. This openness becomes a metaphor for the open coastal spaces. One can argue that many readers of the Sunday magazine supplement did not consciously understand this metaphor. Resonance provides deeper levels of comprehension. The visually illiterate reader who never observes the design of doorknobs and instead only responds to their function as door openers may glance at the lighthouse picture, scan the type, and only touch the surface of Campisi's design. Other readers, with varying degrees of receptivity to the visual world, respond more deeply to the resonance of type, color, space, and scale. A more perceptive reader might enjoy the relationship of the red *O* to the red roofs and the relationship of its circular shape to the yellow circle behind the *N* and further perceive this yellow circle as a sign for the lighthouse spotlight.

On a professional level, an editor or graphic designer might also note the relationship of the dot over the *i* to the red *O* and yellow circle, admire Campisi's use of the dotted line as a compositional device, and note that the title type appears to be slightly condensed relative to most Century fonts.

These levels of understanding about design have been compared to a set of Chinese boxes, with the smallest box fitting inside the second smallest, which fits inside the third smallest, and so on, by architect William Hubbard.[6] In graphic design, the smallest box is the elemental denotation read by the visual illiterate: picture of lighthouse; words saying "On Boston Light." The largest box is the knowledge of a trained designer who understands visual organization, typography, printing processes, photography, content, and meaning. Several levels can exist in between, each fitting inside the next level.

Analysis of three book jackets designed by R. D. Scudellari reveals this principle. The "smallest box" of figure **4-24**, *Baryshnikov at Work,* contains a photograph of the celebrated dancer, the title, and the subtitle of the book. Deeper inspection of "larger

4-24

boxes" reveals that photographer Martha Swope has captured a remarkable moment in Baryshnikov's routine, for his tilted head and facial expression project the sublime emotions that have made dance central to mythic human experience for eons. The photograph expresses the form and counterform relationship between dancer and environmental space that is at the essence of this art form. The calligraphic title, executed by Gow Larson, becomes a visual metaphor for the rhythmic motion of ballet. Its graphic relationship to the horizontal bar of the all-capital subtitle tightly contained by lines echoes the relationship of Baryshnikov to the horizontal bar upon which he strides. This relationship is a contrast between fluid organic motion against gravity and the horizon.

In figure **4-25**, the smallest box contains a photograph of an elderly Chinese woman, the title, *In China,* and the author's name. Larger boxes contain the great humanity of the woman, whose age and experience are captured in her deeply etched face by photographer Eve Arnold. The bracketlike confinement of letterforms moving down the right edge of the space becomes analogous to the vertical flow of Chinese calligraphy. Scudellari's selection of a typeface with extreme thick-and-thin contrast, wide characters, and heavy serifs combines with open letterspacing to emphasize this analogy. The indeterminate space surrounding the

woman has the expansive, undefined space of Oriental landscape painting. Her expression conveys fascination as she gazes back at the stranger, a photographer from a foreign land. The overall resonance of this book jacket promises to reveal fascinating views of China and its people.

In the third Scudellari-designed book jacket, the smallest box also contains a photograph, title, and author's name. Beyond the level of basic denotation, the similarity ends quickly; for the resonance created by graphic forms on the jacket of *Subway* (fig. **4-26**), a photographic essay by renowned photographer Bruce Davidson, shows a subway rider's face shrouded in shadow and an ominous uncertainty. Our vague fears of subway travel, fed by newspaper and television news accounts of robbery and even murder underground, are evoked by this image. The heavy metal jewelry on the unclothed chest connotes social attitudes and background that reinforce the threatening presence. The essence of the book is conveyed: This is a penetrating documentation of social

4-25

behavior and human response to the subterranean environment of subway transportation. The perspective of the lights moving back in space joins with the typography to form a light-streaked triangle, echoing the triangle of the necklace. The larger triangle moves back in space to surround the indistinct head. The white lines behind the white typography strengthen its linear movement. Along with the rightward thrust of the italic type, these lines suggest a horizontal light-against-dark movement and a visual metaphor for the subway rushing through the dark tunnel.

The rich allusions in Scudellari's designs suggest that his problem-solving approach permits him to open his mind and eye to the subject. His book jackets vigorously present their alphasignal messages, but they go beyond that level to create deeper levels of parasignal, connotation, and resonance.

A critical factor about the Chinese-box concept is the nesting process that places each level of information within the next, deeper level. The hasty or unsophisticated browser in a bookstore might completely miss the levels of resonance in these book jackets; however, the basic denotative information is there for that person as well as for the more insightful person who understands and responds more deeply. Those clients and their marketing experts who fail to recognize graphic resonance and the Chinese-box concept and mistakenly believe that shouting down their competition with hard-sell slogans, phosphorescent inks, and strident typography are out of touch with the increased level of visual awareness in contemporary culture.

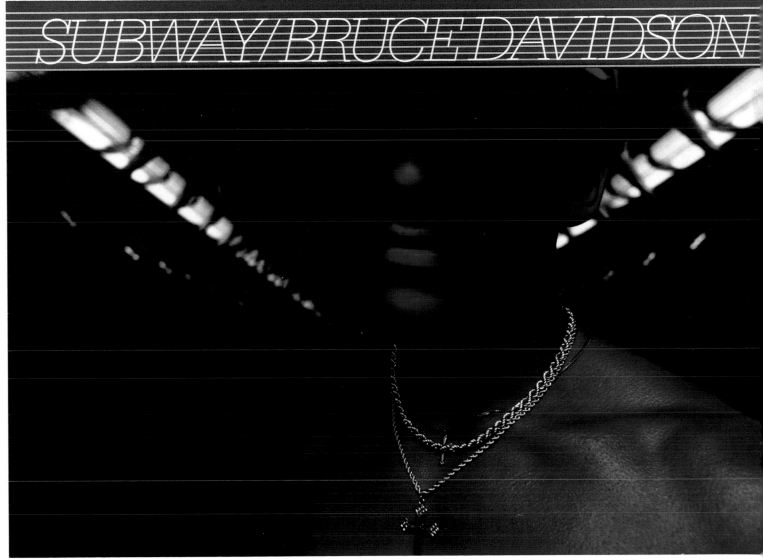

Style as message

In all forms of design, the problem of style is central to the creative process; it cannot be ignored. The belief that decoration is useless or frivolous is invalid, for decorative elements enhance communication with graphic resonance. Ornament is a potent vehicle for heightening the sensory experience and adding connotative expression to denotative forms. As early as 1901, German art historian Alois Riegl argued that stylistic forms in art related to social, cultural, and technological conditions in the culture. This view holds that style is no accident but a vital component of its time. Wassily Kandinsky wrote: "To each spiritual epoch corresponds a new spiritual content, which that epoch expresses as forms that are new, unexpected, surprising and in this way aggressive." [7] In graphic design, this new spiritual content is expressed by resonant visual qualities that collectively manifest a style.

This concept is readily observed in the modernist-functional style that emerged during the 1920s and continues to be a major force in design. This style is characterized by grid structure, sans serif type, and an abhorrence of decoration and ornament. Max Bill's design of *New Swiss Architecture* (see figs. **3-22** through **3-28**) is a paradigm of this style.

The Bauhaus was interested in functional signs stripped of their religious, magical, symbolic, and traditional implications was mentioned in chapter 1. Walter Gropius, the first director of the Bauhaus, advanced the philosophy: "Form follows function." The resulting style of modern design was rational and objective. Photography was favored as machine-made imagery freed from the interference or bias of the individual.

Sans serif types were embraced as basic alphabetical signs stripped bare of serifs and all connotative parasignal. Black letter type styles, based on medieval handwritten forms, were widely used in German printing from the invention of typography until after World War I (see figure **4-17**, *Revolution* cover). Style was propelled by political philosophy, for at the Bauhaus and throughout Germany people were attracted toward socialism. This attraction sprang from a feeling that the Kaiser and capitalist manufacturers had led Germany into disaster during World War I and that a new social order was needed. Sans serif typefaces expressed the spirit of a new era, while black letter styles reverberated with the resonance of an old and outmoded world.

Herbert Bayer, master of the typography workshop at the Bauhaus, designed a universal type style (fig. **4-27**) that reduced the alphabet to lower-case letters only, eliminated capital letters, and only used horizontals, verticals, arcs, and three angles to construct the characters. This "drive toward simplification" addressed four criteria: "simplification in the interest of legibility; clean proportions grounded on basic geometric elements; renunciation of serifs; and adaptation to typewriter or machine print." [8] Ironically, the twentieth-century search for a rational, objective design form denuded of stylistic properties led to an extremely connotative style.

In the late twentieth century, the design dialogue now transcends time and space. For the first time, graphic designers have a comprehensive understanding of their history and use it as a rich resource. *Historicism,* the slavish copying of historical precedents, and *eclecticism,* selecting elements from diverse sources and combining them into an acceptable style, have yielded to *pluralistic reinvention.* This involves extracting—not just from current stylistic tendencies, but from the whole vocabulary of form and expression from other decades and even other epochs—to create graphic resonance. The following discussion of the resonance of style is not intended as a catalog or complete listing of graphic styles; rather it provides selected examples of the contemporary use of style to create resonance.

In the design, illustration, and lettering of a call for entries for an AIGA book exhibition, Dugald Stermer drew upon the humanist tradition of fine printing and publishing (fig. **4-28**) by paraphrasing and reinventing a 1516 title page (fig. **4-29**). Stermer achieves a resonance that relates contemporary book design and production to its five-century tradition. The dolphin (the fastest of sea creatures) and anchor (a weight to stop motion) trademark of Renaissance printer and publisher Aldus Manutius signified the epigram, "Make Haste Slowly," which is as applicable to publishing today as it was 470 years ago.

4-27   **4-28 ▶**

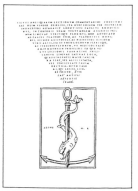

4-29

A CALL FOR ENTRIES TO THE 1986 A.I.G.A. BOOK SHOW
"WHEN A MAN WRITES A BOOK, HE STAMPS IT INDELIBLY WITH THE
MARK OF HIS OWN SPIRIT ~~ THAT IS THE MESSAGE WHICH, AS WE SAY,
WE READ BETWEEN THE LINES ~~ SO IT IS, BVT IN LESSER DEGREE,
WITH THOSE WHO DESIGN & PRINT THE BOOKS, FOR THEY LEAVE THE
IMPRINT OF THEIR PERSONALITIES IN IT IF THEY BE TRVE
CRAFTSMEN ~~ THVS A BOOK IS, MORE THAN MOST THINGS,
A COMPENDIVM OF HVMAN VALVES ~~ SOME OF THESE AP-
PEAL TO THE INTELLECT, SOME TO THE EMOTIONS, SOME
TO THE EYE, & SOME EVEN TO THE SENSE OF TOVCH
SO WROTE BRVCE ROGERS IN 1945; SO IT IS WITH
THE AMERICAN INSTITVTE OF GRAPHIC ARTS
AS IT SEEKS TO HONOR THOSE BOOKS WHICH,
DVRING 1986, CAPTVRED THAT ELVSIVE
SET OF ATTRACTIONS ~~ SO, PLEASE ENTER
YOVR BEST EFFORTS BY THE FIRST OF
JANVARY, 1987 ~ D. STERMER, CHAIRMAN
ALL BOOKS FOR SALE THAT
HAVE ORIGINATED & BEEN
DESIGNED IN THE V.S.
& CANADA DVRING
1986 ARE ELIGIBLE
AWARDED EN-
TRIES WILL
[CON T'D]

D. S.   After ALDVS

The vernacular graphic vocabulary and folklore of the nineteenth century provide a rich inventory of graphic possibilities. It has been widely exploited to create nostalgic and expressive graphics. James Grashow's detailed linear drawing approach for a Charles Ives album cover emulates the floral, decorative complexity of Victorian steel engravings (fig. **4-30**). A signifying relationship exists between the subject matter and historical graphics. Charles Ives was an American composer whose oeuvre, largely written before 1915, included many popular songs and is intimately related to the late nineteenth- and early twentieth-century American historical and musical scene.

4-30

In a similar vein, a record album cover designed by Ed Lee (fig. **4-31**) uses a verbal pun to relate the title "The Badmen" to nineteenth-century wild-West outlaws. Lee paraphrases the woodtype-poster style associated with "Wanted Dead or Alive" notices. Typographic artifact becomes an element in a full-color photograph, and die-cut "bullet holes" complete the parody. A significant difference exists between these album solutions: The Ives and Whiteman (see fig. **4-36**) album covers validate their historical approach through the chronological relationship of graphic style and musical period, but "The Badmen" album cover depends on a rhetorical figure of speech to forge a relationship.

Art nouveau, the late nineteenth- and early twentieth-century style characterized by organic lines, sinuous symbolic forms, and nongeometric curves, is clearly the resource for the letterforms on the book jacket for *Julia Paradise* (fig. **4-32**), designed by Louise Fili. This novel about a disturbed young British woman living in 1927 Shanghai moves between unsettling fantasy and seamy reality. The period photograph gains unmistakable authenticity from its presentation as deckle-edged snapshot. The elegance of this photograph and the decorative pink and white type are contradicted by the viperous snake, signifying ominous psychic forces under the surface opulence. Contrasting and conflicting graphic connotations reflect the intensity of the novel.

In the cover for a biography entitled *Debutante: The Story of Brenda Frazier* (fig. **4-33**), about a young socialite who became an international celebrity in 1938, designer Lorraine Louie closely paraphrases the style of the period to create a rich and authentic graphic resonance. Art deco, the decorative geometric design style derived from cubism and constructivism that emerged in the late 1920s and held sway during the thirties, inspired the ornamentation, pastel hues, and eccentric geometric typography. The black-and-white period photograph of Brenda Frazier conveys the elegance of affluence, even in a depression era. Taken by Horst, it is an authentic example of the refined photographic style of the period. Fili's *Julia Paradise* cover uses an earlier style for symbolic purposes, and Louie's *Debutante* cover uses an earlier style to echo the period when events in the book took place.

Another side of art deco is the geometric and mechanistic expression of the machine age, which was effectively paraphrased in a *Time* magazine cover (fig. **4-34**) designed and illustrated by Michael Doret. The geometric stylization and medallionlike illusion of relief sculpture project the resonance of industrial progress and economic expansion from an earlier era onto a contemporary subject matter.

4-32

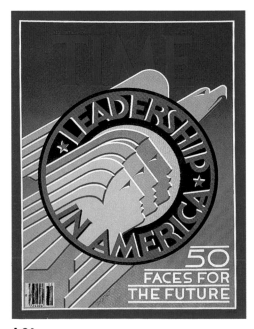

4-34

DEBUTANTE

THE STORY OF
BRENDA FRAZIER

BY
GIOIA DILIBERTO

W·A·R
THE

MARGUERITE
A MEMOIR
DURAS

Even periods such as the 1940s that are not particularly noted for their graphic ambiance offer a vocabulary that can be transformed into effective communications by sensitive designers who select and edit carefully. A lucid eloquence is achieved by designer Louise Fili in a book jacket for French author Marguerite Duras's memoir, *The War* (fig. **4-35**). The graphic resonance is so appropriate that the viewer does not have to ask, "Which war?" Every nuance is carefully considered to convey the spirit of the 1940s and World War II. The photograph of the author, printed in a soft, cool duotone with faded airbrushed edges, expresses the period through connotative imagery: the vintage typewriter, lamp, hairstyle, and dress. An eccentric, boldly geometric sans serif typeface from the period is letterspaced and printed in warm gray. Secondary text is in small type reversed from graduated red bars. The red bar crossing the gray letterform was reversed from the gray printing plate; otherwise, the red overprinting the gray would have produced a very dark gray that would have ruined the effect.

On the record album for a re-release of Paul Whiteman music (fig. **4-36**) designed by John Berg, a large-scale record label reflects the graphic sensibility of the Big Band era of the 1930s and 1940s when Whiteman's music was initially popular. Typefaces, illustration style, organization of space, and color all project the period ambiance.

In the book jacket designed by 212 Associates for *Campus Life* (fig. **4-37**), a serious history of codes of behavior and social structures on American campuses from 1800 to the present, numerous design approaches were possible. Graphic ideas from the 1950s are used as generic symbols of college life: the pennant shape, high-keyed primary colors, bold condensed sans serif type, hand-colored photograph of a coed in a 1950s Ford convertible with almost cliché campus architecture in the background. The turquoise color, a wildly stylish hue in the era of chrome and fins, is the final touch.

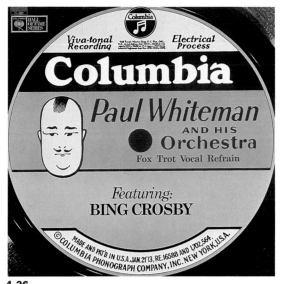

4-36

4-37

4-35

In two posters addressing architectural subjects, letterforms are used as imagery. These exhibit the power of style as content in postmodern design. This term originally designated design that rejected Mies van der Rohe's modernist dictum, "Less is more," and embraced a plurality of influences ranging from classic Greek and Roman columns, forms and shapes from cubist paintings, and decorative geometric patterning. In recent years the term has been used more broadly to encompass design styles of the late twentieth century, including historical revivals, a renewed interest in decoration and ornament, and eccentric expressionism. Figure **4-38** by William Longhauser was created for an exhibition of works by the postmodernist architect Morris Graves. The letterforms of Graves's name are transformed into decorative geometric configurations that evoke the vocabulary of his postmodern design: pale shades of slate blue, light green, pink, and lavender; elemental organic shapes derived from curvilinear cubism, repetitive patterns including tilelike grids, linear stripes, and small squares isolated from one another by relatively large areas of background.

4-38

A poster designed by Massimo Vignelli and Michael Bierut, Vignelli Associates, announcing a lecture by London-based architect James Stirling entitled "The Monumentally Informal: Recent Work by James Stirling, Michael Wilford and Associates" (fig. **4-39**), becomes a visual pun using the connotative power of letterforms as a metaphor for architecture. Bierut executed a pencil drawing of monumental capitals, the classical Roman inscriptional letters carved in the marble bases of monuments, then rendered them informal by transforming an *O* into a sphere, an *I* into a slab placed on the surface, and an *A* into an incised equilateral triangle. Graffiti-like crayon gestures were quickly executed onto each poster in the edition, then the final *O* was silk-screen printed in white ink along with the text type, casting a gray shadow that forces the white *O* to float illusorily in front of the surface of the poster.

4-39

Tupperware

4-40

Consumer and Decorative Products

WEST BEND.

4-41

4-42

Support elements generate resonance

Although graphic support elements lack the denotative properties of typography and images and their connotative properties are frequently vague and unspecific, they can be potent vehicles for creating graphic resonance.

In an annual report for Premark International (figs. **4-40** though **4-42**), a corporation whose trademarks include Tupperware, West Bend, Hobart, and Wilsonart, designer Jacklin Pinsler used color in photography, typography, and support elements to generate a vibrant resonance. In the essay portion of the annual report that discusses the corporation's divisions, Pinsler used red and blue elements in each photograph. These colors were echoed by the vertical blue bar bleeding on the top and side of each left-hand page and the red capital initial that appeared on the opening spread for each division. By closely cropping each photograph so that the products were shown with the hands but not the faces of people using them, attention was directed toward the products rather than the users.

In a poster announcing a series of television ads for a women's clothing manufacturer (fig. **4-43**), Michael Manwaring used supporting elements—color planes, linear gesture, and a torn edge—as the primary vehicles for generating the visual energy and communicative impact of the design. A linear diagonal pattern and the Santa Cruz name appear on a redviolet and purple collage element, formed by a torn edge in the corner of the poster. A vivid, tactile quality is generated by the enlarged halftone dots of the electric guitar and figure. The contours of the images seem to push and form their angular kinetic background shapes. The yellow gesture sweeping through the space generates optical energy through its movement and color vibration as it slips over blue, achromatic gray, and orange. The information level generated by word and picture is minimal: The spirited graphic resonance becomes the dominant message.

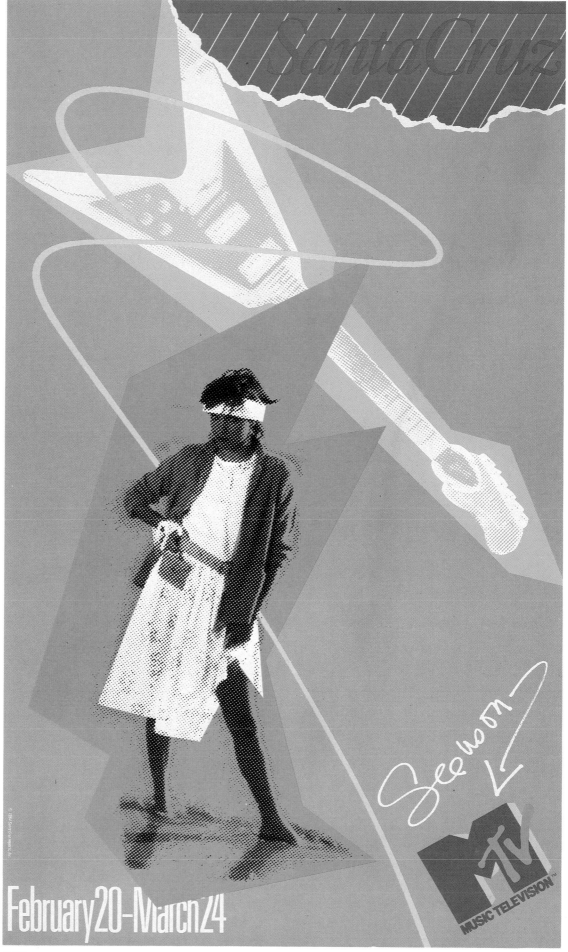

A mailing card designed by William Longhauser for The Fabric Workshop (fig. **4-44**) proves that simple one-color printing can be filled with graphic power and meaningful communication. Rigorous optical contrast is created by the dense black and light white initials placed against a background texture signifying fabrics and woven threads that become written gestures articulating the words, "The Fabric Workshop: a Tradition Continued."

4-44

Resonance as expressive message

Graphic designers often create objective, rational messages; however, some subjects are charged with human emotions and passions and require an intangible element of expressionism to strengthen and heighten the communication.

In a cover article entitled "The Homeless" (fig. **4-45**), designer Ronn Campisi used a Jerry Berndt candid photograph taken at a hospital shelter that captures the pathos of the homeless. The camera is partially blocked by another person, reinforcing a sense that we are eavesdropping on three homeless men whose unaware faces project an emotional immediacy of rare power. The subtitle points responsibility for their plight toward us and further heightens the emotional intensity of the message.

The cover for a biography of Franz Kafka, *The Nightmare of Reason* (fig. **4-46**), designed by Carin Goldberg and illustrated by Anthony Russo, projects a tense emotional power. Heavy black lines trap and contain type and image. The woodcut portrait emerges from darkness, its jagged angular forms echoing and corresponding to the Neuland type. Designed by the German mystic Rudolf Koch and released in 1923, Neuland's pinched angularity of the rounded forms, along with other strokes slashed off obliquely, give it a density magnified by its entrapment. This containment produces slivers and shards of negative space. Type and image evoke the absurdity and alienation in Kafka's work.

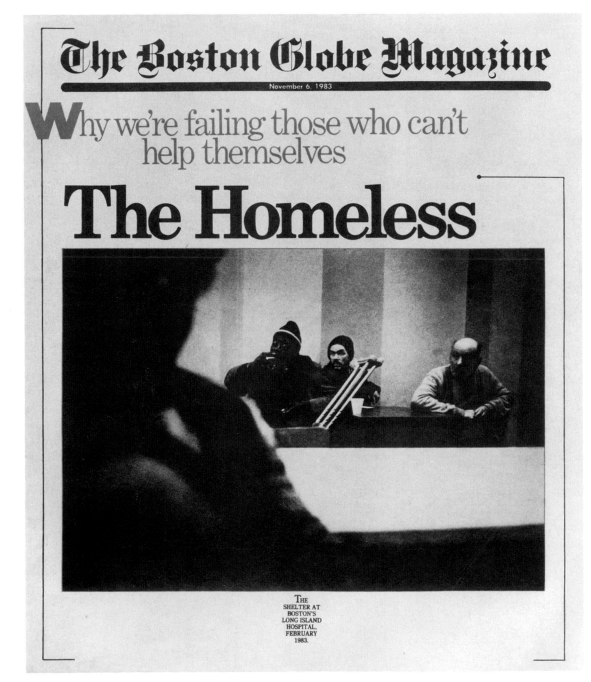

4-45

Just as graphic resonance projects a somber realism appropriate to the plight of the homeless and Kafka's world of absurdity, it can also achieve a sparkling lyricism. In the cover for a book of Raymond Carver's poems, *Where Water Comes Together with Other Water* (fig. **4-47**), designed by Carin Goldberg and illustrated by Gene Greif, the openness and warmth of the cover parallel these qualities in Carver's poems. Some of his poems develop imagery about water, creeks, and rain. Others, including a poem entitled "The Ashtray," involve smoking. The unexpected combination of imagery, with water rather than smoke weaving above the cigarette, is curiously analogous to the unexpected ideas woven into Carver's poems. The wavy blue ornaments on the letterforms express flowing water and echo the wavy line rising from the cigarette.

4-47

An extraordinary lyrical delicacy is realized in Louise Fili's cover for Frederick Barthelme's collection of short stories, *Chroma* (fig. **4-48**). The word becomes an image proclaiming its meaning in visual terms. It is a visual pun, a physical object, and an expression of the spectrum of unexpected characters and events found in Barthelme's stories. An airy space emphasizes the subtle graphic treatment of the title.

4-48

The book *French Fries,* coauthored by Dennis Bernstein and Warren Lehrer and designed by Lehrer, combines type and image in a manner that expands the expressive limits of the book. *French Fries* is presented in the format of a playbook with dialogue and stage directions. It is a form of intermedia: a typographic playbook, which can be read silently; fine art, which can be perceived and enjoyed as graphic compositions; and the script for a play, which can be performed. The story takes place in the Dream Queen fast-food restaurant and is structured as the dialogue of eight characters (employees and regular customers, plus "Flash," a

character taking on different personalities to represent "a psychotic supermarket of fast-food personalities") who hold diverse attitudes and viewpoints prevalent in contemporary culture.

On pages 76 and 77 (fig. **4-49**), Carmen, a Dream Queen order taker, whose voice is signified by type reversed from red bars, and Jack Murphy, a tattooed cab driver who frequents the Dream Queen and whose voice is signified by olive green condensed sans serif type, are having an argument about religion after Jack orders a Dream Fillet fish sandwich with extra tartar sauce. Images of fish and water appear on this spread, signifying Jack's order

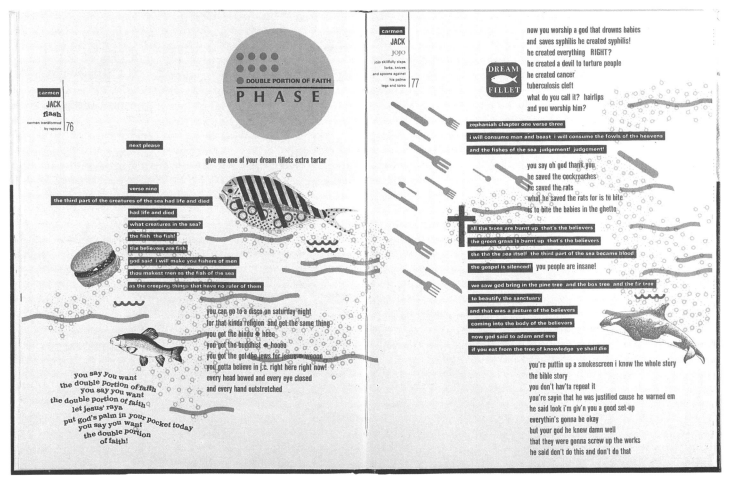

4-49

as well as Carmen's biblical references to "creatures of the sea." The lavender pictographic knives and forks denote JoJo, the Dream Queen's cleanup man, rhythmically slapping eating utensils against his palms, legs, and torso. The horizontal and vertical movements of the conversation and wavelike gestures are energized by overlapping planes and a diagonal movement of fish and forks. A field of spatial tension is created that is delicately balanced yet teetering on the brink of chaos.

Later in the book, Lehrer stages a "shouting match, a brawl of words, an animated dance of polemic confrontation." This erupted as an argument among Louise, who is divorced, fiercely liberal, and a mother of two; Esther, an outspoken, elderly customer with intensely independent views; and Jack. Their wildly divergent views on politicians, communism, and the military escalate into a textured transparency of layered chaos on pages 60 and 61 (fig. **4-50**). *French Fries* achieves an expressionistic resonance and throbbing graphic vitality rarely seen on the printed page. Its space is acoustical (having visual qualities that denote the properties of speech, sound, and music), plastic (possessing the spatial properties of twentieth-century painting), and typographic.

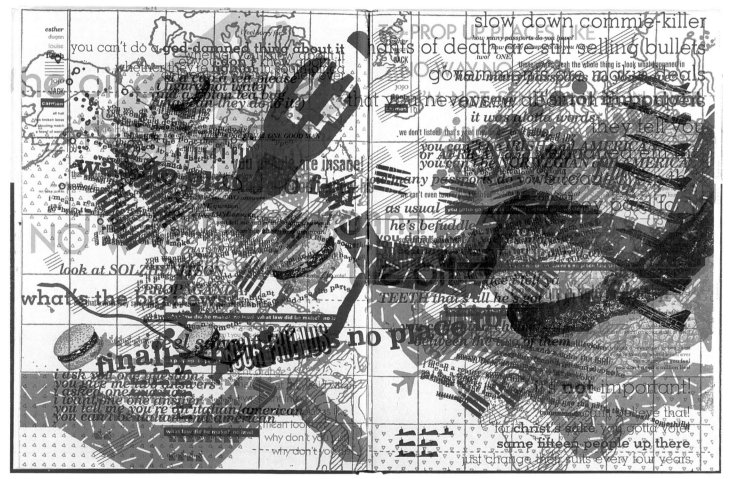

4-50

The scope of graphic expression extends from the perceptual sensation of pure optical phenomenon to traditional illustrative imagery. A poster by David Colley (fig. **4-51**) for a benefit concert, "Performance for Peace," makes its graphic statement with a green rectangle radiating an orange aura against a deep violet field. What symbolic meaning is the viewer to ascribe to this purely visual phenomenon? In his essay *Concerning the Spiritual in Art,* Kandinsky declared, "Form alone, even though abstract and geometrical, has its internal resonance, a spiritual entity whose properties are identical with the form." [9] Colley's color configuration does not carry a specific message; it is devoid of denotative meaning. The typographic message points the viewer toward a meaning, but it does not lock the viewer into a specific message. The viewer can

Performance for Peace

A Benefit Concert

Ian Hobson, *pianist*
William Warfield, *baritone*

Friday March 2 1984 at 8:00 pm
Virginia Theatre
201 West Park, Champaign

readings by Karma Ibsen-Riley

tickets 10.00 public and 5.00 students/low income

Co-sponsored by:
Champaign-Urbana Nuclear Freeze Coalition
and Physicians for Social Responsibility

design: David Colley
typography: Precision Graphics
printing: Andromeda Printing and Graphic Arts Company

respond to color resonance in a subjective, emotional manner or can impose a symbolic interpretation into the abstract configuration.

Philippine artist Renato Habulan's poster entitled "Peasant Farmer—Mangagawang Bukid" (fig. **4-52**) was produced in support of the movement to return democratic government to that country. The man turns to look directly at the viewer who reads the Biblical inscription, "The kind of fasting I want is this: remove the chains of oppression and the yoke of injustice, and let the oppressed go free." An eloquent and universal message moves the viewer toward sympathy and support for those who toil under dictatorial and oppressive regimes. The peasant farmer becomes "every person," a symbolic icon for humanity. The indefinite landscape is filled with darkness, but light begins to break through the sky.

4-52

Both posters address crucial issues in the human community and use graphic resonance to support and intensify the message. Colley's poster dares to use pure color and form to create a graphic resonance, a visual environment in which the call is announced to participate in a fund-raising event sponsored by the nuclear freeze movement. Habulan transforms a peasant farmer into an icon for humanity, a beacon of light against the darkness, to speak eloquently against injustice and oppression.

There is no formula or recipe book for generating appropriate graphic resonance. The designer struggles with the problem at hand and uses type, images, supporting elements, and color to convey a message, to organize the space, and to amplify the message through the expressive power of graphic resonance.

Chapter Five: The Design Process

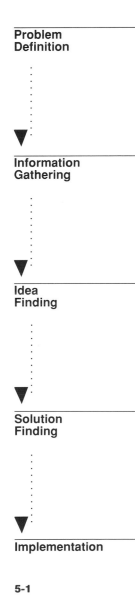

Problem
Definition

Information
Gathering

Idea
Finding

Solution
Finding

Implementation

5-1

In music, literature, art, and design, the creative process is a struggle with the unknown, an attempt to forge a solution to a new problem. The common denominator in all creative arts is the tyranny of the blank page and the challenge of creating something where nothing exists. No infallible theory or guideposts can be offered for tomorrow's creative act, for how-to-do-it instruction is based on past performance. Yesterday's innovation becomes a model not for today's innovation, but for today's imitation. Despite the absence of a blueprint or prescription for the creative process, however, the design process and approaches for generating ideas can be broadly defined.

The design process is a sequence of events that begins when the designer receives an assignment. It continues until the problem is solved and the solution is accepted and implemented. Different individuals and design teams have widely varying approaches to design problem solving. The process can range from *serendipity,* the seemingly accidental discovery of a viable solution without apparent effort, to a protracted trial-and-error process involving numerous client consultations and evaluation of possible solutions with consultants from other disciplines or with focus groups of typical consumers.

Serendipity appeared to be at work when a prominent California graphic designer conceived a new trademark for a Fortune 500 corporation by sketching it on a napkin at a lunch meeting that had been scheduled to brief him on the assignment. A formidable talent focused upon a problem and its parameters and immediately visualized a viable solution. A number of other solutions were explored later, but that initial insight proved to be an exceptional design that has now been in use for a quarter of a century.

Five fundamental steps (fig. **5-1**) are usually involved when solving a design problem. These steps might be compressed into a rapid sequence or even occur simultaneously, as with the logo designed on a napkin, or they might occur over an extended period of time. The design process can be random and intuitive or highly structured and

methodical. The five steps discussed here are one way of looking at the problem-solving process; other schematics are possible. The first three steps— problem definition, information gathering, and idea finding—involve opening the problem to understand and explore it. Solution finding and implementation are closure or resolution.

Problem definition
The first step must always be to define and understand the problem. Sometimes the client has clearly articulated the problem prior to contacting the designer, so the problem is fully defined when the designer receives it. In other situations, the client may only have a vague notion of what the problem is or may even be confused and dependent upon the designer to focus and articulate the problem.

In any event, a problem-solving process usually does not begin until the designer defines the problem and its parameters, including audience, the project goals and objectives, and any constraints, such as time schedule, budget, and production limitations.

During the problem-definition stage, a major impediment is defining the parameters too tightly. Tradition and precedent establish conventions. For example, many clients and designers believe that a corporate annual report must be in an 8½-by-11-inch vertical booklet format. Some advertising managers are convinced that all advertisements must have a large image, a bold headline, body copy, and trademark. Although conventions often develop for logical reasons, such as the need for financial analysts to file annual reports in standard file folders, every rule can have exceptions. Defining a problem should always include testing the problem boundaries and limitations to avoid being locked in by conventional thinking. All conventions, no matter how sacred, must be questioned.

Information gathering

Fact finding involves gathering as much information about the problem as possible. This process includes learning about the client's needs and the sphere of activity, finding out how other designers have solved similar problems, and surveying the communications environment in which the design will function. Some designers make a list of questions about the problem. Library research, consultations with suppliers such as representatives from printers, typesetters, sign fabricators, and paper manufacturers, and detailed discussions with the client are major information-gathering methods. The goal is to know as much as possible about the problem at hand.

Sometimes this step is skipped when a designer feels that he or she received adequate information from the client, has considerable experience with the type of assignment, or is working in an ongoing client-designer relationship. Information gathering is still vital; however, it has already occurred before the assignment is received.

The steps in the design process are not rigidly sequential. Frequently a designer is far along on a project before realizing that more information needs to be gathered before continuing further.

New information stimulates new solutions by pulling the designer away from repetitive thought patterns. Information transfer is invaluable, for ideas and inspiration are often found in film and theater, fine arts, literature, or other design areas, including architecture, fashion, and product design. These inspirations can be reformulated into a graphic design solution. Many designers are curious people who are constantly taking in information from other art forms and the news media.

Idea finding

The search for an effective idea is the most critical step in the design process. Each design problem has many possible solutions. Idea finding is opening the problem to all possible solutions and searching for the most effective ones. Many designers use knowledge-based intuition as their primary approach. Drawing upon their experience and knowledge about design, they intuitively search for a solution without a plan or method. Scores of books about the creative process attempt to define the process and label different idea-generating approaches. These techniques can be useful when ideas don't automatically come to mind.

5-2

Vertical and lateral thinking. Edward de Bono identifies these two approaches to problem solving.[1] *Vertical thinking* follows the most obvious and logical line, proceeding straight up and down. It is the normal way the human brain works, efficiently and logically getting us through our daily routines. *Lateral thinking* is unexpected, sideways thinking. De Bono uses the analogy of digging a hole to explain the difference. Vertical thinking is digging a hole deeper and deeper in the same place, and lateral thinking is trying again somewhere else.

To understand how this applies to graphic design, consider the dozens of trademarks based on a circle with an abstract pattern of lines on it (fig. **5-2**). Effective trademarks were designed this way; therefore, this became a proven approach for designing an effective trademark. Designers dig the "lines and circles trademark hole" bigger and bigger, and clients respond positively to these solutions because they look the way trademarks are supposed to look. More and more designs are made with this approach, until what began as a fresh and innovative approach is turned into a cliché by overuse.[2] An innovative designer working on a trademark must have the courage to abandon the "lines and circles" hole, the "initials" hole (fig. **5-3**), and the "name in bold sans serif type with a line through it" hole (fig. **5-4**), in favor of digging a new hole somewhere else.

SAGA SAM SAMCO S & B S&B S&C
SCAN SCAT SLC SCORE SCRN S&D
SDG SE S&E SEC SFC SFG S&G
SAG SGS SGS S&H SHS SI S&K S&K
SKW SL S&M SMA SMA SMR S & N
S&N SOS SP SPI SPCA SPR SPR SR

5-3

Fashion—not to be confused with style—is created by the herd instinct of vertical thinking. The process begins when a solitary designer observes interesting visual properties in, for example, seldom used typefaces designed in the 1930s but now forgotten and uses them in a fresh and original way. These designs capture attention and are selected for major exhibitions or design annuals. Other designers begin to use these typefaces and they become fashionable.

A useful approach to avoid the dominant ideas and cliché solutions produced by vertical thinking is to write down a list of conventional solutions to the problem. A designer working on an annual report for a bank might list conventional cover solutions for bank annual reports, such as embossed or gold-stamped trademark and headquarters building photograph. The designer can then consciously avoid these solutions or push, exaggerate, combine, or distort them until an original variation emerges. Reinventing a cliché, or looking at it in a fresh and original way can produce original and effective results.

Capitalizing upon the play instinct is another way to break out of vertical thinking. Making collages and montages from printed material as a playful, unassigned activity, making fanciful typographic arrangements from old type proofs, or working with unfamiliar tools and techniques can produce unexpected results that can be incorporated into projects.

Chance, recognized by the Dada movement as a catalyst to creativity, can help designers approach problems in an unfamiliar way. Sometimes designers who are trained to think logically and bring form and order to communications find opening themselves to chance hard. Some of the techniques designers have used to introduce chance into the design process are: randomly selecting typefaces from a specimen book or colors from an ink-swatch book; asking a layman to suggest possible solutions to a problem and being open to even the most naive suggestion, for it may possess the kernel of an insight that can be pushed into a viable solution; and randomly selecting from a list of relevant words and trying to generate form or image combinations from them. Chance is haphazard by nature. Perhaps the best way to allow the unexpected possibilities of chance to enter the design process is being open to unexpected forms or inspirations.

5-4

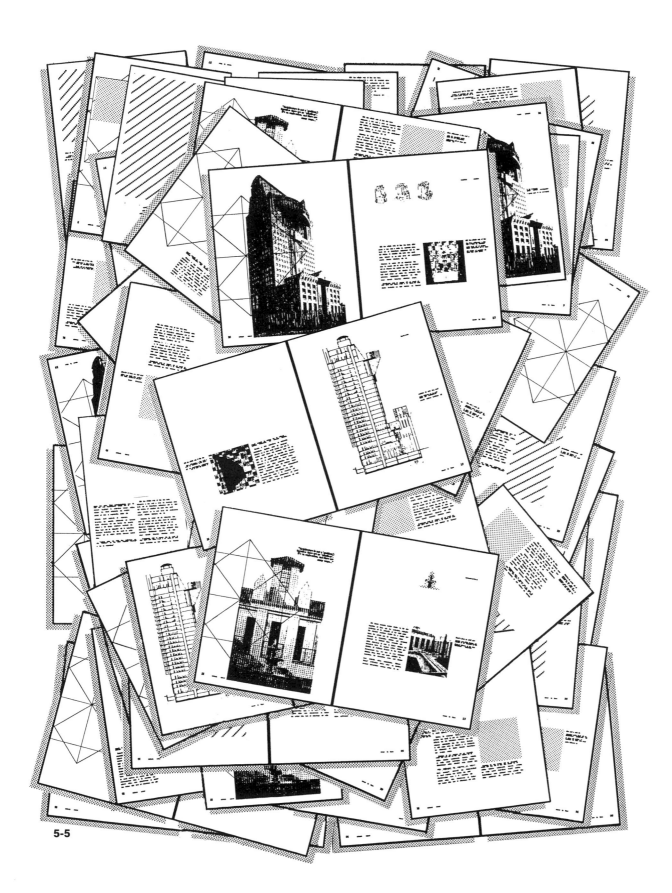

Twisting the problem inside out or turning things upside down can help produce an original solution. If the copy states a fact, what visual possibilities arise if it is changed to a question? If everyone is thinking big, think small. If decoration is out because the fashion of the moment is that "less is more," operate as though "more is better." Contrariwise, in a time of complexity and ornament, seek the essence of the message, period. If most designers have abandoned Helvetica because of its overuse, rethink its possibilities.

At times vertical thinking is important in graphic design. In the design of a visual-identification system, lateral thinking is important when establishing an original trademark and format style; however, when producing vast quantities of material conforming to that system of graphic standards, a high degree of redundancy and continuity is required.

Brainstorming. This process is a classical method of group problem solving.[3] Some designers deplore it because they believe that the individual alone with his or her sketch pad can best tackle problems, but many clients are eager to use this approach. Some people believe that brainstorming involves a group sitting around, throwing out ideas, and accomplishing nothing. Actually, the technique as originally conceived was more structured. It involved preparation, with every participant receiving a copy of the problem and session guidelines or rules beforehand. A group leader and group recorder were designated. Sessions lasted about thirty to forty-five minutes. Later, another group or the same group evaluated the ideas generated. Procedures such as being recognized by the leader before speaking and taking turns to offer ideas and passing if nothing comes to mind are used to keep sessions organized and on track. Sometimes brainstorming sessions can be used effectively to generate a range of possible directions.

Guidelines often used in brainstorming sessions are helpful in any problem-solving process. Defer judgment on each possibility, no matter how weak it seems, for it might inspire a better one. Generate as many ideas as possible. The weak ones provide a benchmark against which stronger ones can be evaluated. Be open to all ideas, no matter how bizarre or stupid they may seem at first. Past experience is the basis for informed judgment, but new ideas cannot always be successfully evaluated by it.

Incubation. After spending time working on a problem, divert attention to something else for a while, letting your thoughts incubate. San Francisco designer Michael Vanderbyl notes that he will work on a problem for a couple of hours, and if a solution does not readily develop, he will shift his attention to something else, returning to the project later with a fresh eye.[4]

The term *black box* has been coined to describe the process of collecting all available data and letting it rummage around in the back of the designer's mind. The information combines and synthesizes until possible solutions begin to emerge intuitively.

Notation. The favored problem-solving method of many designers is simply sitting down with a pad and pencil and generating notations. Small drawings called *thumbnail sketches* permit the exploration of many ideas rather quickly (see figs. **5-72** though **5-75**). Pads of translucent paper allow a designer to stick a sketch or layout under the next sheet and use it as a guide to quickly explore numerous variations. Louise Fili says that her approach to designing a book jacket is "to sketch it over and over again. The type goes from an amorphous thing to being in focus. Once it begins to be focused, I may realize that it is a typeface that doesn't exist."[5] Then, Fili can decide to use a similar typeface, alter a typeface to conform to her sketch, or commission hand-lettering. Lance Hidy makes dozens of color sketches for his posters to explore alternate color possibilities (see figs. **5-13** through **5-67**).

Thumbnails and sketches enable a designer to take a problem through a process of metamorphosis involving change, evaluation, and transformation. The solution evolves through a series of stages. Computer graphics now permit a designer to survey numerous possibilities rather rapidly and spend more time thinking and evaluating and less time simulating typography and doing other routine work. For a capabilities brochure for an architectural firm (fig. **5-5**), designer Les Derby digitized the photographs, quickly drafted diagrams and plans, and then used these elements in small planning layouts on his computer. Derby rapidly changed the size and position of pictures, diagrams, and typography as he explored numerous variations simply by moving, enlarging, and reducing elements. These double-page designs were designed on the computer screen and printed on a 300 DPI (dots per inch) laser printer. Whether on a microprocessor or a sketch pad, notation processes are interactive. A trial-and-error dialogue between the designer and the sketches begins that is a give-and-take process of evaluation and further development.

5-6

Many designers constantly look through design annuals and magazines to stir their thinking. This approach can inspire new ideas but it can also lead to slavish imitation if the designer is not careful and honest about the narrow but deep gulf between influence and plagiarism. Widespread use of design annuals as model books contributes to the rapid development of fashion. While the designer is looking around, a solution for a problem that is incubating can suddenly come to mind, triggered by the composition of a painting, the characters in a play, the cinematography in a film, or even seeing forms briefly created by the chance passing of a girl in a lavender sweater and a man in a green coat walking down the street in opposite directions.

Synthesis. Many major innovations have occurred when artists or designers synthesized and combined diverse and even contradictory influences. The influences of both the Postimpressionist painter Paul Cézanne and African masks were important catalysts for Pablo Picasso in the invention of cubism. The work of Piet Zwart, an innovative pioneer of modern graphic design (see fig. **3-34**), was informed by the structured logical order of the de Stijl movement and the random chance, unexpected associations, and spatial vitality of the Dada movement.

Michael Vanderbyl, trained in a tradition of grid structure, order, and methodology, mentions the colorful, decorative energy of psychedelic posters as one of many influences that inspired his process of "softening the hard edge," which played an important role in the development of the San Francisco approach to postmodern design.[6]

Many designers, writers, and photographers keep a small pad and pencil handy in their pockets, purses, or bedside tables so that they are ready to notate ideas whenever their thinking produces something worth retaining.

Making lists in a fluid and uninhibited manner of every possible thing that comes to mind related to a problem is another way to stimulate thinking. A thesaurus can suggest related concepts. Matrix structures, created by putting items from a list in horizontal and vertical columns and then cross-referencing them, can be a productive approach to generating possible combinations of forms and symbols that might convey the essence of the subject (fig. **5-6**).

Ocular reconnaissance. The visual stimulation of looking, surveying, and inspecting is one of the most fertile sources of inspiration for designers. Wandering through an art museum, a hardware store, or the library can reveal forms, color combinations, and images that enrich the data bank of the brain.

Solution finding

Whereas idea finding involves opening the problem and expanding the possibilities, solution finding is the process of closure or resolution. After generating a series of possible solutions to the problem, the next step is to determine which one (or more) will be executed in a finished form and presented to the client. One tendency is to apply negative, critical judgment, rejecting the less successful ones and declaring winners by default, although this can quickly eliminate the weaker ideas. When a large number of possibilities have been developed, the positive approach—identifying strengths and permitting the best solutions to emerge from the larger group—is more productive. Solution finding can be very objective. When a logical and fully acceptable solution does not readily emerge, a three-phase process can be useful: establish criteria, select a solution, and validate the choice.

Establish criteria. Even if the problem-definition phase established specific criteria, reconsideration of the criteria can be useful because of the knowledge developed during the information-gathering and idea-generation steps. Different kinds of projects have vastly different criteria. Questions relating to message, form and space, and resonance provide one example of a set of criteria against which a solution can be measured.

Message

Do the elements clearly convey appropriate content?

How well does the design position itself relative to similar and competing messages in the communications environment?

Is there any confusion or ambiguity about the message?

Is the typography legible?

Can the typography be read clearly from the appropriate viewing distance?

Do images convey the appropriate information?

Is there anything in the design that the intended audience will have difficulty decoding and understanding?

Do type and image function together as a cohesive message?

Are signs and symbols clear and understandable?

What positive or negative connotations do the colors have?

Are there any undesirable connotations or unintended infrasignals?

Form and space

Do the elements form a cohesive and unified visual whole?

Is the visual hierarchy clear and appropriate?

Are scale relationships between the parts effective?

Do type and image function well together in the space?

Is the visual structure ordered and effective?

Does the viewer's eye move through the design in a desirable sequence?

Do spatial intervals and support elements function appropriately?

Resonance

Do the overall visual aspects express the essence of the subject?

Are the images expressive and engaging?

Do the typefaces used have suitable connotations and design properties?

Is anything unusual or unexpected about the design? If so, does this contribute or detract?

Is the design a Chinese box with several levels of information and meaning? If so, is the movement from the smallest box to the largest box appropriate?

Does the design speak with the right tone of voice for the audience and subject?

Do colors and graphic support elements add to or detract from this tone of voice?

Although the use of a question set introduces logical thinking into the solution-finding process, the nature of human expression is such that a proposed solution might have expressive power not addressed by logic. Innovation is hard to evaluate, for it breaks with the conventional norms of its time. In some cases, a hunch or intuitive response can be the best guide for selecting a solution.

Designers should take responsibility for generating the best possible solutions, for even the most difficult assignments are not impervious to solution. At a medium-sized advertising agency, the staff complained that a young art director was always assigned to the best clients and the most creative projects. After she was shifted from the "best" accounts to the "worst" ones to placate the other art directors, the creative director realized that her ability to generate creative and effective ideas—not being given the best accounts—was the reason her accounts had the most creative work.

Implementation

Implementation involves presenting the solution, gaining its acceptance, and executing the project. The best solutions are worthless if clients do not approve them. Strategies to improve the acceptance rate become critical to the design process. The much touted enthusiasm for the development of new ideas usually does not extend to a bona fide new idea when it is presented, for its unfamiliarity generates uncertainty and reluctance. By becoming an advocate of the solution and enlisting others as advocates, the designer increases the chances of acceptance.

Many clients do not have high visual literacy skills and want the designer to guide them toward acceptance of a solution; therefore, the presentation should emphasize the appropriateness and effectiveness of the message, rather than just visual design properties. The number of individuals or groups who must approve the solution can be a factor. Whenever possible, having one individual with approval authority simplifies gaining acceptance. Enlisting the client as a partner in the problem-solving process, especially in the problem-definition and information-gathering phases, can be an effective strategy, for the client then has a personal investment in the design process and better understands the solution. The list of questions above can be provided to the client, who can consider them one by one to assess the proposed design.

Even the best-planned presentations can go unexpectedly awry. An architectural firm requested a young designer to create a trademark to signify both design and engineering. The architects enthusiastically endorsed the solution: a stylized pen point whose stem was threaded like a bolt. The only board member who did not like it disparagingly panned it as the "stick 'em and screw 'em logo." His comment stuck with the other board members, and several eventually changed their votes.

Many designers find diagrammatic time schedules useful in the implementation process, which involves producing, collecting, and assembling all the elements that go into the design: manuscript text, typesetting, photography or illustration, production art, and other elements. Client responsibility to the time schedule by meeting approval deadlines and supplying materials such as manuscript copy, financial data, and product specifications is essential. Some designers build extensions into their contracts that automatically extend the deadline if the client delays in providing information or approval.

Figure **5-1** presented a simplified diagram of the design process. The more complex process illustrated in figure **5-7** is more typical of how a project really proceeds. The following case studies amplify the design process as documented by actual projects. A poster design, an advertising campaign, and a textbook format design demonstrate a range of problem-solving challenges.

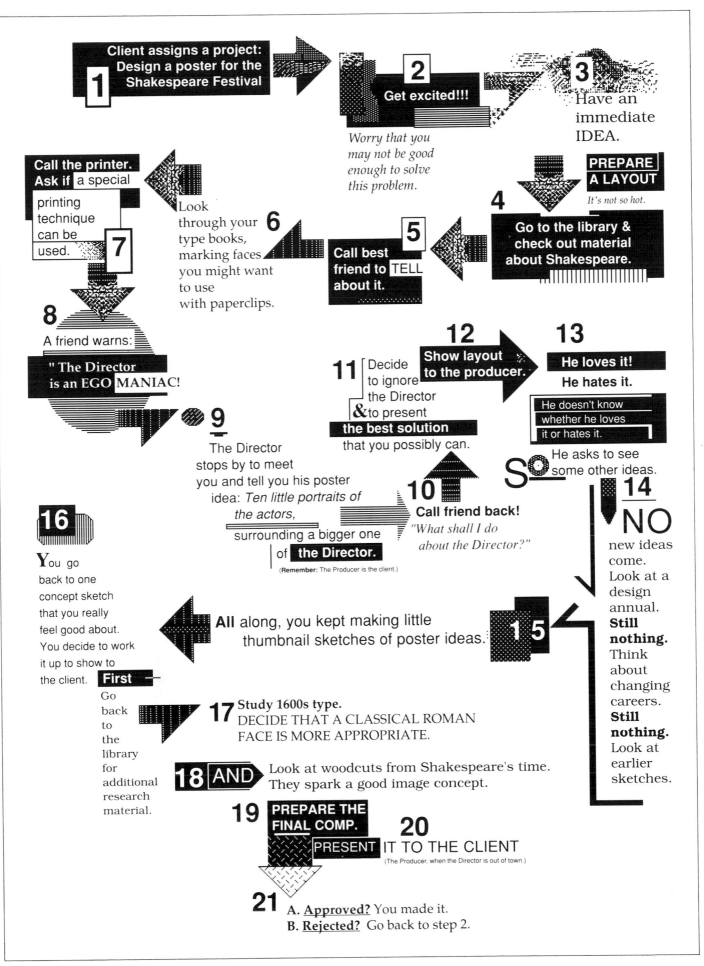

Design process: a social-issue poster

Lance Hidy was commissioned by Women's Action for Nuclear Disarmament (WAND), a Massachusetts organization involved in the movement to reduce nuclear weapons, to design a poster that could be used to publicize the organization and its activities. Also, WAND planned to use the design in fund-raising by reproducing and selling it as a limited-edition silk-screen print, an offset lithographic reproduction, notecards, postcards, and T-shirts. Hidy contributed his time to WAND, carefully stipulating that it could have unlimited use of the design but it was not to make alterations, permit other organizations to use it, or

remove the artist's signature without permission.

Hidy believes that graphic design is a collaboration between designer, sponsor or client, and printer. The initial WAND poster was silk-screen printed by master printer Rob Day, with whom Hidy collaborates. The struggle to satisfy the needs and interests of the client while maintaining the integrity of personal vision is paramount in Hidy's mind. At his initial meetings with a client, Hidy listens carefully to the client's expectations, ideas, and sense of aesthetics. "I am alert for attitudes and ideas that are compatible with my own," Hidy observes, "and I steer the project in that direction." Hidy and the WAND directors agreed at their initial meeting that they wanted to avoid the frightening images of missiles, mushroom clouds, and skulls predominant in antinuclear posters. Hidy believes "terrifying images have limited effectiveness, since they cause us to go numb for awhile. We learn to become insensitive to the meaning of a mushroom cloud; otherwise, we could become disabled by our emotions!" [7]

Hidy's search for a direction became more focused after he attended WAND's Mother's Day event, where one of WAND's fundamental ideas—that nuclear disarmament is for the sake of children and future generations—heightened his appreciation of the movement. As the father of a young daughter, he had great empathy for this concept. Many of Hidy's posters are reductive, presenting only two elements: an image and the sponsor's name. However, he found it difficult to convey the complex concept "nuclear disarmament for the sake of children and future generations" within these simple parameters.

After determining that a slogan was needed to connote the image and function as a rallying cry for the movement, Hidy met with advertising copywriter Margaret Wilcox. Of the thirty ideas they generated during one all-day session, the one that seemed most promising to Hidy was, "They ask the world of you." When Hidy presented this slogan to WAND, the positive response was immediate and unanimous. Hidy sought approval to change this to "Children ask the world of us," because he felt that this version was more specific and personal.

Feeling that an image of a mother and child might be appropriate, Hidy selected his neighbor Sheri Larson and her infant son David as models and shot several rolls of film. From one of the contact sheets (fig. **5-8**), he selected a shot with excellent profile views and a classic maternal gesture (fig. **5-9**).

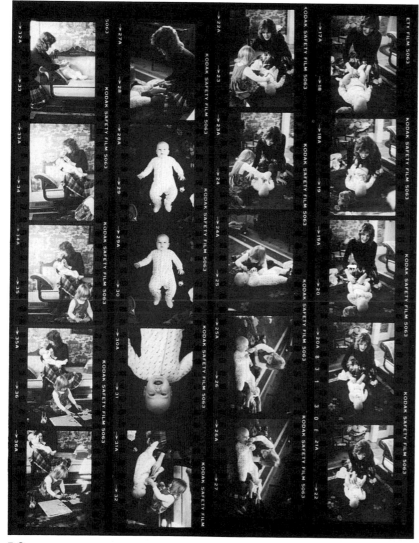

5-8

5-9

Sketches were made from the photograph to develop a feeling for its form and space (fig. **5-10**). The stacks of sketches Hidy had made during the brainstorming session included sketches of the earth as a toy ball. These inspired him to have the mother handing the earth to the child, an eloquent visual metaphor for the concept of passing care of the planet from generation to generation. Additional photography and sketches were made to explore the placement of the continents on the globe and the position of the mother's hand (fig. **5-11**). At this point Hidy felt that he had found the solution and proceeded to the actual artwork.

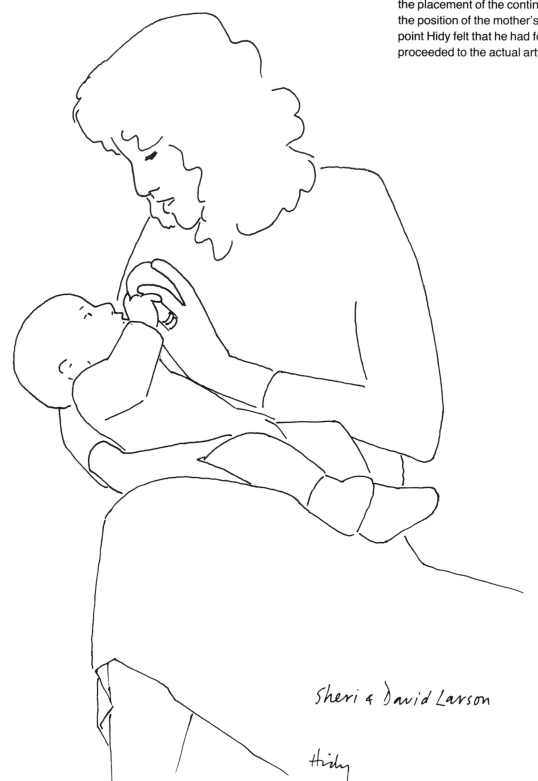

Sheri & David Larson

Hidy

5-10

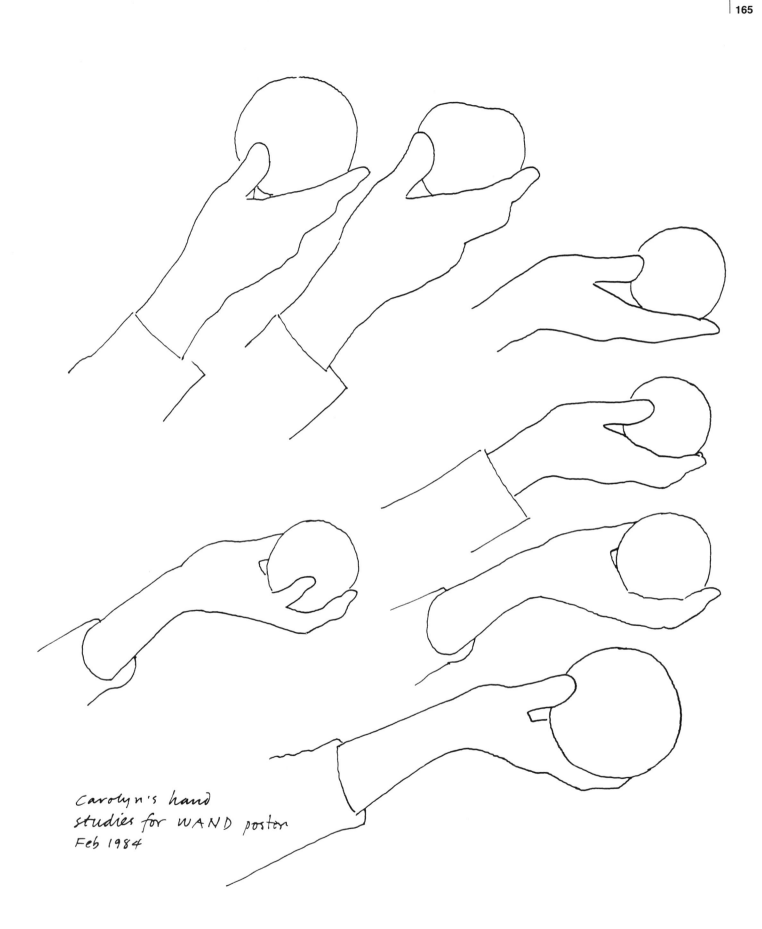

Carolyn's hand
studies for WAND poster
Feb 1984

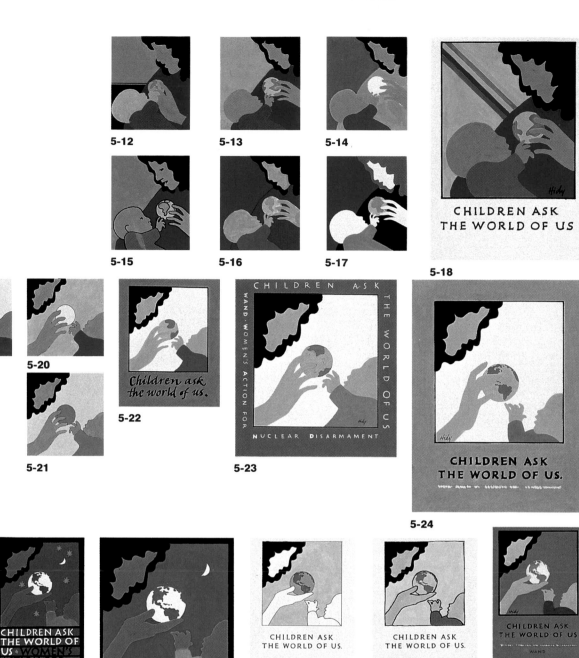

5-12

5-13

5-14

5-15

5-16

5-17

5-18

CHILDREN ASK
THE WORLD OF US

5-19

5-20

5-21

5-22

Children ask
the world of us.

CHILDREN ASK

WAND · WOMEN'S ACTION FOR

THE WORLD OF US

5-23

NUCLEAR DISARMAMENT

CHILDREN ASK
THE WORLD OF US.

5-24

CHILDREN ASK
THE WORLD OF
US · WOMEN'S
ACTION FOR
NUCLEAR
DISARMAMENT

5-28

CHILDREN ASK
THE WORLD OF US

WOMEN'S
ACTION FOR
NUCLEAR
DISARMAMENT

5-31

CHILDREN ASK
THE WORLD OF US.

5-25

CHILDREN ASK
THE WORLD OF US.

5-26

CHILDREN ASK
THE WORLD OF US

WAND

5-27

5-29

5-30

5-32

CHILDREN ASK
THE WORLD OF US.

5-33

CHILDREN ASK
THE WORLD OF US.

5-34

5-35

5-36

CHILDREN ASK
THE WORLD OF US

5-37

CHILDREN ASK
THE WORLD OF US.

5-38

CHILDREN ASK
THE WORLD OF US.

5-39

The three main problems to be resolved were drawing, color, and typography or lettering. Usually Hidy makes from five to fifteen color gouache sketches before solving a poster design problem. For the WAND poster, he made a total of sixty-three sketches, fifty-five of which are reproduced here (figs. **5-12** though **5-66**). Hidy has a policy of showing only one solution at a time to a client. "This forces me to be decisive about what I want," he commented, "and it minimizes the temptation for the client to 'play artist' by picking elements from different designs and asking me to combine these." In the first series of color studies (figs. **5-12** through **5-18**), Hidy worked closely from his line drawing, cropping the figures and simplifying the design into shapes of color. The shape of the mother's shoulder and arm was not satisfactory, for it seemed too dominant and distracted from the mother, child, and globe. Therefore, Hidy abandoned this series without showing it to the client, and he rethought the composition.

In the second series of studies, Hidy simplified the design by stripping away the background and focusing upon the simple silhouettes of the mother and her child, who is reaching up for the globe (figs. **5-19** though **5-24**). The larger study (fig. **5-24**) was presented to the client, who responded favorably except for a few minor reservations.

Hidy returned to his studio and explored this direction further (figs. **5-25** through **5-39**). In the solution presented to WAND a few days later (fig. **5-36**), the color was more intense, and the drawing of the mother's hand was improved. Hidy felt that this was his best shot and was upset when it was flatly rejected. The WAND board did not care for the magenta color used on the skin and feared that the moon and star might have connotations of astrological or Soviet metasymbols. Unsuccessful in his attempts to dissuade them, Hidy "became very discouraged and lost my confidence." Because the deadline was near, he forced himself to continue.

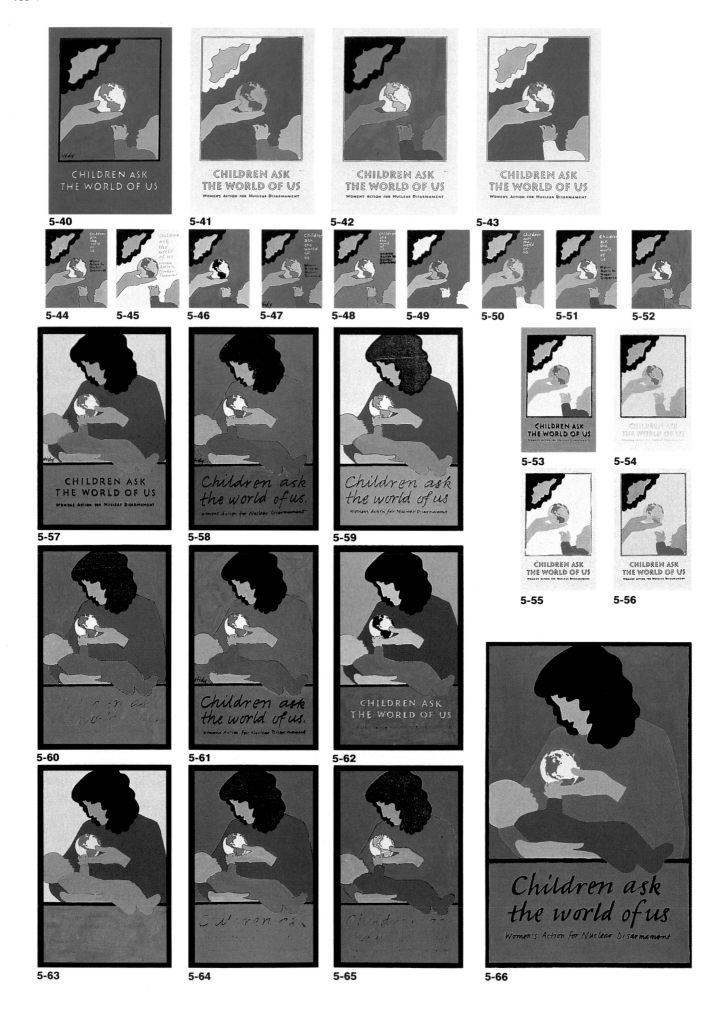

5-40

5-41

5-42

5-43

5-44 **5-45** **5-46** **5-47** **5-48** **5-49** **5-50** **5-51** **5-52**

5-57

5-58

5-59

5-53 **5-54**

5-55 **5-56**

5-60

5-61

5-62

5-63

5-64

5-65

5-66

"I mechanically started doing tiny, two-inch color sketches with a natural skin tone, minus the moon and star," he recalls (figs. **5-40** though **5-56**). "Those were a couple of bad days, since I felt disconnected from the design, and without inspiration. The sketches looked like garbage to me, and with the clock ticking away, I started to panic." Clearly something was bothering Hidy about the solution, and he was struggling to salvage it through the application of color.

Out of desperation, Hidy abruptly stopped making the color sketches and decided to go back to square one. Returning to his photographs, Hidy "tried to salvage the passion he had once had for the project, which was now lost." Looking again at the sketch of Sheri holding David in her arm (see fig. **5-10**), Hidy began to question the rejected design, for "the mother and baby were not touching, which may have been a mistake. So I went back to having the mother hold the baby, making the image more intimate and natural" (figs. **5-57** through **5-66**). The image is less tightly cropped, and both of the mother's hands are shown. This felt right. Hidy quickly regained his enthusiasm and explored two color schemes. Because he felt equally good about them, he broke "his one solution only policy" by showing both to WAND. The client couldn't decide between the two proposed color options either, so they decided to print both versions. The earth-toned palette harmonizes with many domestic interiors, and the brighter palette is more effective in public locations.

In his poster designs, Hidy favors hand-lettering over type, agreeing with British type historian Stanley Morison that typography is a department of calligraphy. The first two lettering approaches (fig. **5-67**) for the WAND poster are formal capitals, with inspiration derived from the typefaces Futura, Albertus, and Neuland. Although a stately and dignified resonance is projected, Hidy finally decided to use his handwriting (fig. **5-68**). The irregularity and informality of it would, Hidy hoped, have the resonance of a personal voice, rather than a distant institutional presence.

5-67

5-68

Hidy

Children ask
the world of us

Women's Action for Nuclear Disarmament

Hidy 263/700

PUBLISHED BY WAND EDUCATION FUND · 691 MASSACHUSETTS AVE · ARLINGTON · MA 02174 · COPYRIGHT © 1984 BY LANCE HIDY · NEWBURYPORT · MA   ·   WRITER: MARGARET WILCOX   ·   PRINTER: ROB DAY · MINK BROOK EDITIONS · W. LEBANON · NH

The simplification of the image enables it to signify every woman and every child, an elemental image speaking to the issue of world peace (fig. **5-69**). The rejected design with the moon and stars has been published by Anthoensen Press in Portland, Maine (fig. **5-70**) and issued as a notecard by Portal Publications. These simple images have become late twentieth-century icons that speak in a gentle voice to universal aspirations. That thousands upon thousands of reproductions of Lance Hidy's "Children Ask the World of Us" graphics for the Women's Action for Nuclear Disarmament have been printed and distributed comes as no surprise.

CHILDREN ASK THE WORLD OF US

5-70

Design process: an advertising campaign

Chicago designer Jeff Barnes was asked by Kieffer-Nolde, Inc., a prominent engraving and four-color-process separation company, to create an advertising campaign. They were celebrating their thirtieth anniversary in the color separation business and wanted a campaign that would attract attention and provoke a reaction within the communications industry.

After the meeting, Barnes saw the dichotomy between old and new as a viable direction. Kieffer-Nolde had been around long enough to develop a tradition of and reputation for reliability and quality; at the same time, they were using the latest high-technology computerized scanners and image processors.

Barnes researched the advertising campaigns for other color separators and found that many of them used garish, neon effects and often printed the four-color process over additional colors to hype up the image. Kieffer-Nolde had been reproducing demonstration photographs, such as food shots, to convey technical perfection. They needed a more creative campaign that would stand out from the crowd. Also, Kieffer-Nolde wanted to restrict their advertising campaign to the four-color process only, allowing potential clients to see the capabilities of the actual four-color printing process that is used in clients' printing and advertising.

While searching for a direction, Barnes recalled the sepia-tone photographs, carefully crafted to look like authentic period images, that had been shown to him by photographer Denis Scott. Barnes, who writes the copy for many of his projects, developed a copy approach based upon a phrase that he heard often in the advertising industry: "what if. . . ."

"What if . . . we do it this way . . . could we get it done by Monday?"

"What if . . . we hand-tint this black-and-white photograph and then adjust the color separation to look like an old sepia-tone photograph?"

"What if . . . we want to superimpose the color photograph of the product over the illustration?"

Thinking about all the things that can go wrong in printing, and knowing that Kieffer-Nolde had a reputation for never missing a single color-separation deadline in thirty years, Barnes generated a list of copy possibilities. Ranging from the fanciful to the practical, these included:

What if . . . you could really do it?

What if . . . you could fly?

What if . . . nothing ever went wrong?

What if . . . you were the boss, and could call the shots?

What if . . . it were up to you to meet the deadline?

What if . . . the party didn't have to end?

What if . . . you knew all the tricks about production?

What if . . . you were there? (Show an exotic, impossible scene that could be reproduced by Kieffer-Nolde technology.)

What if . . . it was yours? (Show something unbelievable.)

Barnes combined his copy concepts with appropriate images by using photographs by Denis Scott. Armed with a set of visual-verbal equations that made almost telegraphic statements about the client's capabilities, Barnes began to search for a format and typographic treatment. He knew that he wanted to achieve a contradiction: vintage, period photographs from an earlier time, used in fresh contemporary layouts.

For this campaign, the photograph and its reproduction were very important. They became a specimen of the client's ability to separate difficult subjects; for example, the black-and-white photograph of a young woman with a hint of pink on the lips had to be separated perfectly to create a black-and-white image by four-color printing. Barnes centered each photograph, using ample surrounding white space and a crisp black line border to separate it from the visual clutter on the opposite page. Typography was placed on colored collage elements that were spontaneously torn, then placed on the page in a dynamic asymmetrical arrangement.

Barnes explored possible arrangements in color sketches in his notebook (figs. **5-71** through **5-74**). These sketches explored color, contrast, balance, and potential composition. Barnes wanted to determine if he could "invade" the photographic space with the collage elements.

Barnes's reputation for creative and original page design stems from this design process. He creates scores of small thumbnail sketches in graph paper notebooks and sometimes explores dozens of possible arrangements.

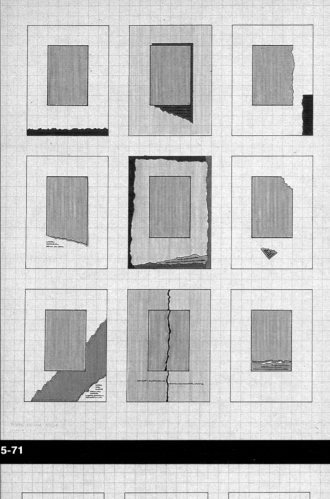

5-71

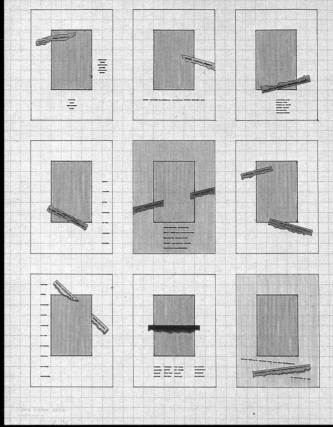

5-72

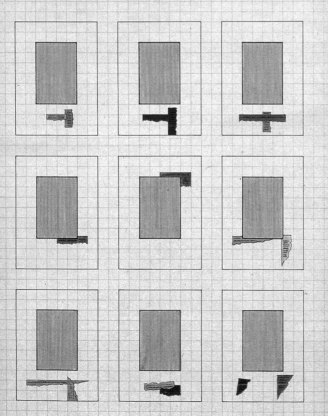

5-73

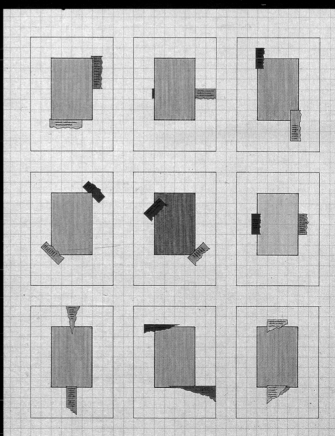

5-74

Photography: Denis Scott Design: Jeff Barnes

what if...nothing ever went wrong...

For thirty years
we've been getting
it there on time.

Kieffer-Nolde, Inc.
Offset & Gravure
Graphics
160 East Illinois
Chicago, IL 60611
312-337-5500
Toll Free
800-621-8314

Call or write for
our complimentary
color calendar.

At first, the choice of typeface had Barnes stumped. Just as the deadline for the first ad approached, Barnes had started work on a visual identity update for Kieffer-Nolde, but it would not be completed in time to use in this campaign. Designer and client both agreed that the old identity, consisting of a mixture of sans serif metal typefaces that Barnes could not even locate in type specimen books, was dated and should not be used. For the campaign Barnes wanted something that was immediate and spontaneous yet would work with nostalgic photographs evoking earlier decades. The typeface should project a strong visual image, yet it should not appear to be part of an identity system because the old visual identity was being phased out but the new one was not yet ready for release. Reasoning that the photograph was the main concern since it demonstrated the client's capabilities, Barnes decided that a spontaneous typographic approach, such as typewriter output, might project the appropriate feeling.

"Somewhere between typography and handwriting, there is the wonderful resonance of the typewriter letter," he observes. "It is an archetype for immediacy. It is today's message . . . today's business communiqué . . . unsophisticated and direct." Barnes studied typefaces based on typewriter type as well as the output from contemporary office typewriters. He determined that they were all "too slick and polished." Thinking that an old typewriter might generate letterforms with the proper resonance and feeling, Barnes purchased a 1913 Underwood typewriter from a friend for eleven dollars. The rhythmic unevenness of its crude letterforms, especially when enlarged to headline size, was an exciting visual discovery.

As Barnes produced the campaign, he tried to keep the ads consistent in format and style yet give each one an individual identity. Short copy creates an immediate message. A participatory effect is generated by the incomplete quality of the copy. The placement of the collage elements serves two purposes: It creates a dynamic asymmetrical composition, and it provides a demonstration of Kieffer-Nolde's skill in producing screen tints that reverse from and overlap four-color process subjects. Throughout, the ads show the subtle graphic humor of Scott's photographic recreations and Barnes's parade of "what ifs."

Figure **5-75** asks, "what if . . . nothing ever went wrong . . ." But something always seems to go wrong, suggests the photograph of a young woman in an old coupe that is out of gas. The text advises, "for thirty years we've been getting it there on time."

Figure **5-76** asks, "what if . . . it were up to you . . ." The concerned young woman obviously has a problem. The viewer wonders, "if what were up to me?" then quickly reads the text, learning that Kieffer-Nolde can take the panic out of production.

"What if . . . you knew all the tricks . . . ," asks a somber magician (fig. **5-77**). "But," thinks the viewer, "I don't know all the tricks." The text proclaims that "for thirty years we've been giving you a great deal." The screen tint area for the body copy is stacked and shifted like playing cards.

A closely cropped profile of a woman smoking a big cigar and wearing the cigar band as a ring (fig. **5-78**) humorously parodies "being the boss." The body copy advises that for "thirty years we've been helping you do it your way." The collage element bearing the body copy is burned in an effective demonstration of graphic reproduction.

In figure **5-79**, Scott's photograph immediately conveys that bittersweet feeling one has after a lively party is over. "What if . . . it didn't have to end . . . ," asks the headline. It doesn't, suggests the text, because "for thirty years we've been helping the good times continue."

The energy of contrast resonates from this ad campaign: refined and elegant photography contrasts with crude old typewriter type, symmetrically placed rectangular photographs contrast with asymmetrically balanced collage elements, and mechanically perfect ruled borders around the photographs contrast with organic torn collage edges.

This advertising campaign proved to be highly effective in meeting its objectives. An image of quality and reliability was communicated, while presenting Kieffer-Nolde as a firm that had been around for three decades *and* was contemporary and up-to-date. Exploring dozens of page layouts and searching for just the right used typewriter whose letterforms would combine with the photographs typifies the involvement and concern of Jeff Barnes's graphic design.

what if...it were up to you...

For thirty years
we've been taking
the panic out of
production.

Kieffer-Nolde,Inc.
Offset & Gravure
Graphics
160 East Illinois
Chicago,IL 60611
312-337-5500
Toll Free
800-621-8314

Call or write for
our complimentary
color calendar.

5-76

what if...you knew all the tricks...

For thirty years
we've been giving
you a great deal.

Kieffer-Nolde,Inc.
Offset & Gravure
Graphics
160 East Illinois
Chicago,IL 60611
312-337-5500
Toll Free
800-621-8314

Call or write for
our complimentary
color calendar.

5-77

what if...you were the boss...

For thirty years
we've been helping
you do it your way.

Kieffer-Nolde,Inc.
Offset & Gravure
Graphics
160 East Illinois
Chicago,IL 60611
312-337-5500
Toll Free
800-621-8314

Call or write for
our complimentary
color calendar.

5-78

what if...it didn't have to end...

For thirty years
we've been helping
the good times
continue.

Kieffer-Nolde,Inc.
Offset & Gravure
Graphics
160 East Illinois
Chicago,IL 60611
312-337-5500
Toll Free
800-621-8314

5-79

Design process: a textbook format

Earlier the purposes of graphic design were identified: to inform or instruct, to motivate, and to delight. Lance Hidy's poster design for WAND informs the public, delights with its color and imagery, and has motivated many persons to support WAND and its antinuclear weapons campaign. The advertising campaign that Jeff Barnes and photographer Denis Scott created for Kieffer-Nolde delights with its sophisticated humor and motivates its audience to inquire further about the firm. In each case, the designer had to create or commission words and images to solve a design problem.

Creating a book format design is quite different. Often the words and images have been produced before the graphic designer becomes involved. The task is to develop a format or package to contain and organize complex information and make the learning process more efficient. A design team consisting of Rob Carter, Steven Chovanec, Ben Day, and Philip Meggs collaborated on the design of a typography textbook, *Typographic Design: Form and Communication.* When designers work in teams, they must suspend egotistical tendencies and focus upon group dialogue and consensus. A 300-page manuscript, 446 illustrations, and 100 pages of type specimens had to be organized into a 272-page book. At a series of initial meetings, the design team developed a set of criteria governing the design of the book:

The diversity of visual material required a neutral format that would not compete with the contents.

To increase the efficiency of the design process and consistency of page design, specific guidelines were needed: grid structure, column-and-margin sizes, flow lines, spatial intervals, line widths, and the like.

The typographic style should be highly legible, harmonize well with a variety of illustrations and typographic examples, and have a clearly defined hierarchy: titles, headings, running text, captions, folios (page numbers).

A grid structure and typographic specifications were the first step. The team studied type specimens and carefully considered: Garamond, a classical Old Style face; Times Roman, a legible, slightly condensed roman face designed for newspapers that permits more characters per line than most text faces; Univers, a sans serif with an excellent black-to-white ratio; and Helvetica, a sans serif face similar to Univers but less geometric in structure. Specimens of the four faces were placed beside a variety of typographic examples that had been selected for the book. Times Roman was eliminated immediately because its denser texture and darker tone conflicted with many of the visual examples. After deciding that the sans serif fonts blended with diverse visual material better than the Garamond, the merits of Univers versus Helvetica were argued and a simple vote (Univers 2, Helvetica 1, abstentions 1) determined that Univers would be used. Before the vote, the team had all agreed that both faces were fully acceptable.

Text-type specimens and copy-fitting charts were evaluated, and a decision was made to use 9-point Univers with 2 points of interline spacing for text and 7-point Univers 55 with 4 points of interline spacing for captions. Because Univers has a large x-height (the size of lower-case characters, determined by measuring the height of the lower-case x), 7-point Univers 55 actually looks as large as 9-point Garamond. Also, the design team knew that legibility research has documented that the additional lead, which enables the caption copy to align with the running text, also increases legibility. The designers discussed Jan Tschichold's recommendation that caption copy should be two points smaller than the running text to insure that readers would not become confused. They agreed that both text and captions should be set in a flush-left, ragged-right configuration, for reasons of both legibility and style. A system of headings was established, using the bolder, 9-point Univers 65. The manuscript has two levels of headings. Both were set in 9-point Univers 65, but major divisions within a chapter were separated from the running text by a spatial interval and the secondary headings were placed within the text column. Later, the team had the typographer set specimens of the captions (fig. **5-80**) and running text (fig. **5-81**) with different kerning (reduction of the spatial interval between letters) so the design team could select the precise kerning desired for legibility and tone. Minus three-eighths of a point kerning was selected for both.

6.

c. 1800-1400 B.C.: Stonehenge, a megalithic monument of thirty-foot-tall stones set into circular patterns.

7.

c. 1570-1349 B.C.: Poly-chromed wood sculpture from New Kingdom Egypt, with hieroglyphic inscriptions.

8.

c. 1450 B.C.: Detail, *The Book of the Dead* of Tuthmosis III, hieroglyphic writing on papyrus.

9.

c. 1500 B.C.: The twenty-two characters of the Phoenician alphabet.

c. 800 B.C.: Homer writes the *Iliad* and *Odyssey.*

540 B.C.: The first public library is established in Athens, Greece.

minus ⅛

6.

c. 1800-1400 B.C.: Stonehenge, a megalithic monument of thirty-foot-tall stones set into circular patterns.

7.

c. 1570-1349 B.C.: Poly-chromed wood sculpture from New Kingdom Egypt, with hieroglyphic inscriptions.

8.

c. 1450 B.C.: Detail, *The Book of the Dead* of Tuthmosis III, hieroglyphic writing on papyrus.

9.

c. 1500 B.C.: The twenty-two characters of the Phoenician alphabet.

c. 800 B.C.: Homer writes the *Iliad* and *Odyssey.*

540 B.C.: The first public library is established in Athens, Greece.

minus ¼

6.

c. 1800-1400 B.C.: Stonehenge, a megalithic monument of thirty-foot-tall stones set into circular patterns.

7.

c. 1570-1349 B.C.: Poly-chromed wood sculpture from New Kingdom Egypt, with hieroglyphic inscriptions.

8.

c. 1450 B.C.: Detail, *The Book of the Dead* of Tuthmosis III, hieroglyphic writing on papyrus.

9.

c. 1500 B.C.: The twenty-two characters of the Phoenician alphabet.

800 B.C.: Homer writes the *Iliad* and *Odyssey.*

540 B.C.: The first public library is established in Athens, Greece.

minus ⅜

6.

c. 1800-1400 B.C.: Stonehenge, a megalithic monument of thirty-foot-tall stones set into circular patterns.

7.

c. 1570-1349 B.C.: Poly-chromed wood sculpture from New Kingdom Egypt, with hier-oglyphic inscriptions.

8.

c. 1450 B.C.: Detail, *The Book of the Dead* of Tuthmosis III, hieroglyphic writing on papyrus.

9.

c. 1500 B.C.: The twenty-two characters of the Phoenician alphabet.

c. 800 B.C.: Homer writes the *Iliad* and *Odyssey.*

540 B.C.: The first public library is established in Athens, Greece.

minus ½

5-80

century. The second timeline covers the long era of the handpress and handset metal types. This period, from Gutenberg's invention of movable type to the end of the eighteenth century, lasted about three hundred and fifty years. In the third timeline, the industrial revolution and nineteenth century are revealed as an era of technological innovation accompanied by an outpouring of new typographic forms. The fourth timeline begins with the year 1900 and continues until

overall kern minus ¼

century. The second timeline covers the long era of the handpress and handset metal types. This period, from Gutenberg's invention of movable type to the end of the eighteenth century, lasted about three hundred and fifty years. In the third timeline, the industrial revolution and nineteenth century are revealed as an era of technological innovation accompanied by an outpouring of new typographic forms. The fourth timeline begins with the year 1900 and continues until the present.

overall kern minus ½

century. The second timeline covers the long era of the handpress and handset metal types. This period, from Gutenberg's invention of movable type to the end of the eighteenth century, lasted about three hundred and fifty years. In the third timeline, the industrial revolution and nineteenth century are revealed as an era of technological innovation accompanied by an outpouring of new typographic forms. The fourth timeline begins with the year 1900 and continues until the pres-

overall kern minus ⅜

5-81

The next step was the development of a grid structure to structure the page designs. Using copier type proofs and photostats of images, the possibilities of three-, four-, and five-column grids were explored. The team decided to use a grid of five columns, each 8 picas wide, with 1-pica gutters between them (fig. **5-82**). A line length of 17 picas (two 8-pica columns plus the gutter between them) was used for the running text. For captions, a one-column line length of 8 picas was specified. A flow line was established 44 picas from the bottom of the page. By keying the page designs to this flow line—which divided the page into two segments, with the lower one forming a perfect square—design continuity could be maintained over 272 extremely diverse pages. A five-column grid is uncommonly flexible. It forces designers to create lively, asymmetrical pages. The area above the flow line was ideal for headings, captions, and small illustrations. Zero, one, or two text columns could be placed on a page, providing areas five, three, or one column wide for illustrations (see figs. **5-87** and **5-93** through **5-100**). Before finalizing the choice of this somewhat unusual five-column grid structure, each member of this design team manipulated type proofs and images on it to develop familiarity with this structure and ways material could be organized upon it.

Having established specifications for the page format and typography, the team proceeded to develop a design proposal and presentation consisting of one double-page spread from each of the eight chapters, a sample chapter title page, and the cover design. Use of dummy type and reductions of the illustrations enabled the team to produce exact facsimile pages rather quickly. A give-and-take dialogue among team members is important in a group design process: All four designers worked together in a large studio and freely collaborated on the designs.

Most books are designed by specialists in book typography and layout, and their jackets are by another designer specializing in book jackets, resulting in covers that have no typographic or visual relationship to their books. The team determined to avoid this graphic anomaly of book

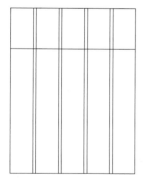

5-82

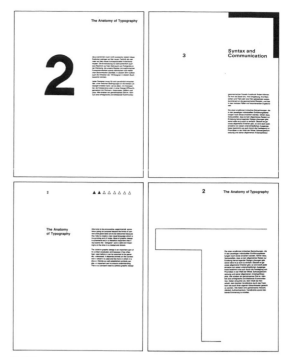

5-87

design at all costs. Because three earlier books on the subject by Emil Ruder, Ben Rosen, and Ruedi Ruegg had all used a capital *T* on the cover, the team decided to continue this tradition. Early roughs were made with cut paper and evaluated. Often strips of white paper were quickly placed on the page to show the size and placement of type.

Some of the roughs, which were discussed and discarded, were rescued from the trash by one of the designers and are reproduced here. The illusionistic space in figure **5-83** was felt to be "untypographic." In figure **5-84** the *T* seemed too static, in spite of efforts to energize the space with a blue bar, yellow *D* shape, and white bar at the bottom. A playful abstraction (fig. **5-85**) was far too whimsical for the subject. Another designer noted that some of the small details were very fascinating. It inspired him to explore simplified versions (fig. **5-86**). The dimensionality of the isometric perspective seemed too architectural.

From a group of sketches made earlier to explore possible designs for the chapter title pages (fig. **5-87**), one team member extracted a study depicting an incompletely drawn large initial *T* and advocated its use as the basis for the cover, title page, and chapter title pages. Its approach to the initial *T* concept differed from the earlier books. The participatory nature of presenting an incomplete letterform that the viewer could decode interested the team, particularly because various portions could be shown on the eight chapter title pages. Possibilities were explored in a series of sketches (figs. **5-88** through **5-91**), culminating in the final cover design (fig. **5-92**), which used bright bits of primary color against a gray field to suggest the structure of the letterforms *T* and *D*.

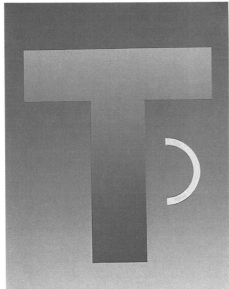

5-83

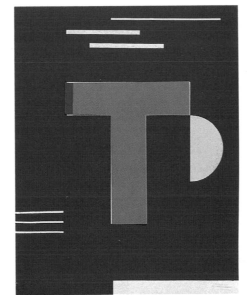

5-84

Rob Carter
Ben Day
Philip Meggs

5-85

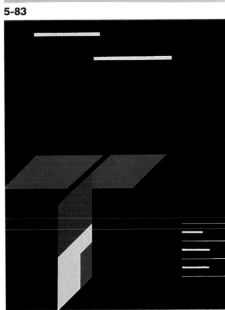

5-86

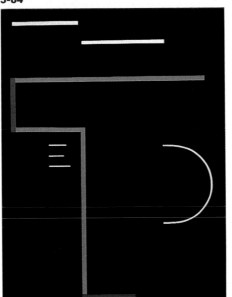

5-88

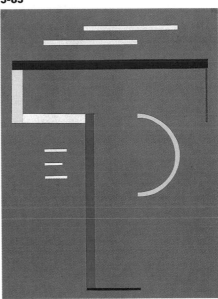

5-89

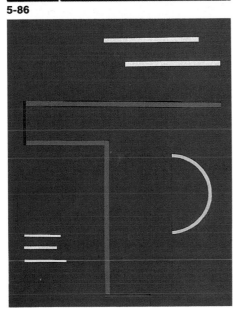

5-90

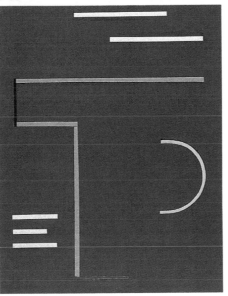

5-91

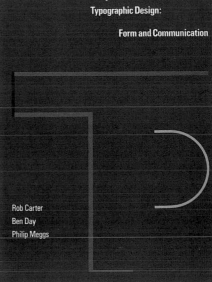

Typographic Design:

Form and Communication

Rob Carter
Ben Day
Philip Meggs

5-92

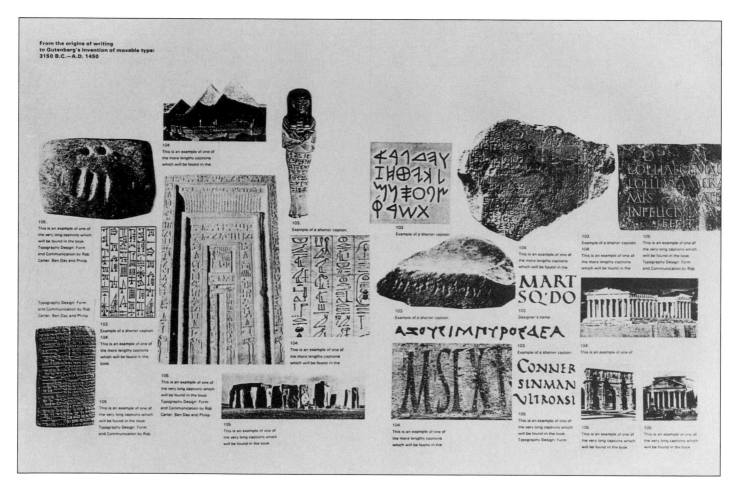

From the origins of writing
to Gutenberg's invention of movable type:
3150 B.C.–A.D. 1450

104.
This is an example of one of
the more lengthy captions
which will be found in the

105.
This is an example of one of
the very long captions which
will be found in the book
Typography Design: Form
and Communication by Rob
Carter, Ben Day and Philip.

103.
Example of a shorter caption.

Typography Design: Form
and Communication by Rob
Carter, Ben Day and Philip.

103.
Example of a shorter caption.
104.
This is an example of one of
the more lengthy captions
which will be found in the
book.

105.
This is an example of one of
the very long captions which
will be found in the book
Typography Design: Form
and Communication by Rob

105.
This is an example of one of
the very long captions which
will be found in the book
Typography Design: Form
and Communication by Rob
Carter, Ben Day and Philip.

105.
This is an example of one of
the more lengthy captions
which will be found in the book

104.
This is an example of one of
the more lengthy captions
which will be found in the

MART
SQ·DO

102.
Designer's name

ΑΞΟΥΓΙΜΠΥΡΟΕΔΕΑ

103.
Example of a shorter caption.

MSEXI

CONNER
SINMAN
ULTROASI

104.
This is an example of one of
the more lengthy captions
which will be found in the

105.
This is an example of one of
the very long captions which
will be found in the book
Typography Design: Form

103.
Example of a shorter caption.
104.
This is an example of one of
the more lengthy captions
which will be found in the

105.
This is an example of one of
the very long captions which
will be found in the book
Typography Design: Form
and Communication by Rob.

104.
This is an example of one of

105.
This is an example of one of
the very long captions which
will be found in the book

105.
This is an example of one of
the very long captions which
will be found in the book

5-93

The design process for three double-page layouts illustrates the group dynamic that occurs when designers collaborate. The first chapter was a bit unusual because it presented a pictorial history of typography with captions but no running text. The first layout mixed images and captions across the page (fig. **5-93**). The group discussed it and decided that putting captions in a horizontal band across the top of the page might be cleaner and less confusing. The second version (fig. **5-94**) was favored because its greater emphasis on the flow line and grid seemed more consistent with the rest of the book.

5-94

An important attitude about the grid developed after one team member prepared a layout for the chapter discussing the anatomy of typography (fig. **5-95**). The illustration depicting the parts of the letterform had an interesting compositional design; however, the team felt that the spatial and scale manipulations actually diverted attention from the subject matter. Also, it departed from the overall format by introducing new visual themes into the format. A quick sketch (fig. **5-96**) prompted agreement that diagrams should be presented in a straightforward manner, conforming to the grid. This sketch became the basis for the final design (fig. **5-97**).

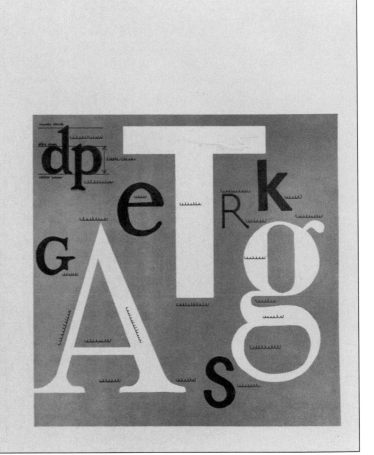

5-95

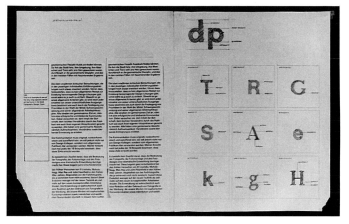

5-96

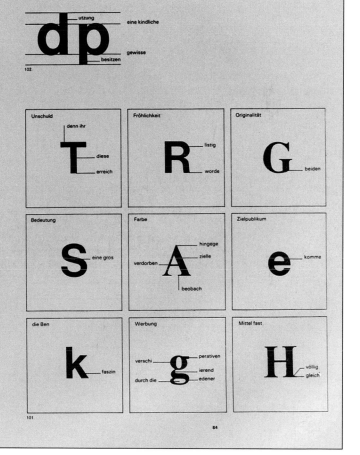

5-97

The typographic specimen sections open with a reproduction of a historical typographic design with the original type style in use, a large letterform, and text discussing the type family. One team member felt strongly that the historical examples should be presented as full-page facsimiles. He developed a layout (fig. **5-98**), which was sharply criticized by another team member who believed that this was unsuccessful because the elements in the example did not align with the book's grid and became visually intrusive. This second team member developed a variation with a smaller illustration (fig. **5-99**). The first member felt that more was lost than gained; therefore, he prepared a revision with a screen tint beneath the facsimile (fig. **5-100**). This separated the facsimile page from the book's format and identified the entire page as an illustration. By making the facsimiles a pale gray, the screen tints isolated these pages from the book format and presented each one as a unified whole rather than as a series of parts. All agreed that this solution was stronger than the two preceding designs.

After the proposal of a dozen sample layout pages and the cover design was approved by the publisher, the entire book was typeset. The four designers paired off into two-person teams to permit each designer to collaborate with each of the others in the design of a chapter. To apportion pages among the chapters, the total area of live space excluding margins was calculated to be 19,720 square inches. The number of square inches of space needed for text and caption type for each chapter was then allocated by measuring the type proofs, leaving a balance (10,348 square inches) for illustrations and white space. This area of space was divided by the number of illustrations and then converted into pages (72.5 square inches equals the live area of one page) to assign each chapter an equitable number of pages. This division accomplished several goals: It permitted an even distribution of text and imagery throughout the book, forced the designers to work within the number of pages agreed upon by the publisher, avoided the cost-overrun that occurs when a book turns out to be more pages than planned, and thwarted that nemesis of book design—a book whose layout becomes cramped in the last chapters because the designer, too generous with white space and large illustrations in the earlier chapters, suddenly

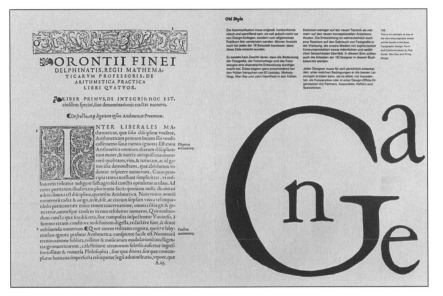

5-98

realizes that the design is going to exceed the allotted number of pages unless drastic economies are taken.

By establishing parameters and attending to details—ranging from the size and placement of page numbers to the thickness of all ruled lines—in the initial design proposal, the group was able to design a 272-page book with a minimum of problems.

Multiple-page assignments and group projects require careful planning at the early stages to avoid unexpected problems. Although graphic design is usually seen as an individual creative effort, team design is often useful. Large projects can be handled in a reasonable length of time, and the critical evaluation of several designers focused upon a project can improve its quality. Of course, the group has to be able to work together in a give-and-take atmosphere and must be compatible in their design philosophies and visual sensibilities; otherwise, the collaboration is doomed to failure.

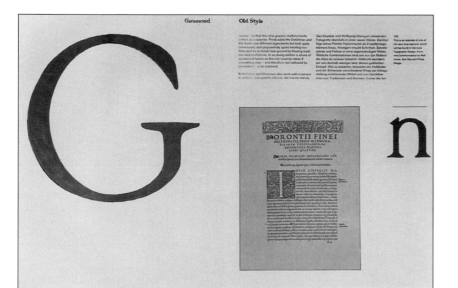

5-99

5-100

Epilogue

Graphic design has a synergistic relationship with the social milieu in which it occurs. It is shaped and formed by its culture. In turn, it helps shape and form the culture. It is neither an art nor a science; rather, it is a hybrid form of public communication that calls upon its practitioners to be visual editors, graphic inventors, and form builders. Because graphic designers speak with a public voice, their signs, symbols, and images are of necessity the signs, symbols, and images of their audience. Arcane language or obscure signification merely cause people in our overcommunicated, postindustrial society to turn away; clear language and spatial order enable graphic designers to transmit messages with clarity and impact.

Graphic design flourishes when cultures invest in the aesthetics of public experience and when a society understands that the resonance from how things are said is as important as what is said. A rigorous attitude toward problem solving and the courage to reach out and risk failure are required from graphic designers *and* their clients if their efforts are to contribute to the advancement of human experience in our time.

Notes

Chapter One

1. Shannon, C. E., and Weaver, W. *Mathematical Theory of Communication.* Champaign-Urbana IL: University of Illinois Press, 1949.
2. Campbell, Jeremy. *Grammatical Man: Information, Entropy, Language, and Life.* New York: Simon and Schuster, 1982, p. 152.
3. Glaser, Milton. *Milton Glaser Graphic Design.* Woodstock: Overlook Press, 1973, p. 15.
4. Woodward, Sylvia Harris. Interview with the author. New York: October 13, 1987.
5. von Franz, Marie-Louise. "The Process of Individualization," in Jung, Carl G., ed., *Man and His Symbols.* London: Aldus, 1964, p. 229.
6. Dunn, Crawford. "Alphasignal, Parasignal, Infrasignal: Notes Toward a Theory of Communication." *Print.* Vol. 24, No. 6, Nov–Dec 1970, pp. 21–28.
7. Ibid., p. 22.
8. Ibid., p. 24.
9. A detailed discussion of semiotics is beyond the scope of this work. An excellent introductory book on this subject is *Structuralism and Semiotics* by Terence Hawkes (Berkeley: University of California, 1977). It has an annotated bibliography for further reading on this subject.
10. Morrison, Philip. "The Modularity of Knowing," in Kepes, Gyorgy, ed. *Module, Proportion, Symmetry, Rhythm.* New York: Braziller, 1966, p. 14.
11. Cossette, Claude. *The Iconic Science: The Still Picture Analysed from the Semiological Point of View.* Paper read at the Icograda Conference, 1975, Winnipeg, Canada, p. 9.
12. Ehses, Hanno H. J. *Design Papers 4: Design and Rhetoric: An Analysis of Theatre Posters.* Nova Scotia: Nova Scotia College of Art and Design, 1987, p. 5.
13. Walsh, Daniel J. Interviewed with author. Alexandria, VA: September 15, 1987.
14. Kince, Eli. *Visual Puns in Design.* New York: Watson Guptill, 1983, p. 31.
15. Campbell, Jeremy. *Grammatical Man: Information, Entropy, Language, and Life.* New York: Simon and Schuster, 1982, p. 91.

Chapter Two

1. Barthes, Roland. *Image Music Text.* New York: Hill and Wang, 1977, p. 26.
2. Ibid., p. 27.
3. Hess, Dick, and Muller, Marion. *Dorfsman and CBS.* New York: American Showcase, 1978, p. 62.
4. Read, Herbert. *A Concise History of Modern Painting.* New York: Praeger, 1959, p. 110.
5. Guercio, James William. Notes in Columbia album GP 8, *The Chicago Transit Authority.* New York: Columbia Records, 1968.
6. This company's French name is La Neuchateloise Assurances. French and German language versions were produced, and examples from each series are illustrated here.

Chapter Three

1. Duke-Elder, W. S. *Text Book of Ophthalmology.* St. Louis: Mosby, 1933, p. 924.
2. Carpenter, Edmund. *They Became What They Beheld.* New York: Ballantine, 1970, p. 78.
3. Frey, Dagobert. "On the Problem of Symmetry in Art." *Studium Generale* (Germany). Vol. 2, July 1949, p. 276.
4. Tschichold, Jan. "El Lissitzky (1890–1941)." Abridged from *Typographische Mitteilungen.* St. Gallen, Switzerland, 1965, in Kuppers-Lissitzky, Sophie. *El Lissitzky: Life, Letters, Text.* Greenwich, CT: New York Graphic Society, 1968, p. 386.
5. The unit is approximately one centimeter in length in these publications. Bill used the Didot type-measurement system that is dominant in most European countries. It is a system of measurement in points based on the French foot (about 30 centimeters), which is divided into 798 points. The Didot point is different from the point used in England and the United States, which has 12 points in a pica, and approximately 6 picas or 72 points in an inch. By comparison, there are approximately 68 Didot points in an inch. This difference is substantial, for in a ten-inch column of type the variance in column depth will be about three picas or one-half inch.
6. Whitehead, Alfred North. *An Enquiry Concerning the Principles of Natural Knowledge.* Cambridge: Cambridge University Press, 1919, p. 198.
7. Related to the author by John Urbain, former assistant to Leo Lionni.
8. Hutchinson, James. *Letters.* New York: Van Nostrand Reinhold, 1983, p. 126.

Chapter Four

1. Birdwhistell, R. L., "Paralanguage Twenty-five Years after Sapir," in Laver, J., and Hutcheson, S., eds., *Communication in Face to Face Interaction.* Harmondsworth: Penguin, 1972.
2. Lange-Seidl, Annemarie. *Approaches to Theories for Nonverbal Signs.* Lisse, The Netherlands: The Peter De Ridder Press, 1977, p. 12.
3. Windsor, Alan. *Peter Behrens: Architect and Designer.* New York: Whitney, 1981, p. 46.
4. Fili, Louise. Interview with the author. New York: October 15, 1987.
5. Gill, Bob. *Forget All the Rules You Ever Learned about Graphic Design Including the Ones in This Book.* New York: Watson-Guptill, 1981, p. 8.
6. Hubbard, William. *Complicity and Conviction: Steps toward an Architecture of Convention.* Cambridge, MA: MIT Press, 1980, pp. 73–75.
7. Kandinsky, Wassily. *Concerning the Spiritual in Art.* New York: Wittenborn, 1947, p. 11.
8. Cohen, Arthur. *Herbert Bayer: The Complete Work.* Cambridge, MA: MIT Press, 1984, p. 215.
9. Kandinsky, p. 47.

Chapter Five

1. De Bono, Edward. *New Think: The Use of Lateral Thinking in the Generation of New Ideas.* New York: Basic Books, 1967.
2. The trademarks depicted in figures 5-2 through 5-4 are hypothetical interpretations. Any duplication of existing trademarks is purely coincidental. See figure 3-8, which is a parody of this genre.
3. Osborn, Alex F. *Applied Imagination.* New York: Scribner's, 1953.
4. Vanderbyl, Michael. Interview with the author. San Francisco: September 4, 1987.
5. Fili, Louise. Interview with the author. New York: October 15, 1987.
6. Vanderbyl, Michael. Interview with the author. San Francisco: September 4, 1987.
7. Hidy, Lance. Unpublished essay prepared to supplement interview with author. October 1987.

Bibliography

Adams, James L. *Conceptual Blockbusting: A Guide to Better Ideas,* 3d ed. Reading, MA: Addison-Wesley, 1986.

Arnheim, Rudolf. *Art and Visual Perception.* Berkeley: University of California Press, 1974.

_____. *The Power of the Center: A Study of Composition in the Visual Arts.* Berkeley: University of California Press, 1982.

Banham, Reyner. *Theory and Design in the First Machine Age,* 2d ed. Cambridge, MA: MIT Press, 1981.

Barthes, Roland. *Image Text Music.* New York: Hill and Wang, 1977.

Birdwhistell, R. L., "Paralanguage Twenty-five Years after Sapir," in Laver, J., and Hutcheson, S., eds. *Communication in Face to Face Interaction.* Harmondsworth: Penguin, 1972.

Campbell, Jeremy. *Grammatical Man: Information, Entropy, Language, and Life.* New York: Simon and Schuster, 1982.

Carpenter, Edmund. *They Became What They Beheld.* New York: Ballantine, 1970.

Carter, Rob; Day, Ben; and Meggs, Philip. *Typographic Design: Form and Communication.* New York: Van Nostrand Reinhold, 1985.

Cohen, Arthur. *Herbert Bayer: The Complete Work.* Cambridge, MA: MIT Press, 1984.

Cossette, Claude. *The Iconic Science: The Still Picture Analysed from the Semiological Point of View.* Paper read at the Icograda Conference, 1975, Winnipeg, Canada.

De Bono, Edward. *New Think: The Use of Lateral Thinking in the Generation of New Ideas.* New York: Basic Books, 1967.

Duke-Elder, William Stewart. *Text Book of Ophthalmology.* St. Louis: Mosby, 1933.

Dunn, Crawford. "Alphasignal, Parasignal, Infrasignal: Notes Toward a Theory of Communication." *Print.* Vol. 24, No. 6, Nov–Dec 1970, pp. 21–28.

Ehses, Hanno H. J. *Design Papers 4: Design and Rhetoric: An Analysis of Theatre Posters.* Nova Scotia: Nova Scotia College of Art and Design, 1987.

Foss, Martin. *Symbol and Metaphor in Human Experience.* Lincoln: University of Nebraska, 1964.

Frey, Dagobert. "On the Problem of Symmetry in Art." *Studium Generale* (Germany), Vol. 2, July, 1949.

Gill, Bob. *Forget All the Rules You Ever Learned about Graphic Design Including the Ones in This Book.* New York: Watson-Guptill, 1981.

Glaser, Milton. *Milton Glaser Graphic Design.* Woodstock: Overlook Press, 1973.

Green, Peter. *Design Education: Problem Solving and Visual Experience.* London: Batsford, 1974.

Hawkes, Terence. *Structuralism and Semiotics.* Berkeley: University of California Press, 1977.

Hayes, John R. *The Complete Problem Solver.* Philadelphia: Franklin, 1981.

Hess, Dick, and Muller, Marion. *Dorfsman and CBS.* New York: American Showcase, 1978.

Hidy, Lance. Unpublished essay prepared to supplement interview with author. October 1987.

Hofmann, Armin. *Graphic Design Manual.* New York: Van Nostrand Reinhold, 1965.

Hubbard, William. *Complicity and Convention: Steps toward an Architecture of Convention.* Cambridge, MA: MIT Press, 1980.

Hurlburt, Allen. *The Design Concept.* New York: Watson-Guptill, 1981.

_____. *Layout: the Design of the Printed Page.* New York: Watson-Guptill, 1977.

_____. *Photo/Graphic Design: The Interaction of Design and Photography.* New York: Watson-Guptill, 1983.

Hutchinson, James. *Letters.* New York: Van Nostrand Reinhold, 1983.

Ivins, William M. *Art and Geometry: A Study in Space Intuitions.* Cambridge, MA: Harvard University Press, 1946.

Kandinsky, Wassily. *Concerning the Spiritual in Art.* New York: Wittenborn, 1947.

_____. *Point and Line to Plane.* New York: Dover, 1979.

Kepes, Gyorgy. *Education of Vision.* New York: Braziller, 1965.

_____. *Language of Vision.* Chicago: Theobald, 1945.

_____. *Module, Proportion, Symmetry, Rhythm.* New York: Braziller, 1966.

Kince, Eli. *Visual Puns in Design.* New York: Watson-Guptill, 1983.

Koberg, Don, and Bagnall, Jim. *The Universal Traveler.* Los Altos, CA: Kaufmann, 1972.

Koestler, Arthur. *The Act of Creation.* New York: Macmillan, 1964.

Koffka, K. *Principles of Gestalt Psychology.* New York: Harcourt, Brace and World, 1935.

Kostelanetz, Richard, ed. *Moholy-Nagy.* London: Allen Lane, 1971.

Kuppers-Lissitzky, Sophie. *El Lissitzky: Life, Letters, Texts.* Greenwich, CT: New York Graphic Society, 1968.

Langer, Susanne K. *Feeling and Form.* New York: Scribner's, 1953.

_____. *Philosophy in a New Key.* New York: Mentor, New American Library, 1957.

_____. *Problems of Art.* New York: Scribner's, 1957.

Lange-Seidl, Annemarie. *Approaches to Theories of Nonverbal Signs.* Lisse: Peter de Ridder,1977.

Leach, Edmund. *Culture and Communication.* Cambridge: Cambridge University Press, 1976.

McLuhan, Marshall. *Understanding Media: The Extensions of Man.* New York: McGraw-Hill, 1964.

Meggs, Philip B. *A History of Graphic Design.* New York: Van Nostrand Reinhold, 1983.

Merrell, Floyd. *Semiotic Foundations.* Bloomington: Indiana University Press, 1982.

Moholy-Nagy, Laszlo. *The New Vision and Abstract of an Artist.* New York: Wittenborn, 1947.

Moholy-Nagy, Sibyl. *Experiment in Totality.* Cambridge, MA: MIT Press, 1969.

Muller-Brockmann, Josef. *The Graphic Artist and His Design Problems.* New York: Hastings House, 1961.

Ogilvy, David. *Ogilvy on Advertising.* New York: Crown, 1983.

Osborn, Alex F. *Applied Imagination.* New York: Scribner's, 1953.

Read, Herbert. *A Concise History of Modern Painting.* New York: Praeger, 1959.

_____. *The Meaning of Art.* Baltimore: Penguin, 1961.

Reis, Al, and Trout, Jack. *Positioning: The Battle for Your Mind.* New York: McGraw-Hill, 1981.

Shannon, C. E., and Weaver, W. *Mathematical Theory of Communication.* Champaign-Urbana: University of Illinois Press, 1949.

Sontag, Susan. *On Photography.* New York: Farrar, Straus and Giroux, 1977.

Spencer, Herbert, ed. *The Liberated Page.* San Francisco: Bedford Press, 1987.

Storr, Anthony. *The Dynamics of Creation.* London: Sacker and Warburg, 1972.

VanGundy, Arthur B. *Creative Problem Solving.* New York: Quorum Books, 1987.

Von Franz, Marie-Louise. "The Process of Individualization," from Jung, Carl G., ed. *Man and His Symbols.* London: Aldus, 1964.

Wade, John W. *Architecture, Problems, and Purposes: Architectural Design as a Basic Problem-Solving Process.* New York: Wiley, 1977.

Weyl, Hermann. *Symmetry.* Princeton: Princeton University Press, 1952.

Whitehead, Alfred North. *The Concept of Nature.* Cambridge: Cambridge University Press, 1926.

_____. *An Enquiry Concerning the Principles of Natural Knowledge.* Cambridge: Cambridge University Press, 1919.

Windsor, Alan. *Peter Behrens: Architect and Designer.* New York: Whitney, 1981.

Woods, Gerald; Thompson, Philip; and Williams, John. *Art without Boundaries.* London: Thames and Hudson, 1972.

Picture Credits

Chapter One

1-1, 1-2. Philip B. Meggs.

1-3. Courtesy of Paul Rand, designer.

1-4. Diagrammatic interpretation of figure 1-3 by Philip B. Meggs.

1-5. Philip B. Meggs.

1-6. Courtesy of Rob Carter.

1-7, 1-8. Philip B. Meggs.

1-9. Photographer: Wallace N. Meggs.

1-10. Courtesy of Eugen Rentsch Verlag, Erlenbach-Zurich, Switzerland.

1-11–1-14. Illustration by Libby P. Meggs.

1-15. Philip B. Meggs.

1-16. Courtesy of Dietmar Winkler, designer.

1-17. Courtesy of Lorraine Louie, designer. Art director: Judith Loeser.

1-18. Courtesy of Jacklin Pinsler, designer.

1-19. Courtesy of Lou Dorfsman, designer.

1-20. Courtesy of Joseph Michael Essex, designer.

1-21. Courtesy of William Longhauser, designer.

1-22. Courtesy of the Sun Company, Inc. Design director: Kenneth Love. Designers: Kenneth Love and Richard Felton. Design firm: Anspach Grossman Portugal Inc.

1-23. Courtesy of Janet Odgis, designer.

1-24. Courtesy of Frank Armstrong, designer. Design firm: Armstrong Design Consultants, Groton, MA.

1-25. Courtesy of Dietmar Winkler, designer.

1-26. Courtesy of Merrill Lynch. Art director: Lauren Deane. Copywriter: Margot Azen. Agency: Young & Rubicam, New York, NY.

1-27. Courtesy of WRXL and Capitol Broadcasting Co., Inc. Art director: Chris Baker. Copywriter: Pat Holstein. Photographer: Dennis Manarchy. Agency: Fricke Associates, Raleigh, NC.

1-28. Designer: J. Breu the Elder. Woodblock cutter: Wolffgang Kosch.

1-29. Courtesy of Kit Hinrichs. Art director: Kit Hinrichs (author). Designers: Kit Hinrichs, D. J. Hyde, Lenore Bartz. Illustration: Kit Hinrichs. Copywriter: Delphine Hirasuna (text), Diane Hirasuna (recipes).

1-30–1-38. Illustrator: Libby P. Meggs.

1-39. Photographer: Philip B. Meggs.

1-40. Courtesy of Hixo, Inc., design firm. Art director: Tom Poth. Copywriter: Guy Bommarito. Illustrator: Larry McIntire.

1-41. Illustrator/designer: Charles B. Falls.

1-42. Courtesy of Sibley/Peteet, design firm.

1-43. Courtesy of David Colley, designer.

1-44. Courtesy of David Colley, designer.

1-45. Courtesy of Jeff Barnes, designer. Photographer: Christopher Hawker.

1-46. Courtesy of Jeff Barnes, designer.

1-47. Courtesy of Jeff Barnes, designer. Photographer: Dennis Manarchy.

1-48. Courtesy of Dietmar Winkler, designer.

1-49. Anonymous nineteenth-century illustrator.

1-50. Courtesy of Frank Armstrong, designer and photographer. Design firm: Armstrong Design Consultants, Groton, MA.

1-51. Courtesy of Dietmar Winkler, designer.

1-52. *Walking Man II* by Alberto Giacometti; The National Gallery of Art, Washington, DC; gift of Enid A. Haupt (date: 1960; bronze; 1.885 × .279 × 1.107 [74¼ × 11 × 43⅝ in.]).

1-53. Courtesy of R. D. Scudellari, designer. Photographer: Eric Meola.

1-54. Illustration by John Tenniel.

1-55. Courtesy of Liberation Graphics, Box 2394, Alexandria, VA 22301, which specializes in the design and distribution of classic oppositional poster art from around the world. Photographer: Yehudah Raviv. Publisher: Twentieth Century Bookstore, Tel Aviv, Israel.

1-56. Courtesy of Frank Armstrong, designer. Photographer: Thomas Wedell. Design firm: Armstrong Design Consultants, Groton, MA.

1-57. Courtesy of Joseph Michael Essex, designer. Photographer: Ira Block.

1-58. Courtesy of Chris Pullman, designer. Photographer: Tom Sumida.

1-59. Courtesy of Jim Jacobs Studio, designer.

1-60. Courtesy of DDB Needham, agency. Art director: Helmut Krone. Copywriter: Julian Koenig.

1-61. Courtesy of *Reader's Digest*. Art director: Tom Roth. Copywriter: Steve Trygg. Agency: Anderson & Lembke, Stamford, CT.

1-62. Courtesy of *The Atlantic*. Art director: Judy Garlan. Illustrator: Theo Rudnak.

1-63. Courtesy of Barry Zaid, designer and illustrator.

1-64. Photographer: Philip B. Meggs.

Chapter Two

2-1. Courtesy of Michael Bierut, Vignelli Associates, designer.

2-2. Courtesy of Bob Gill, designer.

2-3. Reproduced from *The Perfect War: Techowar in Vietnam* by James William Gibson, copyright © 1986 by James William Gibson. By permission of The Atlantic Monthly Press, publisher.

2-4. Courtesy of Adriane Stark, designer.

2-5. Courtesy of Armstrong Design Consultants, Groton, MA. Designer: Frank Armstrong. Photographer: Thomas Wedell. Client: Perkins School for the Blind, Watertown, MA.

2-6. The *B* is by Christine Angus, from *The Studio,* August 1900. The *M* is by C. A. Allen, and the *S* is by Bertha Smith, from *The Studio*, October 1894.

2-7. Courtesy of William Longhauser, designer. Client: Philadelphia College of Art.

2-8. Courtesy of R. D. Scudellari, designer.

2-9. Courtesy of Bradbury Thompson, designer.

2-10. Courtesy of Dugald Stermer, designer.

2-11. Courtesy of Craig Frazier, designer. Firm: Frazier Design, San Francisco, CA.

2-12. Courtesy of Columbia Records.

2-13. Courtesy of Anne Summers, editor-in-chief, *Ms.* magazine.

2-14. Courtesy of Lou Dorfsman. Photographer: Sol Mednick. Client: CBS Radio.

2-15. Courtesy of James McMullan, designer/illustrator.

2-16. Courtesy of The Herb Lubalin Study Center, Cooper Union, New York, NY. Ellen Lupton, curator.

2-17. Courtesy of Sibley/Peteet Design, Dallas, TX.

2-18. Courtesy of Diana Graham, designer.

2-19. Courtesy of Tom Geismar, designer. Firm: Chermayeff and Geismar, New York, NY.

2-20. Courtesy of Diana Graham, designer. Firm: Diagram, New York, NY.

2-21. Courtesy of Ivan Chermayeff, designer. Firm: Chermayeff and Geismar Associates, New York, NY.

2-22–2-30. Courtesy of John Berg, art director. Client: Columbia Records.

2-31. Courtesy of Richard Flint.

2-32. Courtesy of The Office of Michael Manwaring, San Francisco, CA.

2-33. Courtesy of Michael Bierut, designer. Firm: Vignelli Associates, New York, NY.

2-34. Courtesy of Columbia Records.

2-35. Courtesy of Craig Frazier, designer. Firm: Fraizer Design, San Francisco, CA.

2-36–2-41. Courtesy of Odermatt and Tissi, Grafiker AGI, Zurich, Switzerland.

2-42. Courtesy of DDB Needham Worldwide.

2-43. Courtesy of *Reader's Digest.* Art director: Sal DeVito. Copywriter: Jamie Seltzer. Agency: Chiat/Day, New York, NY.

2-44. Courtesy of Jann Church, designer. Firm: Jann Church.

2-45. Courtesy of Lou Dorfsman, designer. Client: CBS Television.

2-46. Courtesy of The Herb Lubalin Study Center, Cooper Union, New York, NY. Ellen Lupton, curator.

Chapter Three

3-1–3-7. Diagrams by Philip B. Meggs.

3-8. Courtesy of Philip B. Meggs, designer.

3-9. Courtesy of Dietmar Winkler, designer.

3-10. Diagram by Philip B. Meggs.

3-11. Courtesy of Kit Hinrichs, art director. Designers: Kit Hinrichs, D. J. Hyde, and Lenore Bartz. Photographer: Tom Tracy. Illustrator: David Stevenson. Copywriters: Delphine Hirasuna (text) and Diane Hirasuna (recipes).

3-12, 3-13. Courtesy of Ronn Campisi, designer.

3-14. Courtesy of Lance Hidy, designer.

3-15. Courtesy of Jeff Barnes, designer. Photographer: Dennis Manarchy.

3-16–3-21. Courtesy of Eugen Rentsch Verlag, Erlenbach-Zurich, Switzerland, publisher. Authors: El Lissitzky and Hans Arp. Designer: El Lissitzky.

3-22. Diagram by Philip B. Meggs.

3-23–3-27. Courtesy of Werner and Bischoff, publisher, Basel, Switzerland. Designer: Max Bill.

3-28. Diagram by Philip B. Meggs.

3-29. Courtesy of John DeMao, designer.

3-30. Courtesy of Rob Carter and Tim Priddy, designers.

3-31. Courtesy of John Massey, designer.

3-32. Courtesy of Don Trousdell, designer.

3-33. Courtesy of Kit Hinrichs, art director. Designers: Kit Hinrichs and Natalie Kitamura. Photographer: Michele Clement. Copywriter: Tom Wrubel. Client: The Nature Company.

3-34. Courtesy of Special Collections and Archives, James Branch Cabell Library, Virginia Commonwealth University, Richmond, VA.

3-35. Courtesy of Cheryl A. Brzezinski, designer.

3-36. Courtesy of Ronn Campisi, designer. Illustrator: Gene Greif.

3-37. Courtesy of Jeff Barnes, designer.

3-38. Courtesy of Malcolm Grear Designers, Providence, RI, design firm. Photographer: Gene Dwiggins.

3-39, 3-40. Courtesy of Jacklin Pinsler, designer.

3-41, 3-42. Courtesy of Jeff Barnes, designer. Photographer: Gordon Meyer. Client: Kieffer-Nolde, Inc.

3-43. Courtesy of Kit Hinrichs, designer. Photographer: Barry Robinson. Copywriter: Delphine Hirasuna. Client: Pentagram Design.

3-44. Courtesy of Lorraine Louie, designer. Art director: Judith Loeser. Client: Vintage Books.

3-45. Diagram by Philip B. Meggs.

3-46. Courtesy of Louise Fili, designer. Illustrator: Robert Goldstrom. Client: Pantheon Books.

3-47. Courtesy of Louise Fili, designer. Illustrator, Susannah Kelly. Client: Pantheon Books.

3-48. Courtesy of Dugald Stermer, designer and illustrator.

3-49. Courtesy of Carin Goldberg, designer.

3-50. Courtesy of Dietmar Winkler, designer.

3-51. Designer: Philip B. Meggs. Illustrator: Libby P. Meggs.

3-52. Courtesy of Ronn Campisi, designer.

3-53. Courtesy of Rob Carter and Tim Priddy, designers.

3-54. Courtesy of Lorraine Louie, designer. Art director: Sara Eisenman. Painting by Giorgio de Chirico.

3-55. Courtesy of The Herb Lubalin Study Center, Cooper Union, New York, NY. Ellen Lupton, curator.

3-56. Courtesy of Armstrong Design Consultants, Groton, MA. Designer: Frank Armstrong. Photographer: Thomas Wedell. Client: Perkins School for the Blind, Watertown, MA.

3-57. Courtesy of Jann Church, designer. Photographer: Walter Urie. Client: Mead Library of Ideas.

3-58. Courtesy of Louise Fili, art director. Designers: Louise Fili and David Tran. Photographer: Lowell Georgia. Client: Pantheon Books.

3-59. Courtesy of Louise Fili, art director. Designers: Louise Fili and David Tran. Photographer: Ellis Herwig. Client: Pantheon Books.

3-60. Courtesy of Dugald Stermer, designer/illustrator. Art director: Louise Fili. Client: Pantheon Books.

3-61. Courtesy of Woody Pirtle, art director. Designers: Woody Pirtle and Jeff Weithman.

3-62. Courtesy of Willi Kunz, designer. Photographer: James B. Abbott. Client: Columbia University School of Architecture and Planning.

Chapter Four

4-1–4-9. Photography and layout by Philip B. Meggs.

4-10–4-15. Typography by Philip B. Meggs, typesetting by Riddick Advertising Art.

4-16. Courtesy of Tom Geismar, designer. Design firm: Chermayeff and Geismar Associates.

4-17. Cover of *Revolution,* Munich, Germany: October, 1913. Private Collection.

4-18. Courtesy of George Tscherny, designer. Photographer: John Naso.

4-19. Courtesy of Jeff Barnes, designer.

4-20. Courtesy of Bob Gill, designer.

4-21. Courtesy of The Herb Lubalin Study Center, Cooper Union, New York, NY. Ellen Lupton, curator.

4-22, 4-23. Courtesy of Ronn Campisi, designer.

4-24. Courtesy of R. D. Scudellari, designer. Photographer: Martha Swope. Calligraphy: Gow Larson.

4-25. Courtesy of R. D. Scudellari, designer. Photographer: Eve Arnold.

4-26. Courtesy of R. D. Scudellari, designer. Photographer: Bruce Davidson.

4-27. Designer: Herbert Bayer.

4-28. Courtesy of Dugald Stermer, designer and illustrator.

4-29. Title page from Ricchieri, Lodovico. *Lectionum Antiquarum Libri XVI.* Venice: Aldus Manutius, 1516.

4-30. Courtesy of CBS Records. Art director: John Berg. Illustrator: James Grashow.

4-31. Courtesy of CBS Records. Art director: John Berg. Designer: Ed Lee.

4-32. Courtesy of Louise Fili, designer.

4-33. Courtesy of Lorraine Louie, designer. Art director: Sara Eisenman. Type design: Daniel Pelavin. Photographer: Horst.

4-34. Courtesy of Michael Doret, designer.

4-35. Courtesy of Louise Fili, designer.

4-36. Courtesy of John Berg, designer.

4-37. Courtesy of 212 Associates, New York, NY, design firm.

4-38. Courtesy of William Longhauser, designer. Client: Goldie Paley Gallery, Moore College of Art, Philadelphia, PA.

4-39. Courtesy of Massimo Vignelli and Michael Bierut, designers. Design firm: Vignelli Associates, New York, NY.

4-40–4-42. Courtesy of Jacklin Pinsler, designer.

4-43. Courtesy of Michael Manwaring, designer. Design firm: The Office of Michael Manwaring, San Francisco, CA.

4-44. Courtesy of William Longhauser, designer. Client: Goldie Paley Gallery, Moore College of Art, Philadelphia, PA.

4-45. Courtesy of Ronn Campisi, designer.

4-46. Courtesy of Carin Goldberg, designer. Illustrator: Anthony Russo.

4-47. Courtesy of Carin Goldberg, designer. Illustrator: Gene Greif.

4-48. Courtesy of Louise Fili, designer.

4-49, 4-50. Courtesy of Warren Lehrer, designer. Writers: Warren Lehrer and Dennis Bernstein. Published by Ear/ Say.

4-51. Courtesy of David Colley, designer.

4-52. Courtesy of Liberation Graphics, Alexandria, VA, Publisher in the United States. Artist: Renato Habulan, The Philippines.

Chapter Five

5-1–5-4. Diagrams by Philip B. Meggs

5-5. Courtesy of Les Derby, designer.

5-6, 5-7. Diagrams by Philip B. Meggs.

5-8–5-70. Courtesy of Lance Hidy, designer/illustrator.

5-71–5-79. Courtesy of Jeff Barnes, designer.

5-80–5-100. Courtesy of Rob Carter, Steven Chovanec, Ben Day, and Philip B. Meggs. Publisher: Van Nostrand Reinhold.

Index

Printing:	Kingsport Press
Binding:	Kingsport Press
Typography:	David E. Seham Associates 9/12 Helvetica with 18/17 Helvetica Bold titles set on the Linotron 202 Digital Phototypesetter
Color separations:	South Sea International Press Ltd.
Art Direction:	Philip B. Meggs
Design:	John DeMao, Libby Phillips Meggs, Philip B. Meggs, and Julie Sebastianelli
Photography:	George Nan